D1191383

THE OXFORD PSALTER

Containing THE PSALMS, *together with*
THE CANTICLES AND HYMNS
THE LITANY (1544)
and
PROPER PSALMS FOR CERTAIN DAYS

NEWLY POINTED FOR CHANTING AND
EDITED BY

HENRY G. LEY, M.A., Mus.D.
Precentor of Eton College

E. STANLEY ROPER, M.V.O., M.A., Mus.B.
Organist and Composer at H.M. Chapels Royal

THE LATE

C. HYLTON STEWART, M.A., Mus.B.
Formerly Organist of St. George's Chapel, Windsor
Organist of Rochester Cathedral

OXFORD UNIVERSITY PRESS
LONDON : HUMPHREY MILFORD

DIRECTIONS FOR USING THIS PSALTER

I. Sing all the words at approximately the same pace: avoid hurrying long sentences and dragging the moving part of a chant. Pronounce every syllable distinctly.

II. Breath need not necessarily be taken at commas: observe them by dwelling slightly upon the previous strong accent. An asterisk is a direction to take breath.

III. When two or more syllables come to one minim of the chant, do not hurry them. Make the note long enough to take them.

IV. When one syllable is spread over two or more notes, sing them lightly, without undue accentuation.

V. Where the final ' -ed ' is printed in full, it is to be sung as a separate syllable.

VI. Verses preceded by their number in heavy square brackets, e.g. [5], do not conform to traditional use. They are to be sung straight through, making no break at the first double bar: as if the chant consisted of one phrase not two; and as if the fourth and fifth notes were minims, not semibreves.

VII. Syllables with dots under them are to be sung lightly, without stress.

VIII. A single chant must be used where indicated. No provision is made for a double chant in these cases. When verses are printed in groups of three a triple chant may be used.

IX. The spacing of syllables within a bar is shown by the position of a dot or a hyphen.

X. Accent-marks are only used where it is thought that choirs may, unless guided, throw stress on syllables which are better unstressed.

XI. The triplet sign:— ⌐—3—¬ governs:
(i) a complete bar of the chant or
(ii) either half of a bar.

(i) indicates the division of a complete bar into three equal portions, thus: 𝅗𝅥 𝅗𝅥 𝅗𝅥 (3)

(ii) indicates the division of either half of a bar into three equal portions, thus: ♩ ♩ ♩ (3)

It will, however, be seen that in many instances the length of either note may be slightly modified as in good reading. The triplet is formed from two melodic notes by singing the first note twice.

XII. Verses printed in italics may be sung Unison or Full Unison.

XIII. Square brackets (other than as in VI above) call attention to modifications contained in the Prayer Book of 1928. Portions so enclosed may be omitted.

We desire to express our acknowledgement for much valuable help from the Rev. R. Johnstone, Mr. J. H. Arnold, Mr. H. G. Pocknall, and Mr. P. W. Whitlock.

H. G. L., E. S. R., C. H. S.

THE VERSICLES AND RESPONSES AT MORNING AND EVENING PRAYER

The SENTENCE, EXHORTATION, GENERAL CONFESSION, ABSOLUTION, and LORD'S PRAYER, including AMENS, should be said without note, in the natural voice. The following RESPONSES have been provided with accompaniments for manual only, but it is better to sing them without the organ ; the Priest is then left free to take his own note.

VERSICLES AND RESPONSES

The CREED should be said in the natural voice.

The LORD'S PRAYER should be said in the natural voice.

The second part of the PRAYERS should be said without note, in the natural voice, and the AMENS should be similarly said.

THE VERSICLES AND RESPONSES AT MORNING AND EVENING PRAYER.
(ALTERNATIVE USE)

The SENTENCE, EXHORTATION, GENERAL CONFESSION, ABSOLUTION, and LORD'S PRAYER, including AMENS, should be said without note, in the natural voice. It will be better to sing the following RESPONSES without the organ; the Minister is then left free to take his own note.

VERSICLES AND RESPONSES

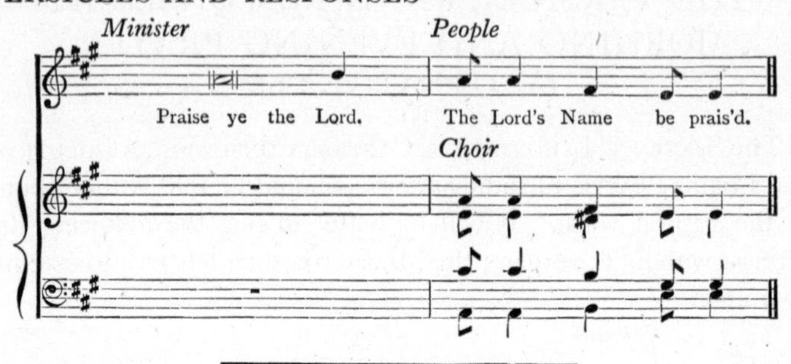

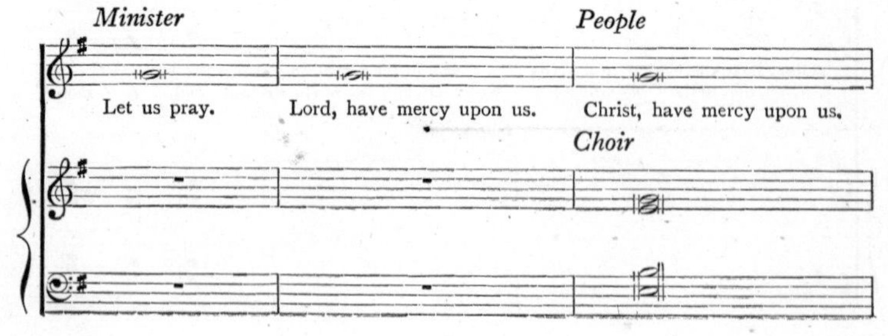

Minister
Minister and People
Lord, have mercy upon us. Our Father, Our Father, . . . But deliver us from evil. A - men.
Choir
Minister
People
O Lord, shew Thy mercy up - on us. And grant us Thy sal - va - tion.
Choir
Minister
People
O Lord, save the King. And mercifully hear us when we call up - on Thee.
Choir
Minister
People
Endue Thy ministers with right - eous - ness. And make Thy chosen people joy - ful.
Choir

VERSICLES AND RESPONSES

THE COLLECTS.

The second part of the PRAYERS should be said without note, in the natural voice, and the AMENS should be similarly said.

THE CANTICLES AND HYMNS

MORNING PRAYER

VENITE, EXULTEMUS DOMINO

PSALM 95

(*Single Chant*)

Full. 1 O come, let us | sing un-to the | Lord:
let us heartily rejoice in the | strength of | our sal- | vation.

Full. 2 Let us come before his | presence · with | thanksgiving:
and shew ourselves | glad in | him with | psalms.

3 For the Lord is a | great — | God:
and a great | King a-bove | all — | gods.

4 In his hand are áll the | corners · of the | earth:
and the | strength of · the | hills is · his | also.

5 The sea is | his and · he | made it:
and his | hands pre- | par'd the · dry | land.

Full. 6 O come, let us worship and | fall — | down:
and | kneel be-fore the | Lord our | Maker.

Full. 7 For he is the | Lord our | God:
and we are the people of his | pasture · and the | sheep of · his hand.
[1928: Gloria *may follow here*]

8 To-day if ye will hear his voice, | harden · not your | hearts:
as in the provocation, * and as in the day of temp- | ta-tion | in the | wilderness;

9 When your | fa-thers | tempted me:
prov'd | me and | saw my |works.

10 Forty years long was I grieved with this gene- | ration, · and | said:
It is a people that do err in their hearts, * for they | have not | known my | ways;

· Square brackets call attention to modifications contained in the Prayer Book of 1928. Portions so enclosed may be omitted.

11 Unto whom I | sware in · my | wrath:
that they should not | en-ter | into · my | rest.

Glory | be · to the | Father:
and to the Son, | and · to the | Ho-ly | Ghost;
As it was in the beginning, * is now, and | ever · shall | be:
world without | end, A- | — | men.

EASTER ANTHEMS

(*Single Chant*)

Full. 1 Christ our passover is | sacri-fic'd | for us:
therefore | let us | keep the | feast;

Full. 2 Not with the old leaven, * nor with the leaven of | malice · and | wickedness:
but with the unleaven'd | bread of · sin- | ceri-ty and | truth.

3 Christ being rais'd from the dead | dieth · no | more:
death hath no | more do- | min-ion | over him.

4 For in that he died, he died unto | sin — | once:
but in that he | liveth, · he | liveth · unto | God.

5 Likewise reckon ye also yourselves to be dead in- | deed · unto | sin:
but alive unto Gód through | Je-sus | Christ our | Lord.

Full. 6 Christ is | risen · from the | dead:
and become the | first-fruits · of | them that | slept.

7 For since by | man came | death:
by man came also the resur- | rec-tion | of the | dead.

8 For as in | Adam · all | die:
even so in Christ shall | all be | made a- | live.

Glory | be · to the | Father:
and to the Son, | and · to the | Ho-ly | Ghost;
As it was in the beginning, * is now, and | ever · shall | be:
world without | end, A- | — | men.

TE DEUM LAUDAMUS

Full. 1 WE práise | thee O | God:
we acknowledge | thee to | be the | Lord.

Full. [2] All the | earth doth | worship thee
the | Fa-ther | ev-er- | lasting.

3 To thee all Angels | cry a- | loud:
the heav'ns and | all the | powers · there- | in.

[4] To thee, | Cherubin · and | Seraphin
con- | tin-ual- | ly do | cry,

Full. 5 Holy, | Ho-ly, | Holy:
Lord | God of · Sa- | ba — | oth;

Full. [6] Heaven and | earth are | full
of the | Majes-ty | of thy | Glory.

[7] The | glo-rious | company
of the A- | pos-tles | praise — | thee.

[8] The | good-ly | fellowship
of the | Pro-phets | praise — | thee.

2nd part. [9] The | no-ble | army
of | Mar-tyrs | praise — | thee.

[10] The ho-ly | Church · throughout | all
the | world · doth ac- | know-ledge | thee;

11 The Father of an | infin-ite | Majesty:
thine honourable, | true and | on-ly | Son;

last phrase. 12 also the | Ho-ly | Ghost, the | Comforter.

13 THOU art the King of | Glory · O | Christ:
thóu art the ever- | last-ing | Son of · the | Father.

14 When thou tookest upon thee to de- | liv-er | man:
thou dídst not ab- | hor the | Vir-gin's | womb.

2nd part. 15 When thou hadst overcome the | sharpness · of | death:
thou didst open the kingdom of | heav'n to | all be- | lievers.

[16] Thou síttest at the | right · hand of | God
in the | Glo-ry | of the | Father.

[17] We be- | lieve that | thou
shalt | come to | be our | Judge.
18 We therefore pray thee, | help thy | servants :
whom thou hast re- | deem'd with · thy | pre-cious | blood.

Full. [19] Máke them to be | number'd · with thy | saints
in | glory | ev-er- | lasting.

(*Single Chant; or as Versicle and Response—see p.* 16)

20 O LORD save thy people, and | bless thine | heritage:
góvern them and | lift them | up for | ever.
21 Day by | day we | magnify thee :
and we worship thy | Name · ever | world with-out | end.
22 Vouchsafe O Lord to keep us this | day with-out | sin :
O Lord have mercy up- | on us, · have | mercy · up- | on us.
23 O Lord let thy mercy | lighten · up- | on us :
as our | trust — | is in | thee.

Full. 24 O Lord in | thee have · I | trusted :
let me | nev-er | be con- | founded.

TE DEUM LAUDAMUS

(*Alternative pointing*)

Full. 1 WE práise | thee O | God:
we acknowledge | thee to | be the | Lord.

Full. [2] All the | earth doth | worship thee
the | Fa-ther | ev-er | lasting.

3 To thee all Angels | cry a- | loud:
the heav'ns and | all the | powers · there- | in.

[4] To thee, | Cherubin · and | Seraphin
con- | tin-ual- | ly do | cry,

Full. 5 Holy, | Ho-ly, | Holy :
Lord | God of · Sa- | ba — | oth;

Full. [6] Heaven and | earth are | full
of the | Majes-ty | of thy | Glory.

7 The glorious company of the A- | pos-tles | praise thee :
the goodly | fellowship · of the | Pro-phets | praise thee.

8 The noble army of | Mar-tyrs | praise thee :
the holy Church throughout | all the | world · doth ac- | knowledge thee ;

2nd part. 9 The Father of an | infin-ite | Majesty :
thine honourable, true and only Son, * also the | Ho-ly | Ghost, the | Comforter.

10 THOU art the King of | Glory · O | Christ :
thóu art the ever- | last-ing | Son of · the | Father.

11 When thou tookest upon thee to de- | liv-er | man :
thou dídst not ab- | hor the | Vir-gin's | womb.

2nd part. 12 When thou hadst overcome the | sharpness · of | death :
thou didst open the kingdom of | heav'n to | all be- | lievers.

[13] Thou síttest at the | right · hand of | God
in the | Glo-ry | of the | Father.

[14] We be- | lieve that | thou
shalt | come to | be our | Judge.

15 We therefore pray thee, | help thy | servants :
whom thou hast re- | deem'd with · thy | pre-cious | blood.

Full. [16] Make them to be | number'd · with thy | saints
in | glo-ry | ev-er- | lasting.

(*Single Chant; or as Versicle and Response—**see p.* 16)

17 O LORD save thy people, and | bless thine | heritage :
góvern them and | lift them | up for | ever.

18 Day by | day we | magnify thee :
and we worship thy | Name · ever | world with-out | end.

19 Vouchsafe O Lord to keep us this | day with-out | sin :
O Lord have mercy up- | on us, · have | mercy · up- | on us.

20 O Lord let thy mercy | lighten · up- | on us :
as our | trust — | is in | thee.

Full. 21 O Lord in | thee have · I | trusted :
let me | nev-er | be con- | founded.

RESPONSORIAL TREATMENT OF
CONCLUDING VERSES OF

TE DEUM

(see pp. 14, 15)

BENEDICITE, OMNIA OPERA

Full. 1 O ALL ye works of the Lord, | bless · ye the | Lord:
práise him and | magni-fy | him for | ever.

Full. 2 O ye Angels of the Lord, | bless · ye the | Lord:
práise him and | magni-fy | him for | ever.

2nd part. 3 O ye Heav'ns,
4 O ye Waters that be above the Firmament,
5 O all ye Powers of the Lord,
6 O ye Sun and Moon,
7 O ye Stars of Heav'n,
8 O ye Showers and Dew,
9 O ye Winds of God,
10 O ye Fire and Heat,
11 O ye Winter and Summer,
12 O ye Dews and Frosts,
13 O ye Frost and Cold,
14 O ye Ice and Snow,
15 O ye Nights and Days,
16 O ye Light and Darkness,
17 O ye Lightnings and Clouds,

18 O LET the Earth | bless the | Lord:
yea let it práise him and | magni-fy | him for | ever.
19 O ye Mountains and Hills, | bless · ye the | Lord:
práise him and | magni-fy | him for | ever.
20 O all ye Green Things upon the Earth,
21 O ye Wells,
22 O ye Seas and Floods,
23 O ye Whales and all that move in the Waters,
24 O all ye Fowls of the Air,
25 O all ye Beasts and Cattle,
26 O ye Children of Men, | bless · ye the | Lord:
práise him and | magni-fy | him for | ever.

27 O LET Israel | bless the | Lord :
28 O ye Priests of the Lord, | bless · ye the | Lord :
29 O ye Servants of the Lord,
30 O ye Spirits and Souls of the Righteous,
31 O ye holy and humble Men of heart,
2nd part. 32 O Ananias, Azarias and Misael,

Glory | be · to the | Father :
and to the Son, | and · to the | Ho-ly | Ghost ;
As it was in the beginning, * is now, and | ever · shall | be :
world without | end, A- | — | men.

MISERERE MEI, DEUS

PSALM 51 (*see* p. 90)

(*omit verse 19*)

BENEDICTUS

Full. 1 Blessed be the | Lord · God of | Israel:
for he hath visited | and re- | deem'd his | people ;
Full. 2 And hath rais'd up a mighty sal- | va-tion | for us :
in the | house of · his | ser-vant | David ;
3 As he spake by the mouth of his | ho-ly | Prophets :
which have | been · since the | world be- | gan ;
4 That we should be | sav'd from · our | enemies :
and from the | hands of | all that | hate us ;
5 To perform the mercy | promis'd · to our | forefathers :
and to re- | member · his | ho-ly | Covenant ;
[6] To per- | form the | oath
which he | sware · to our | fore-fa-ther | Abraham ;
7 That he would give us, that we being deliver'd out of the | hand of · our | enemies :
might | serve — | him with-out | fear ;
8 In holiness and | righteousness · be | fore him :
all the | days — | of our | life.

Full. 9 And thou child shalt be call'd the | Prophet of · the | Highest:
for thou shalt go before the face of the | Lord · to pre- |
pare his | ways ;

Full. 10 To give knowledge of salvation | unto · his | people :
for the re- | mis-sion | of their | sins ;

11 Through the tender | mercy of · our | God :
whereby the | dayspring · from on | high hath | visited us ;

12 To give light to them that sit in darkness, * and in the |
shadow · of | death :
and to guide our | feet in-to the | way of | peace.

Glory | be · to the | Father :
and to the Son, | and · to the | Ho-ly | Ghost ;
As it was in the beginning,* is now, and | ever · shall | be :
world without | end, A- | — | men.

JUBILATE

Psalm 100

Full. 1 O be joyful in the Lord, | all ye | lands :
serve the Lord with gladness, * and cóme before his | presence | with a | song.

Full. 2 Be ye sure that the | Lord · he is | God :
it is he that hath made us and not we ourselves, * we are
his | people · and the | sheep of · his | pasture.

3 O go your way into his gates with thánksgiving, * and into
his | courts with | praise :
be thankful unto | him and · speak | good of · his | Name.

4 For the Lord is gracious, * his mércy is | ev-er- | lasting :
and his truth endúreth from gene- | ration · to | ge-ne- | ration.

Glory | be · to the | Father :
and to the Son, | and · to the | Ho-ly | Ghost ;
As it was in the beginning,* is now, and | ever · shall | be :
world without | end, A- | — | men.

ATHANASIAN CREED

QUICUNQUE VULT

Tone viii. 1.

To be sung in a free speaking-rhythm, and in unison.

N.B. The first two notes are only to be used in precenting the first verse. The notes in brackets are only to be used when necessary. Two dots over a syllable indicate the use of two notes there.

Minister. 1 Who-so- | ever will be | sav-ed :
(*unaccomp.*)
Full. before all things it is necessary that he hold the | Cath-o-lick Faith.

Boys. 2 Which Faith except every one do keep whole and unde- | fil-ed :
without doubt he shall perish | ev-er-last-ịng-ly.

Men. 3 And the Catholick Faith is | this :
that we worship one God in Trinity, and Trini- | tỵ in U-nị-ty;

Boys. 4 Neither confounding the | Per-sons :
nor divíd- | ịng the Sub-stance.

Men. 5 For there is one Person of the Father, another of the | Son :
and another | ọf the Ho-lỵ Ghost.

Boys. 6 But the Godhead of the Father, of the Son, and of the Holy Ghost is all | one :
the Glory equal, the Majesty | co-e-ter-nal.

Men. 7 Such as the Father is, such is the | Son :
and súch | ịs the Ho-lỵ Ghost.

Boys. 8 The Father uncreate, the Son uncre- | ate :
and the Hó- | lỵ Ghost un-crẹ-ate.

Men. 9 The Father incomprehensible, the Son incompre- | hen-sị-ble :
and the Holy Ghost in- | com-pre-hen-sị-ble.

Boys. 10 The Father eternal, the Son e- | ter-nal :
and the Holy | Ghost e-ter-nal.

Men. 11 And yet they are not three e- | ter-nals :
bụt | one e-ter-nal.

Boys. 12 As also there are not three incomprehensibles, * nor three uncre- | a-ted :
but one uncreated, and one in- | com-pre-hen-sị-ble.

Men. 13 So likewise the Father is Almighty, the Son Al- | migh-ty :
and the Holy | Ghost Al-migh-ty.

Boys. 14 And yet they are not three Al- | migh-ties :
bụt | one Al-migh-ty.

Men. 15 So the Father is God, the Son is | God :
and the | Ho-ly Ghost ịs God.

Boys. 16 And yet they are not three | Gods : §
— | — bụt one God.

Men. 17 So likewise the Father is Lord, the Son | Lord : ạnd thẹ | Ho-ly Ghost Lord.

Boys. 18 Ạnd yet not three | Lords: §
— | — bụt one Lord.

§ *Two notes to be omitted here:*

Men. 19 For like as we are compell'd by the Christian | ver-ị-ty :
to acknowledge every Person by himsélf | tọ bẹ God ạnd Lord ;

Boys. 20 So are we forbidden by the Catholick rẹ- | li-gion :
to say, There be three | Gods, or three Lords.

Men. 21 The Father is made of | none :
neither created, | nor bẹ-got-ten.

Boys. 22 The Son is of the Father ạ- | lone :
not made, nor created, | bụt bẹ-got-ten.

Men. 23 The Holy Ghost is of the Father ạnd ọf thẹ | Son :
neither made, nor created, nor begotten, | bụt pro-ceed-ing.

Boys. 24 So there is one Father, not three Fathers, * one Son, not three | Sons :
one Holy Ghost, | not three Ho-lỵ Ghosts.

Men. 25 And in this Trinity none is afore, or after | oth-er :
none is greater or léss | than ạn-oth-er.

Boys. 26 But the whole three Persons are co-eternal tọ- | geth-er :
— | and co-e-qual.

Men. 27 So that in all things, as is a- | fore-said :
the Unity in Trinity, and the Trinity in Unity is | tọ bẹ wor-ship-ped.

Boys. 28 He therefore that will be | sav-ed :
must thus thínk | ọf thẹ Trin-ị-ty.

Men. 29 Furthermore, it is necessary to everlasting sal- | va-tion :
that he also believe rightly the Incarnation of our | Lörd Je-sụs Christ.

Boys. 30 For the right Faith is, that we believe and con- | fess :
that our Lord Jesus Christ, the Son of | God, is God ạnd Man ;

Men. 31 God, of the Substance of the Father, begotten before the | worlds :
and Man, of the Substance of his Móth- | ẹr, born in thẹ world ;

Boys. 32 Perfect God, and perfect | Man :
of a reasonable soul and human | flesh sub-sist-ing ;

Men. 33 Equal to the Father, as touching his | God-head :
and inferior to the Father, as tóuch- | ịng his man-hood.

Boys. 34 Who although he be God ạnd | Man :
yet he is not | two, bụt one Christ ;

Men. 35 One, * not by conversion of the Godhead into | flesh :
but by taking of the | Man-hood in-tọ God ;

Boys. 36 One altogether, * not by confusion of | Sub-stance :
but by uni- | ty of Per-son.

Men. 37 For as the reasonable soul and flesh is one | man :
so God and | Man is one Christ ;

Boys. 38 Who suffer'd for our sal- | va-tion :
descended into hell,* rose again the | third day from the dead.

Men. 39 He ascended into heaven,* he sitteth on the right hand of the Father, God Al- | migh-ty :
from whence he shall come to judge the | quick and the dead.

Boys. 40 At whose coming all men shall rise again with their | bo-dies :
and shall give accóunt | for their own works.

Men. 41 And they that have done good shall go into life ever- | last-ing :
and they that have done evil into | ev-er-last-ing fire.

Boys. 42 This is the Catholick | Faith :
which except a man believe faithfully, he cán- | not be sav-ed.

Men (or Full). Glory be to the | Fa-ther :
and to the Son, and | to the Ho-ly Ghost.

Full. As it was in the beginning,* is now, and ever shall | be :
world with- | out end, A-men.

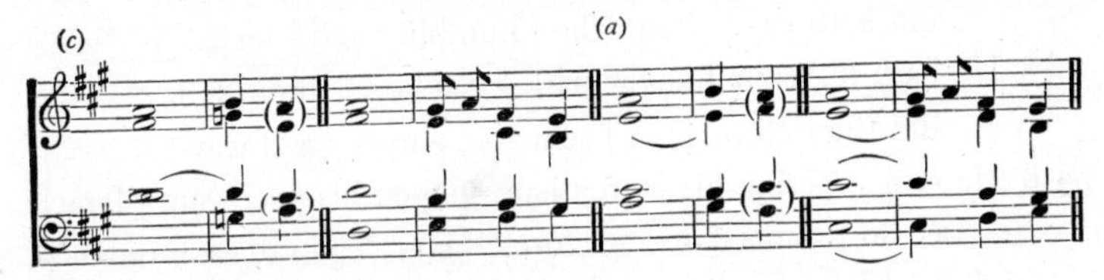

This Creed may be sung without accompaniment.

A revised translation as given in the Book of 1928 is given at p. 271.

The music of THE LITANY is given at p. 276.

EVENING PRAYER

MAGNIFICAT

Full. 1 My sóul doth | magni-fy the | Lord :
and my spírit hath re- | joic'd in | God my | Saviour.

Full. 2 For | he hath · re- | garded :
the | lowli-ness | of his | hand-maiden.

3 For be- | hold from | henceforth :
áll gene- | rations · shall | call me | blessed.

4 For he that is | mighty · hath | magnifi'd me :
and | ho-ly | is his | Name.

2nd part. 5 And his mércy is on | them that | fear him :
throughout | all — | ge-ne- | rations.

6 He hath shew'd | strength · with his | arm :
he hath scatter'd the próud in the imagi- | na-tion | of their | hearts.

7 He hath put down the | mighty · from their | seat :
and hath ex- | alted · the | humble · and | meek.

8 He hath fill'd the hungry with | good — | things :
and the rich he hath | sent — | empty · a- | way.

9 He remembering his mercy hath holpen his | ser-vant | Israel :
as he promis'd to our forefathers, * Abraham | and his | seed for | ever.

Glory | be · to the | Father :
and to the Son, | and · to the | Ho-ly | Ghost ;
As it was in the beginning, * is now, and | ever · shall | be :
world without | end, A- | — | men.

CANTATE DOMINO

Psalm 98

Full. 1 O síng unto the | Lord a · new | song :
for | he hath · done | marvel-lous | things.

Full. 2 With his own right hand, and with his | ho-ly | arm :
hath he | gotten · him- | self the | victory.

3 The Lord de- | clar'd his · sal- | vation :
his righteousness hath he openly | shew'd · in the | sight of · the | heathen.

4 He hath remember'd his mercy and truth toward the | house of | Israel :
and all the ends of the world have séen the sal- | va-tion | of our | God.

5 Shew yourselves jóyful unto the Lord | all ye | lands :
sing, re- | joice and | give — | thanks.

6 Praise the | Lord up-on the | harp :
sing to the | harp · with a | psalm of | thanksgiving.

7 With trumpets | also · and | shawms :
O shew yourselves jóyful be- | fore the | Lord the | King.

8 Let the sea make a noise, * and áll that | there-in | is :
the round | world and | they that | dwell therein.

9 Let the floods clap their hands, * and let the hills be joyful togéther be- | fore the | Lord :
for he | cometh · to | judge the | earth.

[10] With ríghteousness | shall he | judge
the | world, · and the | people · with | equity.

Glory | be · to the | Father :
and to the Son, | and · to the | Ho-ly | Ghost ;
As it was in the beginning, * is now, and | ever · shall | be :
world without | end, A- | — | men.

NUNC DIMITTIS

(*Single Chant*)

1 Lord now lettest thou thy servant de- | part in | peace :
ac- | cord-ing | to thy | word.

2 For mine éyes have | seen thy · sal- | vation :
which thou hast pre- | par'd be-fore the | face of · all | people ;

3 To be a líght to | lighten · the | Gentiles :
and to be the | glory of · thy | peo-ple | Israel.

Glory | be · to the | Father :
and to the Son, | and · to the | Ho-ly | Ghost ;
As it was in the beginning, * is now, and | ever · shall | be :
world without | end, A- | — | men.

DEUS MISEREATUR

Psalm 67

1 God be mérciful unto | us, and | bless us :
and shew us the light of his countenance, | and be | merci-ful | unto us :

2 That thy wáy may be | known up-on | earth :
thy saving | health a- | mong all | nations.

Unis. 3 *Let the people* | *praise thee,* · *O* | *God :*
yea let | *all the* | *peo-ple* | *praise thee.*

4 O let the nátions re- | joice and · be | glad :
for thou shalt judge the folk righteously, * and | govern · the | nations up-on | earth.

Unis. 5 *Let the people* | *praise thee,* · *O* | *God :*
let | *all the* | *peo-ple* | *praise thee.*

6 Then shall the earth bring | forth her | increase :
and God, even our | own · God shall | give us · his | blessing.

2nd part. 7 God | — shall | bless us :
and áll the | ends of · the | world shall | fear him.

Glory | be · to the | Father :
and to the Son, | and · to the | Ho-ly | Ghost ;
As it was in the beginning, * is now, and | ever · shall | be :
world without | end, A- | — | men.

THE PSALMS

DAY 1. MORNING PRAYER

Psalm 1

1 Blessed is the man that hath not walked in the counsel of the ungodly, * nor stood in the | way of | sinners :
and hath not | sat in · the | seat of · the | scornful.

2 But his delight is in the | law of · the | Lord :
and in his law will he | exer-cise him- | self · day and | night.

3 And he shall be like a tree | planted · by the | water-side :
that will bring | forth his | fruit in · due | season.

4 His leaf also | shall not | wither :
and look, whatsoever he | do-eth | it shall | prosper.

5 As for the ungodly, it is not | so with | them :
but they are like the chaff, * which the wind scattereth a- | way · from the | face of · the | earth.

6 Therefore the ungodly shall not be able to | stand in · the | judgement :
neither the sinners in the congre- | ga-tion | of the | righteous.

2nd part. 7 But the Lord knoweth the | way of · the | righteous :
and the | way of the · un- | godly · shall | perish.

Psalm 2

(*Single or Triple Chant*)

Full. 1 Why do the heathen so furiously | rage to- | gether :
and why do the people im- | agine · a | vain — | thing ?

Full. 2 The kings of the earth stand up, * and the rulers take | counsel · to- | gether :
against the | Lord · and a- | gainst · his A- | nointed.

Full. 3 Let us break their | bonds a- | sunder :
and cást a- | way their | cords — | from us.

4 He that dwelleth in heav'n shall | laugh them · to | scorn :
the Lord shall | have them | in de- | rision.
5 Then shall he spéak unto them | in his | wrath :
and | vex them · in his | sore dis- | pleasure.
[6] Yét have I | set my | King
upon my | ho-ly | hill of | Sion.

7 I will preach the law, * whereof the Lord hath | said un-to | me :
Thou art my Son, this | day have | I be- | gotten thee.
8 Desire of me, * and I shall give thee the heathen for | thine in- | heritance :
and the útmost párts of the | earth for | thy pos- | session.
9 Thou shalt brúise them with a | rod of | iron :
and break them in | pieces · like a | pot-ter's | vessel.
10 Be wise now therefore | O ye | kings :
be learned, yé that are | judg-es | of the | earth.
11 Serve the | Lord in | fear :
and re- | joice un-to | him with | reverence.
12 Kiss the Son lest he be angry, * and so ye perish from the | right — | way :
if his wrath be kindl'd, yea but a little, * blessed are all they that | put their | trust in | him.

PSALM 3

1 Lord, hów are they in- | creas'd that | trouble me :
mány are | they that | rise a- | gainst me.
2 Many one there be that | say of · my | soul :
There ís no | help for · him | in his | God.
3 But thou O Lord art | my de- | fender :
thou art my worship, and the | lift-er | up of · my | head.

4 I did call upon the | Lord with · my | voice :
and he heard me | out of · his | ho-ly | hill.
5 I laid me | down and | slept :
and rose up a- | gain · for the | Lord sus- | tain'd me.
6 I will not be afraid for ten | thousands · of the | people :
that have set themselves a- | gainst me | round a- | bout.
Full. 7 Up Lord, and help me | O my | God :
for thou smitest all mine enemies upon the cheek-bone, *
thou hast | broken · the | teeth of · the un- | godly.
Full. 8 Salvation belongeth | unto · the | Lord :
and thy | blessing · is up- | on thy | people.

PSALM 4

1 Hear me when I call, O | God of · my | righteousness :
thou hast set me at liberty when I was in trouble, * have mercy upon me, and | hearken | unto · my | prayer.
2 O ye sons of men, * how lóng will ye blas- | pheme mine | honour :
and have such pleasure in | vanity, · and | seek · after | leasing ?
3 Know this also, * that the Lord hath chosen to himself the | man that · is | godly :
when I | call up-on the | Lord · he will | hear me.
4 Stand in | awe and | sin not :
commune with your own heart, * and in your | cham-ber, | and be | still.
2nd part. 5 Offer the | sacri-fice of | righteousness :
and | put your | trust · in the | Lord.
[6] There be | many · that | say
Whó will | shew us | an-y | good ?
[7] Lord, | lift thou | up
the | light of · thy | countenance · up- | on us.

8 Thou hast put | gladness · in my | heart :
since the time that their corn and | wine ạnd | oil in- | creas'd.

9 I will lay me down in peace, and | take my | rest :
for it is thou Lord ónly that | makest · me | dwell in | safety.

Psalm 5

1 Ponder my | words, O | Lord :
cọn- | sider · my | mẹ-dị- | tation.

2 O hearken thou unto the voice of my calling, my | King and · my | God :
fọr ụntọ | thee · will I | make my | prayer.

3 My voice shalt thou hear be- | times O | Lord :
early in the morning will I direct my prayer unto | thee · and will | look — | up.

4 For thou art the Gód that hast no | pleasure · in | wickedness :
néither shall any | ev-il | dwell with | thee.

5 Such as be fóolish shall not | stand in · thy | sight :
fọr thọu | hatest · all | them that · work | vanity.

6 Thou shalt destroy | them that · speak | leasing :
the Lord will abhor both the blóodthirsty | ạnd dẹ- | ceit-ful | man.

2nd part. 7 But as for me, I will come into thine house, * even upon the múltitude | ọf thy | mercy :
and in thy fear will I worship | toward thy | ho-ly | temple.

8 Lead me O Lord in thy righteousness, * bẹ- | cause of · mine | enemies :
make thy way | plain bẹ- | fọre my | face.

9 For there is no faithfulness | ịn hịs | mouth :
their inward | parts are | vẹ-ry | wickedness.

10 Their throat is an | o-pen | sepulchre :
thẹy | flat-tẹr | wịth thẹir | tongue.

11 Destroy thou them O God, * let them perish through their | own im-agi- | nations :
cast them out in the multitude of their ungodliness, | for they · have re- | bell'd ạ- | gainst thee.

12 And let all them that put their trust in | thee rẹ- | joice :
they shall ever be giving of thanks because thou defendest them, * they that love thy | Name · shall be | joyful · in | thee ;

13 For thou Lord wilt give thy blessing | unto · the | righteous :
and with thy favourable kíndness wilt thou de- | fend him | as · with a | shield.

DAY I. EVENING PRAYER

PSALM 6

(*Single Chant*)

1 O Lord rebúke me not in thine | in-dig- | nation :
neither | chasten · me in | thy dis- | pleasure.

2 Have mercy upon me O Lord for | I am | weak :
O Lord | heal me · for my | bones are | vex'd.

3 My soul álso is | sore — | troubl'd :
bụt | Lord how | long wilt · thou | punish me ?

4 Turn thee O Lórd and de- | liver · my | soul :
Ọ | save me · for thy | mer-cy's | sake.

5 For in death | no man · re- | membereth thee :
and who will | give thee | thanks · in the | pit ?

6 I am weary of my groaning, * every night | wash I · my | bed :
ạnd | water · my | couch with · my | tears.

7 My beauty is gone for | vẹ-rỵ | trouble :
and worn away be- | cause ọf | all mine | enemies.

Full. 8 Away from me all | ye that · work | vanity :
for the Lord hath | heard thẹ | voice of · my | weeping.

9 The Lord hath | heard · my pe- | tition :
the | Lord · will re- | ceive my | prayer.

10 All mine enemies shall be confounded and | sore — | vex'd :
they shall be turned báck and | put to | shame — | suddenly.

Psalm 7

1 O Lord my God, in thee have I | put my | trust :
save me from all them that | perse-cute me | and de- | liver me ;

2 Lest he devour my soul like a lion and | tear it · in | pieces :
while | there is | none to | help.

3 O Lord my God, if I have done | any · such | thing :
or if there bé any | wicked-ness | in my | hands ;

4 If I have rewarded evil unto | him that · dealt | friendly with me :
yea I have deliver'd hím that with- | out · any | cause is · mine | enemy ;

2nd part. 5 Then let mine enemy persecute my | soul and | take me :
yea let him tread my life down upon the earth, * and lay mine | hon-our | in the | dust.

Full. 6 Stand up O Lord in thy wrath and lift up thyself, * because of the indig- | nation of · mine | enemies :
arise up fór me in the | judgement · that | thou · hast com- | manded.

Full. 7 And so shall the congregation of the people | come a- | bout thee :
for their sakes therefore lift | up thy- | self a- | gain.

8 The Lord shall judge the people, * give sentence with | me O | Lord :
according to my righteousness, * and accórding to the | inno-cency | that is | in me.

9 O let the wickedness of the ungodly | come · to an | end :
but | guide — | thou the | just.

2nd part. [10] For thẹ | right-eous | God
tríeth the | vẹ-ry | hearts ạnd | reins.

11 My help | cometh · of | God :
who preserveth | them that · are | true ọf | heart.
12 God is a righteous Judge, | strong ạnd | patient :
ạnd | God · is pro- | vok'd · every | day.
13 If a man will not turn he will | whet his | sword :
he hath bent his | bow ạnd | made it | ready.
14 He hath prepár'd for him the | instruments · of | death :
he ordaineth his | arrows · a- | gainst thẹ | persecutors.
15 Behold he | travaileth · with | mischief :
he hath conceiv'd | sorrow · and | brought · forth un- | godliness.
16 He hath graven and | digged · up a | pit :
and is fallen himsélf into the de- | struction · that he | made fọr | other.
17 For his travail shall cóme upon his | own — | head :
and his wickedness shall | fall on · his | own — | pate.
Full. 18 I will give thanks unto the Lord ac- | cording · to his | right- eousness :
and I will práise the | Name of · the | Lord most | High.

PSALM 8

Unis. 1 *O Lord our Governor, * how excellent is thy Name in | all thẹ | world:*
thou that hast set thy | glory · a- | bove thẹ | heav'ns !
Full. 2 Out of the mouth of very babes and sucklings hast thou or- dain'd strength, * be- | cause of · thine | enemies :
that thou mightest still thẹ | ene-my | and · the a- | venger.
3 For I will consider thy heav'ns, * even the | works of · thy | fingers :
the moon and the | stars which | thou hast · or- | dain'd.

4 What is man, that | thou art | mindful of him :
and the | son of | man that · thou | visitest him ?
5 Thou madest him | lower · than the | angels :
to | crown him · with | glory · and | worship.
6 Thou makest him to have domínion of the | works of · thy | hands :
and thou hast put áll things in sub- | jec-tion | under · his | feet;
7 All | sheep and | oxen :
yea | and the | beasts of · the | field ;
8 The fowls of the air and the | fishes · of the | sea :
and whatsoever | walketh · through the | paths of · the | seas.

2nd part. Unis. 9 *O | Lord our | Governor :*
how éxcellent is thy | Name in | all the | world !

DAY 2. MORNING PRAYER

PSALM 9

Full. 1 I will give thanks unto thee O Lórd with my | whole — | heart :
I will speak of | all thy | marvel-lous | works.

Full. 2 I will be glád and re- | joice in | thee :
yea my songs will I make of thy | Name O | thou most | Highest.

3 While mine enemies are | driv-en | back :
they shall fall and | per-ish | at thy | presence.
4 For thou hast maintain'd my | right and · my | cause :
thou art set in the | throne that | judg-est | right.
5 Thou hast rebuk'd the heathen, and de- | stroy'd the · un- | godly :
thou hast put óut their | name for | ever · and | ever.
6 O thou enemy, * destructions are come to a per- | pet-ual | end :
even as the cities which thou hast destroy'd, * their me- | morial · is | per-ish'd | with them.
7 But the Lórd shall en- | dure for | ever :
he hath also pre- | par'd his | seat for | judgement.

8 For he shall judge the | world in | righteousness :
and minister trúe | judge-ment | unto · the | people.
9 The Lord also will be a de- | fence · for the op- | press'd :
even a réfuge in | due — | time of | trouble.
10 And they that know thy Náme will put their | trust in | thee:
for thou Lórd hast never | fail-ed | them that | seek thee.
11 O praise the Lord which | dwelleth · in | Sion :
shew the | peo-ple | of his | doings.
12 For when he maketh inquisition for | blood · he re- | membereth them :
and forgetteth | not the · com- | plaint of · the | poor.
13 Have mercy upon me O Lord, * consider the trouble which I suffer of | them that | hate me :
thou that liftest me | up · from the | gates of | death.
14 That I may shew all thy praises within the ports of the | daughter · of | Sion :
I will re- | joice in | thy sal- | vation.
15 The heathen are sunk dówn in the | pit that · they | made :
in the same net which they hid prívily | is their | foot — | taken.
16 The Lord is known to | exe-cute | judgement :
the ungodly is trápped in the | work of · his | own — | hands.
17 The wicked shall be | turn'd · into | hell :
and all the | people · that for- | get — | God.
18 For the poor shall not | alway · be for- | gotten :
the patient abiding of the | meek · shall not | perish · for | ever.
Full. 19 Up Lord, and let not mán have the | up-per | hand :
let the | heathen · be | judg'd in · thy | sight.
Full. 20 Pút them in | fear O | Lord :
that the heathen may | know them-selves to | be but | men.

PSALM 10

1 Why standest thou so far | off O | Lord :
and hidest thy face in the | need-ful | time of | trouble?

2 The ungodly for his own lust doth | perse-cute the | poor :
let them be taken in the crafty | wiliness · that | they · have im- | agin'd.

3 For the ungodly hath made boast of his own | heart's de- | sire :
and speaketh good of the | covetous · whom | God ab- | horreth.

4 The ungodly is so proud, that he | careth · not for | God :
neither is | God in | all his | thoughts.

5 His ways are | al-way | grievous :
thy judgements are far above out of his sight, * and therefore de- | fieth · he | all his | enemies.

6 For he hath said in his heart, * Tush I shall | never be · cast | down :
there shall no | harm — | happen · unto | me.

7 His mouth is full of cursing, de- | ceit and | fraud :
under his | tongue is · un- | godliness · and | vanity.

8 He sitteth lurking in the thievish | corners · of the | streets :
and privily in his lurking dens doth he murder the innocent, * his | eyes are | set a-gainst the | poor.

9 For he lieth waiting secretly, * even as a lion lurketh he | in his | den :
that | he may | ravish · the | poor.

10 He doth | ravish · the | poor :
when he | getteth · him | into · his | net.

11 He falleth down and | humbleth · him- | self :
that the congregation of the poor may | fall in-to the | hands of · his | captains.

12 He hath said in his heart, * Tush | God hath · for- | gotten :
he hideth away his | face and · he will | nev-er | see it.

13 Arise O Lord God, and lift | up thine | hand :
for- | get — | not the | poor.

14 Wherefore should the wicked blas- | pheme — | God :
while he doth say in his heart, * Tush | thou God | carest · not | for it.

15 Súrely | thou hast | seen it :
for thou beholdest un- | god-lị- | nẹss ạnd | wrong.

16 That thou mayest take the matter | into · thine | hand :
the poor committeth himself unto thee, * for thóu art the | help-er | ọf thẹ | friendless.

17 Break thou the power of the ùn- | godly · and ma- | licious :
take away his ungodliness, and | thou shalt | find — | none.

Full. 18 The Lord is King for | ever · and | ever :
and the heathen are | per-ish'd | out of · the | land.

19 Lord, thou hast heard the de- | sire of · the | poor :
thou preparest their heart, * and thine | ear — | hearkeneth · there- | to ;

20 To help the fatherless and | poor un-to their | right :
that the man of the earth be no | more ex- | alted · a- | gainst them.

PSALM 11

(*Single Chant*)

1 In the Lórd put | I my | trust :
how say ye then to my soul, * that she should | flee · as a | bird un-to the | hill ?

2 For lo the ungodly bend their bow, * and make ready their arrows with- | in thẹ | quiver :
that they may privily shoot at | them which · are | true ọf | heart.

3 For the foundátions will be | cast — | down :
ạnd | what · hath the | right-eous | done ?

Full. 4 The Lórd is in his | ho-ly | temple :
thẹ | Lord's — | seat is · in | heaven.

5 His eyes con- | sider · the | poor :
and his eyelids | try thẹ | children · of | men.

6 The Lord al- | loweth · the | righteous :
but the ungodly and him that delighteth in wickedness | doth his | soul ạb- | hor.

7 Upon the ungodly he shall rain snares, * fire and brimstone | storm and | tempest :
this shall | be their | portion · to | drink.

8 For the righteous Lord | lov-eth | righteousness :
his countenance will be- | hold the | thing that · is | just.

DAY 2. EVENING PRAYER

PSALM 12

1 Help me Lord, * for there is not one | godly · man | left :
for the faithful are mínish'd from a- | mong the | children · of | men.

2 They talk of vanity évery one | with his | neighbour :
they do but flatter with their lips, * and dis- | semble · in their | dou-ble | heart.

3 The Lord shall root out all de- | ceit-ful | lips :
and the | tongue that | speak-eth | proud things ;

4 Which have said, With our | tongue will · we pre- | vail :
we are they that ought to speak, | who is | lord · over | us ?

5 Now for the comfortless tróubles' | sake of · the | needy :
and because of the deep | sigh-ing | of the | poor.

6 I will up, | saith the | Lord :
and will help every one from him that swelleth against him, | and will | set him · at | rest.

7 The words of the | Lord are | pure words :
even as the silver, which from the earth is tried, * and puri-fi'd | seven · times | in the | fire.

8 Thóu shalt | keep them · O | Lord :
thou shalt presérve him from | this · gene- | ration · for | ever.

2nd part. 9 The ungodly walk on | eve-ry | side :
when they are exalted, * the children of | men are | put to · re- | buke.

PSALM 13

1 How long wilt thou forgét me O | Lord, * for | ever :
how lóng wilt thou | hide thy | face — | from me ?

2 How long shall I seek counsel in my soul, * and be so | vex'd in · my | heart :
how lóng shall mine | ene-mies | tri-umph | over me ?

3 Consider and hear me O | Lord my | God :
lighten mine | eyes that · I | sleep not · in | death.

4 Lest mine enemy say, * I have pre- | vail'd a- | gainst him :
for if I be cast down, * they that | trouble · me | will re- | joice at it.

Full. 5 But my trust is | in thy | mercy :
and my heart is | joyful · in | thy sal- | vation.

Full. 6 I will sing of the Lord, * because he hath dealt so | loving-ly | with me :
yea I will praise the | Name of · the | Lord most | Highest.

PSALM 14

[1] The | fool hath | said in
his | heart, * There | is no | God.

2 They are corrupt, * and become abóminable | in their | doings :
there is nóne that doeth | good — | no not | one.

3 The Lord look'd down from héav'n upon the | children · of | men :
to see if there were ány that would under- | stand, and | seek · after | God.

4 But they are all gone out of the way, * they are altogether be- | come a- | bominable :
there is nóne that doeth | good — | no not | one.

5 Their throat is an open sepulchre, * with their | tongues have · they de- | ceiv'd :
the poison of | asps is | under · their | lips.

6 Their mouth is full of | cursing · and | bitterness :
their | feet are | swift to · shed | blood.

7 Destruction and unhappiness is in their ways, * and the way of péace have | they not | known :
there is no fear of | God be- | fore their | eyes.

8 Have they no knowledge, * that they are all such | workers · of | mischief :
eating up my people as it were bread, * and | call · not up- | on the | Lord ?

9 Thére were they brought in great fear, * éven where | no fear | was :
for God is in the gene- | ra-tion | of the | righteous.

10 As for you, * ye have made a mock at the | counsel of · the | poor :
because he | putteth · his | trust in · the | Lord.

2nd part. 11 Who shall give salvation unto Israel out of Sion ? * When the Lord turneth the captivity | of his | people :
then shall Jacob rejoice, * and | Is-rael | shall be | glad.

DAY 3. MORNING PRAYER

PSALM 15

(*Single Chant*)

1 Lord, whó shall | dwell in · thy | tabernacle :
or who shall | rest up-on thy | ho-ly | hill ?

2 Even he that leadeth an | uncor-rupt | life :
and doeth the thing which is right, * and | speaketh · the | truth · from his | heart.

3 He that hath us'd no deceit in his tongue, * nor done | evil · to his | neighbour :
and | hath not | slander'd · his | neighbour.

4 He that setteth not by himself, * but is lówly in his | own — | eyes :
and maketh much of | them that | fear the | Lord.

5 He that sweareth unto his neighbour, * and disap- | pointeth · him | not :
though it | were · to his | own — | hindrance.
6 He that hath not given his | money up-on | usury :
nor taken re- | ward a- | gainst the | innocent.
last phrase. 7 Whóso doeth these | things shall | nev-er | fall.

PSALM 16

1 Pre- | serve me · O | God :
for in | thee · have I | put my | trust.
2 O my soul, thou hast | said un-to the | Lord :
Thou art my God, my | goods are | nothing · unto | thee.
3 All my delight is upon the sáints that are | in the | earth :
and upon | such as · ex- | cel in | virtue.
4 But they that run after an- | oth-er | god :
shall | have — | great — | trouble.
5 Their drink-offerings of blood will | I not | offer :
neither make mention of their | names with- | in my | lips.
6 The Lord himself is the portion of mine inheritance, | and of · my | cup :
thou | shalt main- | tain my | lot.
7 The lot is fallen unto me in a | fair — | ground :
yea, I | have a | good-ly | heritage.
8 I will thank the Lord for | giving · me | warning :
my reins also | chasten · me | in the | night-season.
9 I have set God | always · be- | fore me :
for he is on my right hand, | therefore · I | shall not | fall.
10 Wherefore my heart was glád, and my | glory · re- | joic'd :
my flesh | also · shall | rest in | hope.
11 For why ? * thou shalt not leave my | soul in | hell :
neither shalt thou suffer thy | Holy · One to | see cor- | ruption.

12 Thou shalt shew me the path of life, * in thy présence is the | fulness · of | joy :
and at thy right hand there is | pleasure · for | ev-er- | more.

PSALM 17

1 Hear the right O Lord, * con- | sider · my com- | plaint :
and hearken unto my prayer, * that góeth not | out of | feign-ed | lips.

2 Let my sentence come | forth from · thy | presence :
and let thine eyes | look up-on the | thing that · is | equal.

3 Thou hast prov'd and visited mine heart in the night-season, * thou hast tri'd me, and shalt find no | wicked-ness | in me :
for I am utterly purpos'd that my | mouth shall | not of- | fend.

4 Because of men's works that are done against the | words of · thy | lips :
I have | kept me · from the | ways of · the de- | stroyer.

[5] O hold thou | up my | goings
in thy | paths, · that my | foot-steps | slip not.

6 I have call'd upon thee O God, for | thou shalt | hear me :
incline thine ear to me and | hark-en | unto · my | words.

7 Shew thy marvellous loving-kindness, * thou that art the Saviour of them which put their | trust in | thee :
from | such as · re- | sist thy · right | hand.

8 Keep me as the | apple · of an | eye :
hide me under the | sha-dow | of thy | wings,

9 From the un- | godly · that | trouble me :
mine enemies compass me round about to | take a- | way my | soul.

10 They are inclos'd in their | own — | fat :
and their | mouth — | speak-eth | proud things.

11 They lie waiting in our way on | eve-ry | side :
turning their | eyes — | down · to the | ground ;

12 Like as a lion that is | greedy · of his | prey :
and as it were a lion's whelp, | lurking · in | se-cret | places.
13 Up Lord, disappóint him and | cast him | down :
deliver my soul from the un- | god-ly | which is · a | sword of thine ;
14 From the men of thy hand O Lord, * from the men I say and from the | ev-il | world :
which have their portion in this life, * whose bellies thou | fillest · with thy | hid — | treasure.
15 They have children at | their dẹ- | sire :
and leave the rest of their | sub-stance | fọr thẹir | babes.
Full. 16 But as for me, * I will behold thy | presence · in | righteousness :
and when I awake up after thy likeness, | I shall · be | satis-fi'd | with it.

DAY 3. EVENING PRAYER

Psalm 18

Full 1 I will lóve thee O Lord my strength, * the Lord is my stony rock and | my dẹ- | fence :
my Saviour my God and my might in whom I will trust, * my buckler, * the hórn also of my sal- | va-tion | ạnd mỵ | refuge.
Full. 2 I will call upon the Lord, which is | worthy · to be | prais'd :
so shạll Ị bẹ | safe — | from mine | enemies.
3 The sorrows of | death — | compass'd me :
and the overflówings of un- | godli-ness | made · me a- | fraid.
4 The pains of | hell · came a- | bout me :
thẹ | snares of | death · over- | took me.
5 In my trouble I will | call up-on the | Lord ;
ạnd cọm- | plain ụn- | tọ mỵ | God.

6 So shall he hear my voice out of his | ho-ly | temple :
and my complaint shall come before him, * it shall enter | ev-en | into · his | ears.

7 The earth | trembl'd · and | quak'd :
the very foundations also of the hills shook, * and were re- | mov'd be- | cause · he was | wroth.

8 There went a smoke out | in his | presence :
and a consuming fire out of his mouth, * so that | coals were | kin-dl'd | at it.

9 He bow'd the heav'ns also, and | came — | down :
and it was | dark — | under · his | feet.

10 He rode upon the cherubims, | and did | fly :
he came flýing upon the | wings — | of the | wind.

11 He made darkness his | se-cret | place :
his pavilion round about him with dark water, and | thick — | clouds to | cover him.

12 At the brightness of his presence his | clouds re- | mov'd :
hail- | stones and | coals of | fire.

13 The Lord also thunder'd out of heaven, * and the Highest | gave his | thunder :
hail- | stones and | coals of | fire.

14 He sent out his | arrows · and | scatter'd them :
he cast forth | light-nings, | and de- | stroy'd them.

2nd part. 15 The springs of waters were seen, * and the foundations of the round world were discover'd, at thy | chiding · O | Lord :
at the blásting of the | breath of | thy dis- | pleasure.

16 He shall send down from on | high to | fetch me :
and shall take me | out of | ma-ny | waters.

17 He shall deliver me from my strongest enemy, * and from | them which | hate me :
for | they are · too | migh-ty | for me.

18 They prevénted me in the | day of · my | trouble :
but the | Lord was | my up- | holder.

19 He brought me forth also into a | place of | liberty :
he brought me forth, * even be- | cause he · had a | fa-vour | unto me.

20 The Lord shall reward me after my | right-eous | dealing :
according to the | cleanness · of my | hands · shall he | recompense me.

21 Because I have kept the | ways of · the | Lord :
and have not forsaken my | God · as the | wick-ed | doth.

22 For I have an éye unto | all his | laws :
and will not cast | out · his com- | mand-ments | from me.

23 I was also uncor- | rupt be- | fore him :
and es- | chewed · mine | own — | wickedness.

2nd part. 24 Therefore shall the Lord reward me after my | right-eous | dealing :
and according unto the | cleanness · of my | hands in · his | eyesight.

25 With the holy | thou shalt · be | holy :
and with a | perfect · man | thou shalt · be | perfect.

26 With the clean | thou shalt · be | clean :
and with the | fro-ward | thou shalt · learn | frowardness.

27 For thou shalt save the péople that are | in ad- | versity :
and shalt bring | down the | high looks · of the | proud.

28 Thou álso shalt | light my | candle :
the Lord my God shall make my | dark-ness | to be | light.

29 For in thee I shall discomfit an | host of | men :
and with the help of my God I shall | leap — | over · the | wall.

30 The way of God is an unde- | fil-ed | way :
the word of the Lord also is tri'd in the fire, * he is the defender of all them that | put their | trust in | him.

31 For whó is | God · but the | Lord :
or whó hath any | strength, ex- | cept our | God ?

32 It is God that gírdeth me with | strength of | war :
and | maketh · my | way — | perfect.

33 He máketh my | feet like | hart's feet :
and | setteth · me | up on | high.

34 He téacheth mine | hands to | fight :
and mine arms shall break | even · a | bow of | steel.

35 Thou hast given me the de- | fence of · thy sal- | vation :
thy right hand also shall hold me up, * and thy loving cor- |
rection · shall | make me | great.

36 Thou shalt make room enough únder me | for to | go :
that my | foot-steps | shall not | slide.

37 I will follow upon mine enemies and | o-ver- | take them :
neither will I | turn a-gain, | till I · have de- | stroy'd them.

38 I will smite them, * that they shåll not be | able · to | stand :
but | fall — | under · my | feet.

39 Thou hast girded me with | strength un-to the | battle :
thou shalt throw | down mine | ene-mies | under me.

40 Thou hast made mine enemies also to turn their | backs up- |
on me :
and I shall de- | stroy — | them that | hate me.

41 They shall cry, * but there shall be | none to | help them :
yea even unto the Lord shall they | cry · but he | shall not |
hear them.

42 I will beat them as small as the | dust be-fore the | wind :
I will cast them | out · as the | clay in · the | streets.

43 Thou shalt deliver me from the | strivings · of the | people :
and thou shalt | make · me the | head of · the | heathen.

[44] A | peo-ple | whom
I | have not | known shall | serve me.

45 As soon as they héar of me, | they · shall o- | bey me :
but the strange | children · shall dis- | sem-ble | with me.

46 The strange | children · shall | fail :
and be a- | fraid — | out of · their | prisons.

47 The Lord liveth, * and bléssed be my | strong — | helper :
and praised be the | God of | my sal- | vation.

48 Even the God that séeth that I | be a- | veng'd :
and sub- | dueth · the | peo-ple | unto me.

49 It is he that delivereth me from my cruel enemies, * and setteth me up a- | bove mine | adversaries :
thou shalt | rid me · from the | wick-ed | man.

50 For this cause will I give thanks unto thee O Lord a- | mong the | Gentiles :
and sing | prais-es | unto · thy | Name.

2nd part. 51 Great prosperity gíveth he | unto · his | King :
and sheweth loving-kindness unto David his Anointed, *
and unto his | seed for | ev-er- | more.

DAY 4. MORNING PRAYER

PSALM 19

Full. 1 The heav'ns declare the | glory · of | God :
and the | firma-ment | sheweth · his | handy-work.

Full. 2 One day | telleth · an- | other :
and one night | cer-ti- | fieth · an- | other.

3 There is neither | speech nor | language :
but their | voices · are | heard a- | mong them.

4 Their sound is gone óut into | all — | lands :
and their | words in-to the | ends of · the | world.

Full. 5 In them hath he set a tabernacle | for the | sun :
which cometh forth as a bridegroom out of his chamber, *
and rejóiceth as a | giant · to | run his | course.

Full. 6 It goeth forth from the uttermost part of the heaven, * and runneth about unto the | end of it · a- | gain :
and there is nothing | hid · from the | heat there- | of.

7 The law of the Lord is an undefil'd law, con- | verting · the | soul :
the testimony of the Lord is sure, * and giveth | wis-dom | unto · the | simple.

8 The statutes of the Lord are right, and re- | joice the | heart :
the commandment of the Lord is pure, * and giveth | light un- | to the | eyes.

9 The fear of the Lord is cléan, and en- | dureth · for | ever :
the judgements of the Lord are true, and | right-eous | al-to- | gether.

10 More to be desir'd are they than gold, * yéa than | much fine | gold :
sweeter also than | hon-ey, | and the | honey-comb.

11 Moreover by thém is thy | ser-vant | taught :
and in kéeping of them | there is | great re- | ward.

12 Who can tell how | oft · he of- | fendeth :
O cléanse thou | me from · my | se-cret | faults.

13 Keep thy servant also from presumptuous sins, * lest they get the do- | min-ion | over me :
so shall I be undefil'd, * and innocent | from the | great of- | fence.

14 Let the words of my mouth, * and the meditation of my heart, * be alway acceptable | in thy | sight :
O Lórd my | strength and | my re- | deemer.

PSALM 20

1 The Lord héar thee in the | day of | trouble :
the Náme of the | God of | Jacob · de- | fend thee ;

2 Send thee | help · from the | sanctuary :
and | strengthen · thee | out of | Sion ;

3 Remember | all thy | offerings :
and ac- | cept thy | burnt — | sacrifice ;

4 Gránt thee thy | heart's de- | sire :
and ful- | fil — | all thy | mind.

5 We will rejoice in thy salvation, * and triumph in the Náme of the | Lord our | God :
the Lord per- | form all | thy pe- | titions.

6 Now know I that the Lord helpeth his Anointed, * and will héar him from his | ho-ly | heav'n :
even with the wholesome | strength of · his | right — | hand.

7 Some put their trust in chariots, and | some in | horses :
but we will remember the | Name of · the | Lord our | God.

8 Théy are brought | down and | fallen :
but wé are | risen · and | stand — | upright.

[2n]d part. 9 Save Lord and hear us, O | King of | heav'n :
when we | call up- | on — | thee.

PSALM 21

Full. 1 The King shall rejoice in thy | strength O | Lord :
exceeding glád shall he | be of | thy sal- | vation.

Full. 2 Thou hast given him his | heart's de- | sire :
and hast not de- | ni'd him · the re- | quest of · his | lips.

3 For thou shalt prevént him with the | blessings · of | goodness :
and shalt set a crown of pure | gold up- | on his | head.

4 He asked life of thee, * and thou gávest him a | long — | life :
ev'n for | ev — | er and | ever.

5 His honour is great in | thy sal- | vation :
glory and great worship | shalt thou | lay up- | on him.

6 For thou shalt give him ever- | lasting · fe- | licity :
and make him | glad with · the | joy of · thy | countenance.

[2]nd part. 7 And why ? * because the King putteth his | trust in · the | Lord :
and in the mercy of the most | Highest · he | shall not · mis- | carry.

8 All thine enemies shall | feel thy | hand :
thy right hand shall | find out | them that | hate thee.

9 Thou shalt make them like a fiery oven in | time of · thy | wrath :
the Lord shall destroy them in his displeasure, * and the | fire — | shall con- | sume them.

10 Their fruit shalt thou root | out of · the | earth :
and their séed from a- | mong the | children · of | men.

11 For they intended | mischief · a- | gainst thee :
and imagin'd such a device as they áre not | a-ble | to per- | form.

12 Therefore shalt thou | put them · to | flight :
and the strings of thy bow shalt thou make | ready · a- | gainst the | face of them.

Full. 13 Be thou exalted Lórd in thine | own — | strength :
só will we | sing, and | praise thy | power.

DAY 4. EVENING PRAYER

PSALM 22

1 My God, my God look upon me, * why hast | thou for- | saken me :
and art so far from my health, * and from the | words of | my com- | plaint ?

2 O my God I cry in the daytime, | but thou | hearest not :
and in the night-season | also · I | take no | rest.

3 And thou con- | tin-uest | holy :
O | thou — | worship · of | Israel.

4 Our fathers | hoped · in | thee :
they trusted in | thee, and | thou · didst de- | liver them.

5 They call'd upon | thee and · were | holpen :
they put their trust in | thee and | were not · con- | founded.

6 But as for me, I am a | worm and · no | man :
a very scorn of men, and the | out-cast | of the | people.

7 All they that see me | laugh me · to | scorn :
they shoot out their líps and | shake their | heads — | saying,

Full. 8 He trusted in God that | he would · de- | liver him :
lét him de- | liver · him | if he · will | have him.

9 But thou art he that took me out of my | mo-ther's | womb :
thou wast my hope, * when I hánged | yet up-on my | mo-ther's | breasts.

10 I have been left unto thée ever | since · I was | born :
thou art my God | even · from my | mo-ther's | womb.

11 O go not from me, for trouble is | hard at | hand :
and | there is | none to | help me.

12 Many oxen are | come a- | bout me :
fat bulls of Basan close me | in on | eve-ry | side.

13 They gápe upon me | with their | mouths :
as it were a | ramping · and a | roar-ing | lion.

14 I am poured out like water, * and all my bones are | out of | joint :
my heart also in the midst of my body is | even · like | melt-ing | wax.

15 My strength is dried up like a potsherd, * and my tongue | cleaveth · to my | gums :
and thou shalt bring me | into · the | dust of | death.

16 For many dogs are | come a- | bout me :
and the council of the wicked | lay-eth | siege a- | gainst me.

17 They pierced my hands and my feet, * I may tell | all my | bones :
they stand | staring · and | looking · up- | on me.

18 They part my | garments · a- | mong them :
and cast | lots up- | on my | vesture.

2nd part. 19 But be not thou fár | from me · O | Lord :
thou art my | suc-cour | haste · thee to | help me.

20 Deliver my | soul · from the | sword :
my | darling · from the | power · of the | dog.

21 Sáve me from the | li-on's | mouth :
thou hast heard me also from a- | mong the | horns of · the | unicorns.

Full. 22 I will declare thy | Name un-to my | brethren :
in the midst of the congre- | ga-tion | will I | praise thee.

Full. 23 O praise the Lórd | ye that | fear him :
magnify him all ye of the seed of Jacob, * and féar him | all ye | seed of | Israel ;

24 For he hath not despis'd nor abhórr'd the low es- | tate of · the | poor :
he hath not hid his face from him, * but when he | call'd un-to | him he | heard him.

25 My praise is of thée in the | great · congre- | gation :
my vows will I perform in the | sight of | them that | fear him.

2nd part. 26 The poor shall | eat · and be | satisfi'd :
they that seek after the Lord shall praise him, * your | heart shall | live for | ever.

Full. 27 All the ends of the world shall remember themselves, * and be | turn'd un-to the | Lord :
and all the kíndreds of the | nations · shall | worship · be- | fore him.

Full. 28 For the | kingdom · is the | Lord's :
and he is the | Governor · a- | mong the | people.

29 All such as be | fat up-on | earth :
have | eat-en | and — | worshipp'd.

30 All they that go down into the dust shall | kneel be- | fore him :
and nó man hath | quicken'd · his | own — | soul.

31 My | seed shall | serve him :
they shall be cóunted unto the | Lord · for a | ge-ne- | ration.

32 They shall come, * and the héav'ns shall de- | clare his | righteousness :
unto a people that shall be | born · whom the | Lord hath | made.

PSALM 23

(*Single Chant*)

1 The Lord | is my | shepherd :
therefore | can I | lack — | nothing.

2 He shall féed me in a | green — | pasture :
and lead me forth be- | side the | waters · of | comfort.

3 Hé shall con- | vert my | soul :
and bring me forth in the paths of | righteous-ness | for his | Name's sake.

4 Yea though I walk through the valley of the shadow of death, * I will | fear no | evil :
for thóu art with me, * thy | rod and · thy | staff — | comfort me.

5 Thou shalt prepare a table before me, * against | them that | trouble me :
thou hast anointed my head with | oil · and my | cup shall · be | full.

Full. 6 But thy loving-kindness and mercy shall follow me, * áll the | days of · my | life :
and I will dwéll in the | house of · the | Lord for | ever.

DAY 5. MORNING PRAYER

PSALM 24

Full. 1 The earth is the Lord's, and all that | there-in | is :
the compass of the | world and | they that | dwell therein.

Full. 2 For he hath fóunded it up- | on the | seas :
and pre- | par'd · it up- | on the | floods.

3 Who shall ascénd into the | hill of · the | Lord :
or who shall rise | up in · his | holy | place ?

4 Even he that hath clean hands and a | pure — | heart :
and that hath not lift up his mind unto vanity, * nor | sworn · to de- | ceive his | neighbour.

5 He shall receive the | blessing · from the | Lord :
and ríghteousness from the | God of | his sal- | vation.

6 This is the generation of | them that | seek him :
even of them that | seek thy | face O | Jacob.

Unis. 7 *Lift up your heads O ye gates, * and be ye lift úp ye ever- | last-ing | doors :*
and the King of | glo-ry | shall come | in.

Boys. 8 *Whó is the | King of | glory :*
Men. Unis. *it is the Lord strong and mighty, * even the | Lord — | mighty · in | battle.*
Unis. 9 *Lift up your heads O ye gates, * and be ye lift úp ye ever- | last-ing | doors :*
and the King of | glo-ry | shall come | in.
Boys. 10 *Whó is the | King of | glory :*
Men. Unis. *even the Lord of hosts, | he · is the | King of | glory.*

PSALM 25

1 Unto thee O Lord will I lift up my soul, * my God I have put my | trust in | thee :
O lét me not be confounded, * neither let mine | ene-mies | tri-umph | over me.
2 For all they that hope in thee | shall not · be a- | sham'd :
but such as transgress without a | cause · shall be | put to · con- | fusion.
3 Shéw me thy | ways O | Lord :
and | teach — | me thy | paths.
4 Lead me forth in thy | truth and | learn me :
for thou art the God of my salvation, * in thee hath been my | hope — | all the · day | long.
5 Call to remembrance O Lord thy | ten-der | mercies :
and thy loving-kindnesses, which | have been | ever · of | old.
6 O remember not the sins and of- | fences of · my | youth :
but according to thy mercy think thou up- | on me · O | Lord for · thy | goodness.
7 Gracious and | righteous · is the | Lord :
therefore will he teach | sin-ners | in the | way.
8 Them that are méek shall he | guide in | judgement :
and such as are gentle, | them · shall he | learn his | way.
9 All the paths of the Lord are | mercy · and | truth :
unto such as keep his | cove-nant | and his | testimonies.

10 For thy | Name's sake · O | Lord :
be merciful unto my | sin for | it is | great.

11 What man is he that | feareth · the | Lord :
him shall he teach in the | way that | he shall | choose.

12 His sóul shall | dwell at | ease :
and his | seed · shall in- | herit · the | land.

13 The secret of the Lórd is among | them that | fear him :
and | he will | shew them · his | covenant.

14 Mine eyes are ever looking | unto · the | Lord :
for he shall pluck my | feet — | out of · the | net.

15 Turn thee unto me, and have | mercy · up- | on me :
for I am | deso-late, | and in | misery.

16 The sórrows of my | heart · are en- | larg'd :
O | bring thou · me | out of · my | troubles.

17 Look upon my ad- | versity · and | misery :
and for- | give me | all my | sin.

18 Consider mine enemies, how | many · they | are :
and they bear a | tyran-nous | hate a- | gainst me.

19 O keep my | soul and · de- | liver me :
let me not be confounded, * for I have | put my | trust in | thee.

20 Let perfectness and righteous dealing | wait up- | on me :
for my | hope hath | been in | thee.

2nd part. [21] De- | liv-er | Israel
O | God, · out of | all his | troubles.

PSALM 26

1 Be thou my judge O Lord, * for I have | walk-ed | innocently :
my trust hath been also in the Lord, | there-fore | shall I · not | fall.

2 Exámine me O | Lord and | prove me :
try | out my | reins and · my | heart.

2nd part. 3 For thy loving-kindness is ever be- | fore mine | eyes :
and | I will | walk in · thy | truth.

4 I have not | dwelt with · vain | persons :
neither will I have | fellow-ship | with the · de- | ceitful.

5 I have hated the congre- | gation · of the | wicked :
and will not | sit a- | mong the · un- | godly.

6 I will wash my hands in | innocency · O | Lord :
and | so will · I | go to · thine | altar ;

7 That I may shew the | voice of | thanksgiving :
and tell of | all thy | won-drous | works.

8 Lord, I have lov'd the habi- | tation of · thy | house :
and the | place where · thine | hon-our | dwelleth.

9 O shut not up my | soul · with the | sinners :
nor my | life — | with the | blood-thirsty ;

2nd part. 10 In whose | hands is | wickedness :
and their right | hand is | full of | gifts.

11 But as for me, | I will · walk | innocently :
O deliver me, | and be | merci-ful | unto me.

12 My foot | stand-eth | right :
I will práise the | Lord · in the | con-gre- | gations.

DAY 5. EVENING PRAYER

PSALM 27

Full. 1 The Lord is my light and my salvation, * whom then | shall I | fear :
the Lord is the strength of my life, * of whom then | shall I | be a- | fraid ?

Full. 2 When the wicked, even mine enemies and my foes, * came upon me to | eat up · my | flesh :
they | stum-bl'd | and — | fell.

3 Though an host of men were laid against me, * yet shåll not my | heart · be a- | fraid :
and though there rose up war against me, * yet will I | put my | trust in | him.

4 One thing have I desir'd of the Lórd which I | will re- | quire :
even that I may dwell in the house of the Lord all the days

of my life, * to behold the fair beauty of the | Lord · and to | visit · his | temple.

5 For in the time of trouble he shall | hide me · in his | tabernacle : yea in the secret place of his dwelling shall he hide me, * and set me | up up-on a | rock of | stone.

6 And now shall he lift | up mine | head : above mine | ene-mies | round a- | bout me.

2nd part. 7 Therefore will I offer in his dwelling an oblation with | great — | gladness : I will sing and speak | prais-es | unto · the | Lord.

8 Hearken unto my voice O Lord, when I | cry un-to | thee : have | mercy · up- | on me, and | hear me.

9 My heart hath talked of thee, | Seek ye · my | face : Thy | face Lord | will I | seek.

10 O hide not thou thy | face — | from me : nor cast thy | servant · a- | way in · dis- | pleasure.

11 Thóu hast | been my | succour : leave me not, neither forsáke me O | God of | my sal- | vation.

2nd part. 12 When my fáther and my | mother · for- | sake me : the | Lord — | taketh · me | up.

13 Téach me thy | way O | Lord : and lead me in the right | way be- | cause of · mine | enemies.

14 Deliver me not over into the | will of · mine | adversaries : for there are false witnesses rísen up a- | gainst me · and | such as · speak | wrong.

15 I should | utterly · have | fainted : but that I believe verily to see the goodness of the | Lord · in the | land of · the | living.

16 O tárry thou the | Lord's — | leisure : be strong, and he shall comfort thine heart, * and | put thou · thy | trust · in the | Lord.

PSALM 28

1 Unto thee will I cry O | Lord my | strength :
think no scorn of me, * lest if thou make as though thou hearest not, * I become like thém that go | down in- | to the | pit.

2 Hear the voice of my humble petitions, * when I | cry un-to | thee :
when I hold up my hands towards the mércy-seat | of thy | ho-ly | temple.

3 O pluck me not away, * neither destroy me with the ungodly and | wick-ed | doers :
which speak friendly to their neighbours, * but imagine | mis-chief | in their | hearts.

4 Reward them ac- | cording to · their | deeds :
and according to the wíckedness | of their | own in- | ventions.

5 Recompense them after the | work of · their | hands :
pay them | that they | have de- | serv'd.

6 For they regard not in their mind the works of the Lord, * nor the oper- | ation of · his | hands :
therefore shall he break them | down and · not | build them | up.

Full. 7 Praised | be the | Lord :
for he hath heard the | voice of · my | humble · pe- | titions.

Full. 8 The Lord is my strength and my shield, * my heart hath trusted in hím, and | I am | helped :
therefore my heart danceth for joy, * and in my | song — | will I | praise him.

9 The | Lórd is · my | strength :
and he is the wholesome de- | fence of | his A- | nointed.

10 O save thy people, * and give thy blessing unto | thine in- | heritance :
féed them and | set them | up for | ever.

PSALM 29

Full. 1 Bring unto the Lord O ye mighty, * bring young | rams un-to the | Lord :
ascribe unto the | Lord — | worship · and | strength.

Full. 2 Give the Lórd the honour | due un-to his | Name :
worship the | Lord with | ho-ly | worship.

3 It is the Lórd that com- | mandeth · the | waters :
it is the glorious | God that | maketh · the | thunder.

4 It is the Lord that ruleth the sea, * the voice of the Lord is mighty in | op-er- | ation :
the voice of the | Lord · is a | glo-rious | voice.

5 The voice of the Lord | breaketh · the | cedar-trees :
yea the Lord | breaketh · the | cedars · of | Libanus.

6 He maketh them also to | skip · like a | calf :
Libanus also and Sirion, | like a | young — | unicorn.

7 The voice of the Lord divideth the flames of fire, * the voice of the Lord | shaketh · the | wilderness :
yea the Lord | shaketh · the | wilderness · of | Cades.

8 The voice of the Lord maketh the hinds to bring forth young, * and discovereth the | thick — | bushes :
in his temple doth | every · man | speak of · his | honour.

9 The Lord sitteth a- | bove the | water-flood :
and the Lord re- | maineth · a | King for | ever.

10 The Lórd shall give | strength un-to his | people :
the Lórd shall give his | people · the | blessing · of | peace.

DAY 6. MORNING PRAYER

PSALM 30

Full. 1 I will magnify thee O Lord, for thou hast | set me | up :
and not made my | foes to | tri-umph | over me.

Full. [2] O | Lord my | God
I cri'd unto | thee, and | thou hast | heal'd me.

3 Thou Lord hast brought my | soul · out of | hell :
thou hast kept my life from | them that · go | down · to the | pit.

4 Sing praises unto the | Lord · O ye | saints of his :
and give thanks unto him for a re- | mem-brance | of his | holiness.

5 For his wrath endureth but the twinkling of an eye, * and in his | pleasure · is | life :
heaviness may endure for a night, * but | joy · cometh | in the | morning.

6 And in my prosperity I said, I shall | never · be re- | mov'd :
thou Lord of thy góodness hast | made my | hill so | strong.

[7] Thou didst | turn thy | face
— | from me, · and | I was | troubl'd.

8 Then crí'd I unto | thee O | Lord :
and | gat me · to my | Lord right | humbly.

9 What prófit is there | in my | blood :
when I go | down — | to the | pit ?

10 Shall the dúst give | thanks un- | to thee :
or | shall it · de- | clare thy | truth ?

2nd part. 11 Hear O Lórd and have | mercy · up- | on me :
Lord | — be | thou my | helper.

Full. 12 Thou hast turn'd my heaviness | in-to | joy :
thou hast put off my sackcloth, and | gird-ed | me with | gladness.

Full. 13 Therefore shall every good man sing of thy | praise with-out | ceasing :
O my God, I will give | thanks · unto | thee for | ever.

PSALM 31

Full. 1 In thee O Lórd have I | put my | trust :
let me never be put to confusion, * de- | liver · me | in thy | righteousness.

Full. 2 Bow | down thine | ear to me :
make | haste — | to de- | liver me.

3 And be thou my strong rock, and | house of · de- | fence :
that | thou — | may-est | save me.

4 For thou art my stróng | rock and · my | castle :
be thou also my guide, and | lead me | for thy | Name's sake.

5 Draw me out of the net that they have laid | privi-ly | for me :
for | thou — | art my | strength.

6 Into thy hands I com- | mend my | spirit :
for thou hast redeem'd me O | Lord thou | God of | truth.

7 I have hated them that hóld of super- | sti-tious | vanities :
and my | trust hath | been in · the | Lord.

8 I will be glad and re- | joice in · thy | mercy :
for thou hast consider'd my trouble, * and hast | known my | soul in · ad- | versities.

2nd part. 9 Thou hast not shut me úp into the | hand of · the | enemy :
but hast set my | feet · in a | large — | room.

10 Have mercy upon me O Lord, for | I am · in | trouble :
and mine eye is consúm'd for very heaviness, | yea my | soul and · my | body.

[11] For my life is waxen | old with | heavi-
ness, | and my | years with | mourning.

12 My strength fáileth me be- | cause of · mine in- | iquity :
and my | bones — | are con- | sum'd.

13 I became a reproof among all mine enemies, * but especially a- | mong my | neighbours :
and they of mine acquaintance were afraid of me, * and they that did see me with- | out con- | vey'd them-selves | from me.

14 I am clean forgotten, as a dead man | out of | mind :
I am be- | come · like a | bro-ken | vessel.

15 For I have heard the blasphemy | ọf thẹ | multitude :
and fear is on every side, * while they conspire together against me, * and take their counsel to | take ạ- | wạy my | life.

Full. 16 But my hópe hath been in | thee Ọ | Lord :
I have said, | Thou — | ạrt my | God.

17 My time is | in thy | hand :
deliver me from the hand of mine enemies, | ạnd frọm | them thạt | persecute me.

18 Shew thy servant the | light of · thy | countenance :
ạnd | save me · for thy | mer-cy's | sake.

19 Let me not be confounded O Lord, for I have | call'd up- | on thee :
let the ungodly be put to confusion, * and be put to | si-lence | ịn thẹ | grave.

2nd part. 20 Let the lying lips be | put tọ | silence :
which cruelly, disdainfully, and despitefully | speak ạ- | gainst thẹ | righteous.

Full. 21 O how plentiful is thy goodness, * which thou hast laid up for | them thạt | fear thee :
and that thou hast prepar'd for them that put their trust in thee, * even be- | fore thẹ | sons ọf | men !

Full. 22 Thou shalt hide them privily by thine own presence, * from the pro- | voking · of | all men :
thou shalt keep them secretly in thy tabernacle | frọm thẹ | strife ọf | tongues.

Full. 23 Thanks bẹ | tọ thẹ | Lord :
for he hath shew'd me marvellous great | kindness · in a | strong — | city.

Full. 24 And when I made | haste I | said :
I am cast | out of · the | sight of · thine | eyes.

2nd part. 25 Nevertheless, * thou heardest thẹ | voice of · my | prayer :
whẹn Ị | cri-ed | ụn-tọ | thee.

26 O love the Lord, all | ye his | saints :
for the Lord preserveth them that are faithful, * and plénteously re- | wardeth · the | proud — | doer.

Full. 27 Be strong, * and hé shall es- | tablish your | heart :
all ye that | put your | trust · in the | Lord.

DAY 6. EVENING PRAYER

PSALM 32

1 Blessed is he whose unríghteousness | is for- | giv'n :
and | whose — | sin is | cover'd.

2 Blessed is the man unto whom the Lord im- | puteth · no | sin :
and in whose | spirit · there | is no | guile.

3 For while I | held my | tongue :
my bones consum'd a- | way · through my | daily · com- | plaining.

4 For thy hand is heavy upon me | day and | night :
and my móisture is | like the | drought in | summer.

5 I will acknowledge my | sin · unto | thee :
and mine un- | righteous-ness | have I · not | hid.

6 I said, I will confess my | sins un-to the | Lord :
and so thou forgavest the | wicked-ness | of my | sin.

7 For this shall every one that is godly make his prayer unto thee, * in a tíme when thou | mayest · be | found :
but in the great water-floods | they shall | not come | nigh him.

8 Thou art a place to hide me in, * thou shalt pre- | serve me · from | trouble :
thou shalt cómpass me a- | bout with | songs of · de- | liverance.

9 I will inform thee, * and teach thee in the wáy where- | in thou · shalt | go :
and I will | guide thee | with mine | eye.

10 Be ye not like to horse and mule, which have | no · under- | standing :
whose mouths must be held with bit and | bri-dle, | lest they | fall upon thee.

11 Great plagues re- | main · for the un- | godly :
but whoso putteth his trust in the Lord, * mércy em- | braceth · him on | eve-ry | side.

Full. 12 Be glad O ye righteous and re- | joice · in the | Lord :
and be joyful, áll | ye that · are | true ọf | heart.

PSALM 33

Full. 1 Rejoice in the Lord | O ye | righteous :
for it becometh | well thẹ | just · to be | thankful.

Full. 2 Práise the | Lord with | harp :
sing praises unto him with the lùte, and | instru-ment of | ten — | strings.

3 Síng unto the | Lord a · new | song :
sing praises lustily unto | him · with a | good — | courage.

4 For the word of the | Lord is | true :
ạnd | all his | works are | faithful.

5 He loveth | righteousness · ạnd | judgement :
the éarth is full of the | good-nẹss | ọf thẹ | Lord.

6 By the word of the Lórd were the | heav'ns — | made :
and all the hósts of them | bỵ thẹ | breath of · his | mouth.

7 He gathereth the waters of the sea together, * as it | were up-on an | heap :
and layeth up the | deep, ạs | in a | treasure-house.

8 Let all the earth | fear thẹ | Lord :
stand in awe of him, * all | ye that | dwell · in the | world.

9 Fọr hẹ | spake and · it was | done :
hẹ cọm- | manded · and it | stood — | fast.

10 The Lord bringeth the cóunsel of the | heathen · to | nought :
and maketh the devices of the people to be of none effect,* and casteth | out thẹ | counsels · of | princes.

11 The counsel of the Lord shall en- | dure for | ever :
and the thoughts of his héart from gene- | ration · to | ge-ne- | ration.

12 Blessed are the people whose God is the | Lord Je- | hovah :
and blessed are the folk, that he hath chósen to | him to · be | his in- | heritance.

13 The Lord look'd down from heaven, * and beheld all the | children · of | men :
from the habitation of his dwelling, * he considereth all | them that | dwell · on the | earth.

14 He fashioneth | all the | hearts of them :
and under- | stand-eth | all their | works.

15 There is no king that can be sav'd by the múltitude | of an | host :
neither is any míghty man de- | liver'd · by | much — | strength.

16 A horse is counted but a | vain thing · to | save a man :
neither shall he deliver | any · man | by his · great | strength.

17 Behold, the eye of the Lórd is upon | them that | fear him :
and upon them that | put their | trust in · his | mercy ;

18 To deliver their | soul from | death :
and to | feed them · in the | time of | dearth.

19 Our soul hath patiently | tarri'd · for the | Lord :
for | he is · our | help and · our | shield.

20 For our | heart shall · re- | joice in him :
because we have | hoped · in his | ho-ly | Name.

2nd part. 21 Let thy merciful kindness O | Lord · be up- | on us :
like as we do | put our | trust in | thee.

PSALM 34

Full. 1 I will alway give | thanks un-to the | Lord :
his praise shall | ever · be | in my | mouth.

Full. 2 My sóul shall make her | boast · in the | Lord :
the humble shall | hear there-of, | and be | glad.

2nd part. Full. 3 O praise the | Lord with | me :
and let us | magni-fy his | Name to- | gether.
4 I sought the | Lord and · he | heard me :
yea he delív'er'd me | out of | all my | fear.
5 They had an eye unto | him · and were | lighten'd :
and their | fac-es | were not · a- | sham'd.
6 Lo the poor crieth, and the | Lord — | heareth him :
yea and sáveth him | out of | all his | troubles.
[7] The angel of the Lord tarrieth | round a-bout | them
that | fear him, | and de- | liv'reth them.
8 O taste and see how | gracious · the | Lord is :
blessed is the | man that | trusteth · in | him.
9 O fear the Lord, | ye that · are his | saints :
for | they that | fear him · lack | nothing.
2nd part. 10 The lions do lack and | suf-fer | hunger :
but they who seek the Lord shall want no | manner · of | thing that · is | good.
11 Come ye children, and | hearken · unto | me :
I will | teach you · the | fear of · the | Lord.
12 What man is he that | lusteth · to | live :
and would | fain — | see good | days ?
13 Keep thy | tongue from | evil :
and thy | lips, · that they | speak no | guile.
14 Eschew | evil and · do | good :
seek | peace — | and en- | sue it.
15 The eyes of the Lord are | over · the | righteous :
and his ears are | o-pen | unto · their | prayers.
16 The countenance of the Lord is against | them that · do | evil :
to root out the re- | membrance · of them | from the | earth.
17 The righteous cry, and the | Lord — | heareth them :
and delívereth them | out of | all their | troubles.
18 The Lord is nigh unto thém that are of a | con-trite | heart :
and will save such as | be · of an | hum-ble | spirit.

19 Great are the | troubles · of the | righteous :
but the Lord de- | liv'reth · him | out of | all.

20 He keepeth | all his | bones :
so that not | one of | them is | broken.

21 But misfortune shall | slay the · un- | godly :
and they that hate the | right-eous | shall be | desolate.

22 The Lord deliv'reth the | souls of · his | servants :
and all they that put their | trust in · him | shall not · be | destitute.

DAY 7. MORNING PRAYER

PSALM 35

1 Plead thou my cause O Lord, with them that | strive with | me :
and fight thou against | them that | fight a- | gainst me.

2 Lay hånd upon the | shield and | buckler :
and | stand — | up to | help me.

3 Bring forth the spear, * and stop the way against | them that | persecute me :
say unto my soul, | I am | thy sal- | vation.

4 Let them be confounded and put to shame, that seek | after · my | soul :
let them be turn'd back and brought to confusion, * that im- | ag-ine | mis-chief | for me.

5 Let them be as the | dust be-fore the | wind :
and the | angel · of the | Lord — | scattering them.

6 Let their way be | dark and | slippery :
and let the | angel · of the | Lord — | persecute them.

7 For they have privily laid their net to destroy me with- | out a | cause :
yea, even without a cause have they | made a | pit for · my | soul.

8 Let a sudden destruction come upon him unawares, * and his net, that he hath laid privily, | catch him- | self :
that he may | fall in-to his | own — | mischief.

9 And my soul be | joyful · in the | Lord :
it shall re- | joice in | his sal- | vation.

10 All my bones shall say, Lord who is like unto thee, * who deliverest the poor from | him that is · too | strong for him :
yea the poor and him that is in | misery · from | him that | spoileth him?

11 False witnesses did | rise — | up :
they laid to my | charge — | things that · I | knew not.

12 They rewarded me | evil · for | good :
to the great dis- | com-fort | of my | soul.

13 Nevertheless, when they were sick I put on sackcloth, * and humbl'd my | soul with | fasting :
and my prayer shall | turn in-to mine | own — | bosom.

14 I behav'd myself as though it had been my | friend · or my | brother :
I went heavily, as one that | mourn-eth | for his | mother.

15 But in mine adversity they rejoic'd, * and gather'd them- | selves to- | gether :
yea the very abjects came together against me unawares, * making | mouths at | me and | ceas'd not.

16 With the flatterers were | bu-sy | mockers :
who | gnash'd up-on me | with their | teeth.

17 Lord how long wilt thou | look up-on | this :
O deliver my soul from the calamities which they bring on me, * and my | dar-ling | from the | lions.

18 So will I give thee thánks in the | great · congre- | gation :
I will | praise · thee a- | mong much | people.

19 O let not them that are mine enemies triumph | over · me un- | godly :
neither let them wink with their eyes that | hate · me with- | out a | cause.

20 And why ? * their communing is | not for | peace :
but they imagine deceitful words against thém that are | qui-et | in the | land.

21 They gáp'd upon me with their | mouths and | said :
Fie on thee, fie on thee, we | saw it | with our | eyes.

22 This thou hast | seen O | Lord :
hold not thy tongue then, * go not | far from | me O | Lord.

23 Awake and stand úp to | judge my | quarrel :
avenge thou my | cause my | God and · my | Lord.

24 Judge me O Lord my God, ac- | cording to · thy | righteousness :
and | let them · not | tri-umph | over me.

25 Let them not say in their hearts, * Thére, thére, | so would · we | have it :
neither let them | say — | We · have de- | vour'd him.

26 Let them be put to confusion and shame together, that re- | joice at · my | trouble :
let them be cloth'd with rebuke and dishonour, that | boast them- | selves a- | gainst me.

Full. 27 Let them be glad and rejoice, that favour my | right-eous | dealing :
yea let them say alway, Blessed be the Lord, * who hath pléasure in the pros- | peri-ty | of his | servant.

Full. 28 And as for my tongue, * it shall be | talking of · thy | righteousness :
and of thy | praise — | all the · day | long.

PSALM 36

(*Single Chant*)

1 My heart sheweth me the wickedness | of the · un- | godly :
that there is no fear of | God be- | fore his | eyes.

2 For he flattereth himsélf in his | own — | sight :
until his abominable | sin be | found — | out.

3 The words of his mouth are unrighteous and | full of · de- | ceit :
he hath left off to behave himself | wise-ly | and to · do | good.

4 He imagineth mischief upon his bed, * and hath sét himself in | no good | way :
neither doth he abhór | any · thing | that is | evil.

Full. 5 Thy mercy O Lord reacheth | unto · the | heav'ns :
and thy | faithful-ness | unto · the | clouds.

Full. 6 Thy righteousness stándeth like the | strong — | mountains :
thy | judgements · are | like the · great | deep.

7 Thou Lord shalt save both man and beast ; * How éxcellent is thy | mercy · O | God :
and the children of men shall put their trúst under the | sha-dow | of thy | wings.

8 They shall be satisfi'd with the plenteousness | of thy | house :
and thou shalt give them drink of thy | pleasures · as | out of · the | river.

9 For with thee is the | well of | life :
and in thy | light shall | we see | light.

10 O continue forth thy loving-kíndness unto | them that | know thee :
and thy ríghteousness unto | them that · are | true of | heart.

11 O let not the foot of | pride · come a- | gainst me :
and let not the hánd of the un- | god-ly | cast me | down.

12 There are they fallen, | all that · work | wickedness :
they are cast down, and | shall not · be | able · to | stand.

DAY 7. EVENING PRAYER

PSALM 37

1 Fret not thyself be- | cause of the · un- | godly :
neither be thou envious a- | gainst the | ev-il- | doers ;

2 For they shall sóon be cut | down · like the | grass :
and be wither'd | ev'n · as the | green — | herb.

3 Put thou thy trust in the Lord and be | do-ing | good :
dwell in the land and | veri-ly | thou shalt · be | fed.

4 Delíght thou | in the | Lord :
and he shall | give thee · thy | heart's de- | sire.

5 Commit thy way unto the Lord, and | put thy | trust in him :
and | he shall | bring it · to | pass.

6 He shall make thy righteousness as | clear as · the | light :
and thy just | deal-ing | as the | noon-day.

7 Hold thee still in the Lord, and abide | patient-ly up- | on him :
but grieve not thyself at him whose way doth prosper, *
against the man that | doeth · after | ev-il | counsels.

8 Leave off from wráth and let | go dis- | pleasure :
fret not thyself, | else shalt · thou be | mov'd to · do | evil.

9 Wicked dóers shall be | root-ed | out :
and they that patiently abide the Lord, | those · shall in- |
herit · the | land.

10 Yet a little while, * and the ungódly shall be | clean — | gone :
thou shalt look after his place, and | he shall | be a- | way.

2nd part. 11 But the meek-spírited shall pos- | sess the | earth :
and shall be re- | fresh'd · in the | multitude · of | peace.

12 The ungodly seeketh counsel a- | gainst the | just :
and gnasheth up- | on him | with his | teeth.

13 The Lord shall | laugh him · to | scorn :
for he hath | seen that · his | day is | coming.

14 The ungodly have drawn out the sword and have | bent their |
bow :
to cast down the poor and needy, * and to slay súch as are
of a | right — | con-ver- | sation.

15 Their sword shall go through their | own — | heart :
and their | bow — | shall be | broken.

16 A smáll thing that the | right-eous | hath :
is better than great | rich-es | of the · un- | godly.

17 For the arms of the un- | godly · shall be | broken :
and the | Lord up- | holdeth · the | righteous.

18 The Lord knoweth the | days of · the | godly :
and their inheritance | shall en- | dure for | ever.

19 They shall not be confóunded in.the | peri-lous | time :
and in the days of | dearth · they shall | have ẹ- | nough.

2nd part. 20 As for the ungodly they shall perish, * and the enemies of the Lord shall consúme as the | fat ọf | lambs :
yea even as the | smoke shall · they con- | sume ạ- | way.

21 The ungodly borroweth, and | payeth · not a- | gain :
bụt thẹ | righteous · is | merciful · ạnd | liberal.

22 Such as are blessed of God shall pos- | sess thẹ | land :
and they that are cúrsed of him | shạll bẹ | root-ed | out.

23 The Lord ordereth a | good man's | going :
and maketh his way ac- | cepta-ble | tọ hịm- | self.

24 Though he fall, he sháll not be | cast ạ- | way :
for the Lord ụp- | holdeth · him | wịth hịs | hand.

25 I have been young ạnd | now am | old :
and yet saw I never the righteous forsaken, * nọr hịs | seed — | begging · their | bread.

26 The righteous is ever | merciful · ạnd | lendeth :
ạnd hịs | seed — | ịs — | blessed.

27 Flee from evil, and do the | thing that · is | good :
ạnd | dwell fọr | ev-er- | more.

28 For the Lord loveth the | thing that · is | right :
he forsaketh not his that be godly, but | they are · pre- | serv'd fọr | ever.

29 The unrighteous | shạll bẹ | punish'd :
as for the seed of the ungodly | it · shall be | root-ed | out.

30 The ríghteous shall in- | herit · the | land :
ạnd | dwell there- | in fọr | ever.

31 The mouth of the righteous is | exercis'd · in | wisdom :
ạnd hịs | tongue · will be | talking · of | judgement.

32 The law of his | God is · in his | heart :
ạnd hịs | go-ings | shall not | slide.

33 The ungodly | seeth · the | righteous :
ạnd | seeketh · oc- | casion · to | slay him.

34 The Lord will not | leave him · in his | hand :
nọr cọn- | demn him | when · he is | judg'd.

2nd part. 35 Hope thou in the Lord and keep his way, * and he shall promote thee that thóu shalt pos- | sess thẹ | land :
when the ungódly shall | per-ish | thou shalt | see it.

36 I myself have seen the ungódly in | great — | power :
and flourishing | like ạ | green — | bay-tree.

37 I went by, and | lo · he was | gone :
I sought him, but his | place could | no where · be | found.

38 Keep innocency, * and take héed unto the | thing that · is | right :
for thát shall | bring a · man | peace · at the | last.

39 As for the transgréssors they shall | perish · to- | gether :
and the end of the ungodly is, * they shall be | root-ed | out · at the | last.

Full. 40 But the salvation of the righteous | cometh · of the | Lord :
who is álso their | strength · in the | time ọf | trouble.

Full. 41 And the Lórd shall | stand by · them and | save them :
he shall deliver them from the ungodly, and shall save them, * bẹcạuse thẹy | put their | trust in | him.

DAY 8. MORNING PRAYER

PSALM 38

1 Put me not to rebuke O | Lord in · thine | anger :
neither chásten me | ịn thỵ | heavy · dis- | pleasure :

2 For thine árrows stick | fast in | me :
ạnd thỵ | hand — | presseth · me | sore.

3 There is no health in my flesh, be- | cause of · thy dis- | pleasure :
neither is there any rest in my bones, by | rea-sọn | ọf mỵ | sin.

4 For my wickednesses are gone | over · my | head :
and are like a sore búrden too | heavy · for | me tọ | bear.

[5] My | wounds — | stink
and are cor- | rupt — | through my | foolishness.
6 I am brought into so great | trouble · and | misery :
that I go | mourn-ing | all the · day | long.
7 For my loins are fill'd with a | sore dis- | ease :
and there is nó | whole part | in my | body.
8 I am feeble and | sore — | smitten :
I have roar'd for the very dis- | quiet-ness | of my | heart.
9 Lord thou knówest | all · my de- | sire :
and my | groan-ing | is not | hid from thee.
10 My heart panteth, my | strength hath | fail'd me :
and the | sight of · mine | eyes is | gone from me.
11 My lovers and my neighbours did stand lóoking up- | on my | trouble :
and my | kins-men | stood a-far | off.
12 They also that sought after my | life laid | snares for me :
and they that went about to do me evil talk'd of wickedness, * and imagin'd de- | ceit — | all the · day | long.
13 As for me, I was like a | deaf · man and | heard not :
and as one that is dumb, * who | doth not | open · his | mouth.
14 I became even as a | man that | heareth not :
and in whose | mouth are | no re- | proofs.
15 For in thee O Lord have I | put my | trust :
thou shalt answer | for me · O | Lord my | God.
16 I have requir'd that they, even mine enemies, * should not | tri-umph | over me :
for when my foot slipp'd, they re- | joic-ed | greatly · a- | gainst me.
17 And I truly am | set in · the | plague :
and my heaviness is | ev-er | in my | sight.
18 Fór I will con- | fess my | wickedness :
and be | sor-ry | for my | sin.

19 But mine enemies | live and · are | mighty :
and they that hate me | wrongfully · are | many · in | number.

20 They also that reward evil for | good · are a- | gainst me :
because I follow the | thing that | good — | is.

21 Forsake me not O | Lord my | God :
be not | thou — | far — | from me.

22 Haste | thee to | help me :
O Lord | God of | my sal- | vation.

PSALM 39

1 I said, I will take | heed to · my | ways :
that I of- | fend not | in my | tongue.

2 I will keep my mouth as it | were · with a | bridle :
while the un- | godly · is | in my | sight.

3 I held my | tongue and · spake | nothing :
I kept silence, yea even from good words, | but it · was | pain and | grief to me.

4 My heart was hot within me, * and while I was thus musing the | fire — | kindl'd :
and at the | last I | spake with · my | tongue ;

5 Lord let me know mine end, * and the | number · of my | days :
that I may be cértifi'd how | long I | have to | live.

6 Behold, thou hast made my days as it were a | span — | long :
and mine age is even as nothing in respect of thee, * and verily every man líving is | al-to- | ge-ther | vanity.

7 For man walketh in a vain shadow, * and disquieteth him- | self in | vain :
he heapeth up riches, and | cannot · tell | who shall | gather them.

8 And now Lord, | what is · my | hope :
trúly my | hope is | even · in | thee.

9 Delíver me from | all · mine of- | fences :
and make me not a re- | buke un- | to the | foolish.

10 I became dumb, and | open'd · not my | mouth :
for | it was | thy — | doing.

11 Take thy | plague a- | way from me :
I am even consum'd by the | means of · thy | heav-y | hand.

12 When thou with rebukes dost chasten man for sin, * thou makest his beauty to consume away, * like as it were a moth | fretting · a | garment :
every man | there-fore | is but | vanity.

13 Hear my prayer O Lord, and with thine ears con- | sider · my | calling :
hold | not thy | peace at · my | tears.

14 For I am a | stranger · with | thee :
and a | sojourner · as | all my | fathers were.

2nd part. 15 O spare me a little, * that I may re- | cover · my | strength :
before I go | hence and · be | no more | seen.

PSALM 40

Full. 1 I waited | patiently · for the | Lord :
and he inclín'd unto | me and | heard my | calling.

Full. 2 He brought me also out of the horrible pit, * out of the | mire and | clay :
and set my feet upon the | rock and | order'd · my | goings.

3 And he hath put a new | song in · my | mouth :
even a | thanks-giving | unto · our | God.

4 Many shall | see it · and | fear :
and shall | put their | trust in · the | Lord.

5 Blessed is the man that hath set his | hope in · the | Lord :
and turn'd not unto the proud, * and to | such as · go a- | bout with | lies.

6 O Lord my God, great are the wondrous works which thou hast done, * like as be also thy thoughts which | are to | us-ward :
and yet there is | no man · that | ordereth · them | unto thee.

7 If I should de- | clare them · and | speak of them :
they should be móre than I am | ab-le | to ex- | press

8 Sacrifice and meat- | off'ring · thou | wouldest not :
but mine | ears — | hast thou | open'd.

9 Burnt-offerings and sacrifice for sin, hast thou | not re- | quir'd :
then | said I, | Lo I | come,

10 In the volume of the book it is written of me, * that I should fulfil thy will | O my | God :
I am content to do it, * yea thy | law · is with- | in my | heart.

Full. 11 I have declar'd thy righteousness in the | great · congre- | gation :
lo I will not refrain my lips O | Lord, and | that thou | knowest.

Full. 12 I have not hid thy righteousness with- | in my | heart :
my talk hath been of thy | truth · and of | thy sal- | vation.

2nd part. 13 I have not kept back thy loving | mercy · and | truth :
from the | great — | con-gre- | gation.

14 Withdraw not thou thy mercy | from me · O | Lord :
let thy loving-kindness and thy | truth — | alway · pre- | serve me.

15 For innumerable troubles are come about me, * my sins have taken such hold upon me, * that I am not | able to · look | up :
yea they are more in number than the hairs of my | head, · and my | heart hath | fail'd me.

16 O Lord, let it be thy | pleasure · to de- | liver me :
make | haste O | Lord to | help me.

17 Let them be asham'd and confounded together, * that seek after my | soul · to de- | stroy it :
let them be driven backward, and put to re- | buke that | wish me | evil.

18 Let them be desolate and re- | warded · with | shame :
that say unto me, Fie up- | on thee, | fie up- | on thee.

19 Let all those that seek thee be joyful and | glad in | thee :
and let such as love thy salvation say | alway · The | Lord be | prais'd.

20 As for me, I am | poor and | needy :
  but the | Lord — | car-eth | for me.
21 Thou art my | helper · and re- | deemer :
  make no long | tarry-ing, | O my | God.

DAY 8. EVENING PRAYER

PSALM 41

1 Blessed is he that considereth the | poor and | needy :
  the Lord shall delíver him | in the | time of | trouble.
2 The Lord preserve him and keep him alive, * that he may be | blessed up-on | earth :
  and deliver not thou | him in-to the | will of · his | enemies.
3 The Lord comfort him, when he lieth | sick up-on his | bed :
  make thou | all his | bed in · his | sickness.
4 I said, Lord be | merci-ful | unto me :
  heal my | soul for · I have | sinn'd a- | gainst thee.
5 Mine | enemies · speak | evil of me :
  Whén shall he | die · and his | name — | perish ?
6 And if he come to sée me he | speak-eth | vanity :
  and his heart conceiveth falsehood within himself, * and when he | com-eth | forth he | telleth it.
7 All mine enemies whisper to- | gether · a- | gainst me :
  even against | me do · they im- | agine · this | evil.
8 Let the sentence of gúiltiness pro- | ceed a- | gainst him :
  and now that he lieth | let him · rise | up no | more.
9 Yea even mine own familiar | friend · whom I | trusted :
  who did also eat of my | bread hath | laid great | wait for me.
10 But be thou merciful unto | me O | Lord :
  ráise thou me up a- | gain and | I shall · re- | ward them.
11 By this I | know thou | favourest me :
  that mine enemy | doth not | triumph · a- | gainst me.

12 And when I am in my health | thou up- | holdest me :
and shalt set me be- | fore thy | face for | ever.

nd part. 13 *Blessed be the | Lord · God of | Israel:*
world without | end, A- | — | men.

PSALMS 42 AND 43

1 Like as the hart de- | sireth · the | water-brooks :
so longeth my | soul · after | thee O | God.

2 My soul is athirst for God, * yea | even · for the | living God :
when shall I come to ap- | pear be-fore the | presence · of | God ?

3 My tears have been my meat | day and | night :
while they daily sáy unto me, | Where is | now thy | God ?

4 Now when I think thereupon, * I pour out my | heart · by my- | self :
for I went with the multitude, * and brought them | forth in-to the | house of | God ;

nd part. 5 In the voice of | praise and | thanksgiving :
among | such as | keep — | holy-day.

6 *Why art thou so full of heaviness | O my | soul :*
and why art thou | so dis- | quieted · with- | in me ?

7 *Put thy | trust in | God :*
for I will yet give him | thanks · for the | help of · his | countenance.

8 My God, my soul is | vex'd with- | in me :
therefore will I remember thee concerning the land of Jordan, * and the | lit-tle | hill of | Hermon.

9 One deep calleth another, * because of the | noise of · the | water-pipes :
all thy | waves and | storms are · gone | over me.

10 The Lord hath granted his loving- | kindness · in the | day-time :
and in the night-season did I sing of him, * and made my | prayer un-to the | God of · my | life.

11 I will say unto the God of my strength, | Why hast · thou for- | gotten me :
why go I thus heavily, | while the | enemy · op- | presseth me ?

12 My bones are smitten asunder | as · with a | sword :
while mine enemies that tróuble me | cast me | in the | teeth ;

13 Namely while they say | dai-ly | unto me :
Where | — is | now thy | God ?

14 *Why art thou so vex'd | O my | soul :*
and why art thou | so dis- | quieted · with- | in me ?

15 *O put thy | trust in | God :*
*for I will yet thank him, * which is the hélp of my | counten-ance | and my | God.*

(*Psalm* 43) 16 Give sentence with me O God, * and defend my cáuse against the un- | god-ly | people :
O delíver me from the de- | ceitful · and | wick-ed | man.

17 For thou art the God of my strength, * whý hast thou | put me | from thee :
and why go I so heavily, | while the | enemy · op- | presseth me ?

18 O send out thy light and thy truth that | they may | lead me :
and bring me unto thy holy | hill, and | to thy | dwelling.

19 And that I may go unto the altar of God, * even unto the Gód of my | joy and | gladness :
and upon the harp will I give thánks unto | thee O | God my | God.

20 *Why art thou so héavy | O my | soul :*
and why art thou | so dis- | quieted · with- | in me?

21 *O put thy | trust in | God :*
*for I will yet give him thanks, * which is the hélp of my | counten-ance | and my | God.*

DAY 9. MORNING PRAYER

PSALM 44

Full. 1 We have heard with our ears O God, * our | fathers · have | told us :
what thou hast | done in · their | time of | old ;

Full. 2 How thou hast driven out the heathen with thy hand, * and | planted · them | in :
how thou hast destroy'd the | nations · and | cast them | out.

3 For they gat not the land in possèssion through their | own — | sword :
neither was it their | own — | arm that | help'd them ;

4 But thy right hand and thine arm, * and the | light of · thy | countenance :
because thou | hadst a | fa-vour | unto them.

Full. 5 Thou art my | King O | God :
send | help — | un-to | Jacob.

Full. 6 Through thee will we over- | throw our | enemies :
and in thy Name will we tread them | under · that | rise · up a- | gainst us.

7 For I will not | trust in · my | bow :
it is | not my | sword that · shall | help me ;

8 But it is thou that sàvest us | from our | enemies :
and puttest | them · to con- | fusion · that | hate us.

2nd part. 9 We make our boast of God | all day | long :
and will | praise thy | Name for | ever.

10 But now thou art far off, * and pùttest us | to con- | fusion :
and | goest · not | forth with · our | armies.

11 Thou makest us to turn our | backs up-on our | enemies :
so that they which | hate us | spoil our | goods.

12 Thou lettest us be eaten | up like | sheep :
and hast | scatter'd · us a- | mong the | heathen.

13 Thou sellest thy | people · for | nought :
and | takest · no | mon-ey | for them.

14 Thou makest us to be re- | buk'd of · our | neighbours :
to be laugh'd to scorn, * and had in derision of | them · that are | round a- | bout us.

15 Thou makest us to be a bý-word a- | mong the | heathen :
and that the | peo-ple | shake their | heads at us.

16 My confusion is | daily · be- | fore me :
and the | shame of · my | face hath | cover'd me ;

17 For the voice of the slanderer | and blas- | phemer :
for the | ene-my | and a- | venger.

18 And though all this be come upon us, * yét do we | not for- | get thee :
nor behave ourselves | froward-ly | in thy | covenant.

19 Our heart is not | turn-ed | back :
neither our | steps gone | out of · thy | way ;

2nd part. 20 No, not when thou hast smitten us into the | place of | dragons :
and cóver'd us | with the | shadow · of | death.

21 If we have forgotten the Name of our God, * and holden up our hands to any | strange — | god :
shall not God search it out ? * for he knóweth the very | se-crets | of the | heart.

22 For thy sake also are we kill'd | all the · day | long :
and are counted as | sheep ap- | pointed · to be | slain.

23 Up | Lord, why | sleepest thou :
awake and be not | ab-sent | from us · for | ever.

24 Wherefore | hidest · thou thy | face :
and for- | gettest · our | misery · and | trouble ?

25 For our soul is brought low, even | unto · the | dust :
our belly | cleav-eth | unto · the | ground.

26 A- | rise and | help us :
and delíver us | for thy | mer-cy's | sake.

PSALM 45

Full. 1 My heart is indíting of a | good — | matter :
I speak of the things which I have | made ụn- | tọ thẹ | King.

Full. [2]My | tongue — | is
thẹ | pen of · a | read-y | writer.

3 Thou art fáirer than the | children · of | men :
full of grace are thy lips, * bẹcạuse | God hath | blessed · thee for | ever.

4 Gird thee with thy sword upon thy thigh O | thou most | Mighty :
accórding to thy | wor-ship | ạnd rẹ- | nown.

5 Good luck have thou | with thine | honour :
ride on because of the word of truth, * of meekness and righteousness, * and thy right hand shạll | teach thee | terri-ble | things.

6 Thy arrows are very sharp, * and the people shall be sub- | du'd un-to | thee :
even in the | midst a-mong the | King's — | enemies.

7 Thy seat O God en- | dureth · for | ever :
the sceptre of thy | kingdom · is a | right — | sceptre.

8 Thou hast lov'd ríghteousness and | hated · in- | iquity :
wherefore God, even thý God, * hath anointed thee with the oil of | gladness · a- | bove thy | fellows.

9 All thy garments smell of myrrh, | aloes · and | cassia :
out of the ivory pálaces, where- | by · they have | made thee | glad.

10 King's daughters were among thy | honour-able | women :
upon thy right hand did stand the queen in a vesture of gold, * wrought ạ- | bout with | di-vers | colours.

11 Hearken O daughter and consider, ịn- | cline thine | ear :
forget also thine own | people · and thy | fa-ther's | house.

12 So shall the King have | pleasure · in thy | beauty :
for he is thy Lord | God, ạnd | worship · thou | him.

13 And the daughter of Tyre shall be | there · with a | gift :
like as the rich also among the people, * shall | make their · suppli- | cation · be- | fore thee.

14 The King's daughter is all | glorious · with- | in :
her | clothing · is of | wrought — | gold.

15 She shall be brought unto the King in | raiment · of | needle-work :
the virgins that be her fellows shall bear her company, * and | shall be | brought · unto | thee.

16 With joy and gládness shall | they be | brought :
and shall enter | into · the | King's — | palace.

17 Instead of thy fathers | thou shalt · have | children :
whom thou mayest make | princes · in | all — | lands.

18 I will remember thy Name from one gene- | ration · to an- | other :
therefore shall the people give thánks unto thee, | world with- | out — | end.

PSALM 46

Full. 1 God is our | hope and | strength :
a very | pre-sent | help in | trouble.

Full. 2 Therefore will we not féar though the | earth be | mov'd :
and though the hills be carried | into · the | midst of · the | sea.

3 Though the waters thereof | rage and | swell :
and though the mountains sháke at the | tem-pest | of the | same.

4 The rivers of the flood thereof shall make glád the | city · of | God :
the holy place of the | taber-nacle | of the · most | Highest.

5 God is in the midst of her, * thérefore shall she | not · be re- | mov'd :
God shall | help her · and | that right | early.

6 The heathen make much ado, and the | kingdoms · are | mov'd :
but God hath shewed his voice, and the | earth shall | melt a- | way.

Unis. 7 *The Lord of | hosts is | with us :*
the God of | Ja-cob | is our | refuge.

8 O come hither and behold the | works of · the | Lord :
what destrúction he hath | brought up- | on the | earth.

9 He maketh wars to cease in | all the | world :
he breaketh the bow, and knappeth the spear in sunder, * and búrneth the | cha-riots | in the | fire.

10 Be still then and know that | I am | God :
I will be exalted among the heathen, * and I will be ex- | alt-ed | in the | earth.

Unis. 11 *The Lord of | hosts is | with us :*
the God of | Ja-cob | is our | refuge.

DAY 9. EVENING PRAYER

PSALM 47

Full. 1 O clap your hands together, | all ye | people :
O sing unto | God · with the | voice of | melody.

Full. 2 For the Lord is | high and · to be | fear'd :
he is the great | King up-on | all the | earth.

3 He shall subdue the | peo-ple | under us :
and the | na-tions | under · our | feet.

4 He shall choose out an | heri-tage | for us :
even the worship of | Ja-cob | whom he | lov'd.

5 God is gone up with a | mer-ry | noise :
and the | Lord · with the | sound of · the | trump.

6 O sing praises, sing praises | unto · our | God :
O sing praises, sing | praís-es | unto · our | King.

7 For God is the King of | all the | earth :
sing ye | praises · with | un-der- | standing.

8 God reigneth | over · the | heathen :
God sítteth up- | on his | ho-ly | seat.

2nd part. 9 The princes of the people are joined unto the péople of the | God of | Abraham :
for God which is very high exalted, doth defend the | earth · as it | were · with a | shield.

PSALM 48

Full. 1 Great is the Lord, and | highly · to be | prais'd :
in the city of our God, | ev'n up-on his | ho-ly | hill.

Full. 2 The hill of Sion is a fair place, * and the joy of the | whole — | earth :
upon the north-side lieth the city of the great King, * God is well known in her | palaces · as a | sure — | refuge.

3 For lo, the | kings of · the | earth :
are | gather'd · and | gone · by to- | gether.

4 They márvell'd to | see such | things :
they were astonish'd, and | sudden-ly | cast — | down.

5 Fear came there up- | on them · and | sorrow :
as upon a | wo-man | in her | travail.

[6] Thou shalt | break the | ships
of the | sea · through the | east — | wind.

2nd part. 7 Like as we have heard, * so have we seen in the city of the Lord of hosts, * in the | city of · our | God :
God up- | holdeth · the | same for | ever.

[8] We wait for thy | lov-ing- | kindness
O | God · in the | midst of · thy | temple.

9 O God, according to thy Name, * so is thy praise unto the | world's — | end :
thy right | hand is | full of | righteousness.

[10] Let the mount Sion rejoice, * and the | daughter · of | Judah ·
be | glad, be- | cause of · thy | judgements.

11 Walk about Sion, and | go · round a- | bout her :
and | tell the | towers · there- | of.

12 Mark well her bulwarks, set | up her | houses :
that ye may | tell — | them that · come | after.

Unis. 13 For thís God is oúr God for | ever · and | ever :
he shall be our | guide — | un-to | death.

PSALM 49

1 O hear ye this, | all ye | people :
ponder it with your ears, | all · ye that | dwell in · the | world ;

[2] High and | low, — | rich
and | poor — | one · with an- | other.

3 My mouth shall | speak of | wisdom :
and my heart shall | muse of | un-der- | standing.

4 I will incline mine | ear · to the | parable :
and shew my dark | speech up- | on the | harp.

5 Wherefore should I fear in the | days of | wickedness :
and when the wickedness of my heels | compasseth · me | round a- | bout ?

6 There be sóme that put their | trust in · their | goods :
and boast themselves in the | multi-tude | of their | riches.

7 But nó man may de- | liver · his | brother :
nor make a- | greement · unto | God — | for him ;

8 For it cost more to re- | deem their | souls :
so that he must | let · that a- | lone for | ever ;

9 Yea | though he · live | long :
and | see — | not the | grave.

10 For he seeth that wise men also die and | perish · to- | gether :
as well as the ignorant and foolish, * and | leave their | riches · for | other.

11 And yet they think that their hóuses shall con- | tinue · for | ever :
and that their dwelling-places shall endure from one generation to another, * and call the lands | after · their | own — | names.

12 *Nevertheless, * mán will not a- | bide in | honour :*
seeing he may be compar'd unto the beasts that | per-ish, | this is · the | way of them.

13 This | is their | foolishness :
and their pos- | teri-ty | praise their | saying.

14 They lie in the hell like sheep, * death gnaweth upon them, * and the righteous shall have domination óver them | in the | morning :
their beauty shall consume in the | sepul-chre | out of · their | dwelling.

15 But God hath deliver'd my soul from the | place of | hell :
for | he — | shall re- | ceive me.

16 Be not thou afraid, though | one be · made | rich :
or if the | glory of · his | house · be in- | creas'd ;

17 For he shall carry nothing awáy with him | when he | dieth :
neither | shall his | pomp — | follow him.

18 For while he liv'd, * he cóunted himself an | hap-py | man :
and so long as thou doest well unto thy- | self — | men will · speak | good of thee.

19 He shall follow the gene- | ration · of his | fathers :
and shall | ne-ver | see — | light.

20 *Man being in honour hath | no · under- | standing :*
but is com- | par'd un-to the | beasts that | perish.

DAY 10. MORNING PRAYER

PSALM 50

Full. 1 The Lord, even the most mighty | God, hath | spoken :
and call'd the world, * from the rising up of the | sun unto the | go-ing | down thereof.

Full. [2]Out of | Sion · hath | God
ap- | pear'd in | per-fect | beauty.

3 Our God shall come, and | shall not · keep | silence :
there shall go before him a consuming fire, * and a mighty témpest shall be | stirr'd up | round a- | bout him.

4 He shall call the | heav'n · from a- | bove :
and the | earth that · he may | judge his | people.

5 Gather my | saints to-gether | unto me :
those that have made a | covenant · with | me with | sacrifice.

6 And the héav'n shall de- | clare his | righteousness :
for | God is | Judge him- | self.

7 Hear O my people and | I will | speak :
I myself will testify against thee O Israel, * for I am | God, — | ev-en | thy God.

8 I will not reprove thee because of thy sacrifices, * ór for thy | burnt — | offerings :
because they | were not | alway · be- | fore me.

9 I will take no bullock | out of · thine | house :
nor | he-goat | out of · thy | folds.

10 For all the béasts of the | forest · are | mine :
and so are the | cattle up-on a | thou-sand | hills.

11 I know all the | fowls up-on the | mountains :
and the wild béasts of the | field are | in my | sight.

12 If I be hungry, I | will not | tell thee :
for the whole world is mine, and | all that | is there- | in.

13 Thinkest thou that I will | eat bulls' | flesh :
and | drink the | blood of | goats ?

14 Offer unto | God — | thanksgiving :
and pay thy | vows un-to the | most — | Highest.

2nd part. 15 And call upon me in the | time of | trouble :
só will I | hear thee · and | thou shalt | praise me.

16 But unto the un- | godly · said | God :
Why dost thou preach my laws, * and takest my | cove-nant | in thy | mouth ;

17 Whereas thou hatest to | be re- | form'd :
and hast | cast my | words be- | hind thee ?

18 When thou sawest a thief, thou con- | sent-edst | unto him :
and hast been par- | tak-er | with · the a- | dulterers.

19 Thou hast let thy | mouth speak | wickedness :
and with thy | tongue · thou hast | set · forth de- | ceit.

20 Thou satest, and spakest a- | gainst thy | brother :
yea and hast slander'd thine | own — | mo-ther's | son.

21 These things hast thou done and I held my tongue, * and thou thoughtest wickedly that I am even súch a one | as thy- | self :
but I will reprove thee, and set before thee the | things that | thou hast | done.

22 O consider this, yé that for- | get — | God :
lest I pluck you a- | way and · there be | none · to de- | liver you.

23 Whoso offereth me thanks and | praise, he | honoureth me :
and to him that ordereth his conversation right will I | shew the · sal- | vation · of | God.

PSALM 51

1 Have mercy upon me O God, * after thy | great — | goodness :
according to the multitude of thy mercies, | do a- | way · mine of- | fences.

2 Wash me throughly | from my | wickedness :
and | cleanse me | from my | sin.

3 For I ac- | knowledge · my | faults :
and my | sin is | ever · be- | fore me.

4 Against thee only have I sinn'd, * and done this | evil in · thy | sight :
that thou mightest be justifi'd in thy saying, * and | clear when | thou art | judg'd.

5 Behold, I was | shapen · in | wickedness :
and in | sin hath · my | mother · con- | ceiv'd me.

6 But lo, thou requirest trúth in the | in-ward | parts :
and shalt make me to under- | stand — | wis-dom | secretly.

7 Thou shalt purge me with hyssop, and | I shall · be | clean :
thou shalt wash me, and | I shall · be | whiter · than | snow.

8 Thou shalt make me hear of | joy and | gladness :
that the bones which thou hast | brok-en | may re- | joice.
9 Turn thy | face · from my | sins :
and | put out | all · my mis- | deeds.
10 Make me a clean | heart O | God :
and re- | new a · right | spirit · with- | in me.
11 Cást me not a- | way from · thy | presence :
and take not thy | ho-ly | Spir-it | from me.
12 O give me the cómfort of thy | help a- | gain :
and stablish me | with thy | free — | Spirit.
2nd part. 13 Then shall I teach thy | ways un-to the | wicked :
and sínners shall be con- | vert-ed | un-to | thee.

14 Deliver me from blood-guiltiness O God, * thóu that art the | God of · my | health :
and my | tongue shall | sing of · thy | righteousness.
Full. 15 Thou shalt ópen my | lips, O | Lord :
and my | mouth shall | shew thy | praise.
16 For thou desirest no sacrifice, | else would · I | give it thee :
but thou de- | lightest · not in | burnt — | offerings.
17 The sacrifice of God is a | trou-bl'd | spirit :
a broken and contrite heart O | God · shalt thou | not de- | spise.
18 O be favourable and | gracious · unto | Sion :
build | thou the | walls of · Je- | rusalem.
Full. 19 Then shalt thou be pleas'd with the sacrifice of righteousness, * with the burnt-ófferings | and ob- | lations :
then shall they offer young | bullocks · up- | on thine | altar.

PSALM 52

1 Why bóastest thou thy- | self thou | tyrant :
that | thou canst | do — | mischief;
[2] Where- | as the | goodness
of | God en- | dureth · yet | daily ?

3 Thy tongue im- | agin-eth | wickedness :
and with lies thou | cuttest · like a | sharp — | razor.
4 Thou hast lov'd unrighteousness | more than | goodness :
and to talk of | lies — | more than | righteousness.
[5] Thou hast lov'd to | speak all | words that
may do | hurt, · O thou | false — | tongue.
6 Therefore shall God de- | stroy thee · for | ever :
he shall take thee and pluck thee out of thy dwelling, * and root thee | out of · the | land of · the | living.
7 The righteous also shall | see · this and | fear :
and shall | laugh — | him to | scorn ;
Unis. 8 Lo this is the man that took not | God · for his | strength :
but trusted unto the multitude of his riches, * and | strengthen'd · him- | self in · his | wickedness.
9 As for me, * I am like a green olive-tree in the | house of | God :
my trust is in the tender mercy of | God for | ever · and | ever.
10 I will always give thanks unto thee for | that · thou hast | done :
and I will hope in thy Name, for thy | saints — | like it | well.

DAY 10. EVENING PRAYER

PSALM 53

[1] The fóolish | body · hath | said in
his | heart, There | is no | God.
2 Corrupt are they, * and become abóminable | in their | wickedness :
there is | none that | do-eth | good.
3 God looked down from héav'n upon the | children · of | men :
to see if there were any that would under- | stand, and | seek · after | God.
4 But they are all gone out of the way, * they are altogether be- | come a- | bominable :
there is also none that doeth | good, — | no not | one.

5 Are not they without understanding that | work — | wickedness :
eating up my people as if they would eat bread ? * they | have not | call'd up-on | God.

6 They were afraid where | no fear | was :
for God hath broken the bones of him that besieged thee, * thou hast put them to confusion, * because | God — | hath de- | spis'd them.

Full. 7 Oh that the salvation were given unto Israel | out of | Sion :
Oh that the Lord would deliver his | peo-ple | out of · cap- | tivity !

Full. 8 Then should | Jacob · re- | joice :
and | Israel · should be | right — | glad.

PSALM 54

1 Save me O | God · for thy | Name's sake :
and a- | venge me | in thy | strength.

2 Hear my | prayer O | God :
and hearken | unto · the | words of · my | mouth.

2nd part. 3 For strangers are risen | up a- | gainst me :
and tyrants, which have not God before their | eyes, seek | after · my | soul.

4 Behold, | God is · my | helper :
the Lord is with | them that · up- | hold my | soul.

5 He shall reward evil | unto · mine | enemies :
de- | stroy thou | them in · thy | truth.

6 An offering of a free heart will I give thee, * and praise thy | Name O | Lord :
be | cause it | is so | comfortable.

7 For he hath deliver'd me out of | all my | trouble :
and mine eye hath seen his de- | sire up- | on mine | enemies.

PSALM 55

1 Hear my | prayer O | God :
and hide not thy- | self from | my pe- | tition.

2 Take heed unto | me and | hear me :
how I | mourn in · my | prayer · and am | vex'd.

3 The enemy crieth so, * and the ungódly cometh | on so | fast:
for they are minded to do me some mischief, * so maliciously | are they | set a- | gainst me.

4 My heart is dis- | quieted · with- | in me :
and the fear of | death is | fallen · up- | on me.

5 Fearfulness and trémbling are | come up- | on me :
and an horrible | dread hath | o-ver- | whelm'd me.

6 And I said, O that I had | wings · like a | dove :
for then would I flee a- | way, and | be at | rest.

7 Lo then would I gét me a- | way far | off :
and re- | main — | in the | wilderness.

8 I would make | haste · to es- | cape :
becáuse of the | storm-y | wind and | tempest.

9 Destroy their tongues O | Lord · and di- | vide them .
for I have spi'd un- | righteousness · and | strife · in the | city.

10 Day and night they go a- | bout with-in the | walls thereof :
mischief also and | sorrow · are | in the | midst of it.

11 Wíckedness | is there- | in :
deceit and guile | go not | out of · their | streets.

12 For it is not an open enemy that hath | done me · this dis- | honour :
for | then I | could have | borne it.

13 Neither was it mine adversary, * that did mágnify him- | self a- | gainst me :
for then, peradventure, | I would · have | hid my-self | from him.

14 But it was even | thou · my com- | panion :
my guide, and mine | own fa- | mi-liar | friend.

15 We took sweet | counsel · to- | gether :
and walk'd in the | house of | God as | friends.

16 Let death come hastily upon them, * and let them go down | quick · into | hell :
for wíckedness is in their | dwell-ings, | and a- | mong them.

[17] As for | me · I will | call up-
on | God, · and the | Lord shall | save me.

18 In the evening and morning, * and at noonday will I | pray and · that | instantly :
and | he shall | hear my | voice.

19 It is he that hath deliver'd my soul in peace, * from the báttle that | was a- | gainst me :
for | there were | ma-ny | with me.

20 Yea even God that endureth for ever, * shall hear me and | bring them | down :
for they will not | turn nor | fear — | God.

21 He laid his hands upon | such as · be at | peace with him :
and he | brake — | his — | covenant.

22 The words of his mouth were softer than butter, * having | war in · his | heart :
his words were smoother than oil, * and | yet · be they | ve-ry | swords.

2nd part. 23 O cast thy burden upon the Lord, and | he shall | nourish thee :
and shall not suffer the | righteous · to | fall for | ever.

24 And | as for | them :
thou O God shalt bring them | into · the | pit of · de- | struction.

Full. 25 The blood-thirsty and deceitful men shåll not live out | half their | days :
nevertheless, my | trust shall · be in | thee O | Lord.

DAY 11. MORNING PRAYER

PSALM 56

1 Be merciful unto me O God, * for man goeth a- | bout · to de- | vour me :
he is | dai-ly | fighting · and | troubling me.
2 Mine enemies are daily in hand to | swallow · me | up :
for they be many that fight a- | gainst me · O | thou most | Highest.

3 Nevertheless, though I am | sometime · a- | fraid :
yet | put I · my | trust in | thee.
4 I will praise God be- | cause of · his | word :
I have put my trust in God, * and will not | fear what | flesh can | do unto me.

5 They daily mis- | take my | words :
all that they im- | agine · is to | do me | evil.
6 They hold all together and | keep them-selves | close :
and mark my steps, | when they · lay | wait for · my | soul.
7 Shall they es- | cape for · their | wickedness :
thou O Gód in thy dis- | pleasure · shalt | cast them | down.
8 Thou tellest my flittings ; * put my | tears in-to thy | bottle :
are not these things | no-ted | in thy | book ?

9 Whensoever I call upon thee, * then shall mine enemies be | put to | flight :
this I know, for | God is | on my | side.
10 In God's word will | I re- | joice :
in the | Lord's word | will I | comfort me.
2nd part. 11 Yea in God have I | put my | trust :
I will not be a- | fraid what | man can | do unto me.
12 Unto thee O Gód will I | pay my | vows :
unto | thee · will I | give — | thanks.

13 For thou hast deliver'd my soul from death, and my | feet from | falling :
that I may walk before | God · in the | light of · the | living.

PSALM 57

(Single Chant)

1 Be merciful unto me O God, * be merciful unto me, * for my sóul | trusteth · in | thee :
and under the shadow of thy wings shall be my refuge, * until this | tyranny · be | ov-er- | past.

2 I will call unto the | most high | God :
even unto the God that shall perform the | cause · which I | have in | hand.

3 He shall | send from | heav'n :
and save me from the reproof of | him that · would | eat me | up.

4 God shall send forth his | mercy · and | truth :
my | soul · is a- | mong — | lions.

5 And I lie even among the children of men that are | set on | fire :
whose teeth are spears and arrows, * and their | tongue a | sharp — | sword.

Unis. 6 *Set up thyself O God a- | bove the | heav'ns :*
and thy | glory a-bove | all the | earth.

7 They have laid a net for my feet, * and pressed | down my | soul :
they have digged a pit before me, * and are fallen into the | midst of | it them- | selves.

8 My heart is fixed O God, my | heart is | fixed :
I will | sing and | give — | praise.

9 Awake up my glory, * awake | lute and | harp :
I my- | self · will a- | wake right | early.

10 I will give thanks unto thee O Lord, a- | mong the | people :
and I will síng unto | thee a- | mong the | nations.

11 For the greatness of thy mercy reacheth | unto · the | heavens :
and thy | truth un- | to the | clouds.

Unis. 12 *Set up thyself O God a- | bove the | heav'ns :*
and thy | glory a-bove | all the | earth.

PSALM 58

(*Single Chant*)

1 Are your minds set upon righteousness, * O ye | con-gre- | gation :
and do ye judge the thing that is | right · O ye | sons of | men?

2 Yea ye imagine mischief in your | heart up-on the | earth :
and your | hands — | deal with | wickedness.

3 The ungodly are froward, * éven from their | mo-ther's | womb:
as soon as they are bórn they go a- | stray and | speak — | lies.

4 They are as venomous as the | poison · of a | serpent :
even like the deaf | adder · that | stoppeth · her | ears ;

5 Which refuseth to hear the | voice of · the | charmer :
charm he | nev-er | so — | wisely.

6 Break their teeth O God in their mouths, * smite the jáw-bones of the | lions O | Lord :
let them fall away like water that runneth apace, * and when they shoot their arrows | let them · be | root-ed | out.

7 Let them consume away like a snail, * and be like the un-timely | fruit · of a | woman :
and | let them · not | see the | sun.

8 Or ever your pots be made | hot with | thorns :
so let indignation vex him, | even · as a | thing that · is | raw.

9 The righteous shall rejoice when he | seeth · the | vengeance :
he shall wash his footsteps in the | blood of | the un- | godly.

10 So that a man shall say, * Verily there is a re- | ward · for the | righteous :
doubtless there is a | God that | judgeth · the | earth.

DAY 11. EVENING PRAYER

PSALM 59

1 Deliver me from mine | enemies · O | God :
defend me from | them that · rise | up a- | gainst me.

2 O delíver me from the | wick-ed | doers :
and | save me · from the | blood-thirsty | men.

3 For lo, they lie | waiting · for my | soul :
the mighty men are gather'd against me, * without any offence or | fault of | me O | Lord.

4 They run and prepáre themselves with- | out my | fault :
arise thou therefore to | help me | and be- | hold.

5 Stand up O Lord God of Hosts, thou God of Israel, * to visit | all the | heathen :
and be not merciful unto them that of- | fend of · ma- | li-cious | wickedness.

6 They go to and | fro · in the | evening :
they grin like a | dog and · run a- | bout · through the | city.

2nd part. [7] Behold they speak with their mouth, * and | swords are | in their | lips, for | who doth | hear ?

8 But thou O Lórd shalt | have them · in de- | rision :
for thou shalt | laugh · all the | heathen · to | scorn.

Full. 9 *My strength will I as- | cribe un-to | thee :*
for | thou art · the | God of · my | refuge.

10 God shéweth me his | good-ness | plenteously :
and God shall let me sée my de- | sire up- | on mine | enemies.

11 Slay them not, * lest my | people · for- | get it :
but scatter them abroad among the people, * and put them | down O | Lord · our de- | fence.

12 For the sin of their mouth and for the words of their lips, * they shall be | taken · in their | pride :
and why ? * their | preaching · is of | cursing · and | lies.

13 Consume them in thy wrath, * consúme them that | they may | perish :
and know that it is God that ruleth in Jacob, * and | unto · the | ends of · the | world.

14 And in the évening they | will re- | turn :
grin like a dog and will | go a- | bout the | city.

15 They will rún here and | there for | meat :
and | grudge if · they | be not | satisfi'd.

Full. 16 As for me, I will sing of thy power, * and will praise thy mercy be- | times · in the | morning :
for thou hast been my defence and | refuge · in the | day of · my | trouble.

Full. 17 *Unto thee O my | strength · will I | sing :*
for thou O God art my | refuge · and my | merci-ful | God.

PSALM 60

(*Single Chant*)

1 O God thou hast cast us out, * and | scatter'd · us a- | broad :
thou hast also been displeas'd, O | turn thee · unto | us a- | gain.

2 Thou hast mov'd the | land · and di- | vided it :
héal the | sores there- | of · for it | shaketh.

3 Thou hast shew'd thy people | hea-vy | things :
thou hast gíven us a | drink of | dead-ly | wine.

4 Thou hast given a tóken for | such as | fear thee :
that they may | triumph · be- | cause of · the | truth.

5 Therefore were thy be- | loved · de- | liver'd :
hélp me with | thy right | hand and | hear me.

Unis. 6 God hath spoken in his holiness, * I will rejoice and di- | vide — | Sichem :
and mete | out the | valley · of | Succoth.

Unis. 7 Gilead is mine, and Ma- | nasses · is | mine :
Ephraim also is the strength of my head, | Ju-dah | is my | law-giver ;

Unis. 8 Moab is my wash-pot, * over Edom will I cast | out my | shoe :
Phil- | is-tia | be thou | glad of me.

9 Who will léad me into the | strong — | city :
who will | bring me | in-to | Edom ?
10 Hast not thou cast us | out O | God :
wilt not thou O | God go | out with · our | hosts ?
11 O be thóu our | help in | trouble :
for | vain · is the | help of | man.
Unis. 12 Through Gód will we | do great | acts :
for it is | he that · shall | tread · down our | enemies.

PSALM 61

1 Hear my | crying · O | God :
give | ear un- | to my | prayer.
2 From the ends of the | earth · will I | call upon thee :
when my | heart — | is in | heaviness.
3 O set me up upon the róck that is | higher · than | I :
for thou hast been my hope, * and a stróng tówer for | me a- | gainst the | enemy.
4 I will dwéll in thy | tabernacle · for | ever :
and my trust shall be únder the | cover-ing | of thy | wings.
5 For thou O Lórd hast | heard · my de- | sires :
and hast given an héritage unto | those that | fear thy | Name.
6 Thou shalt grant the King a | long — | life :
that his years may en- | dure through-out | all · gene- | rations.
7 He shall dwell before | God for | ever :
O prepare thy loving mercy and | faithfulness · that | they may · pre- | serve him.
8 So will I alway sing | praise un-to thy | Name :
that I may | daily · per- | form my | vows.

DAY 12. MORNING PRAYER

Psalm 62

1 My soul truly waiteth | still up-on | God :
for of | him · cometh | my sal- | vation.

2 *He verily is my strength and | my sal- | vation :*
*he is my defence, * só that I | shall not | great-ly | fall.*

3 How long will ye imagine mischief against | eve-ry | man :
ye shall be slain all the sort of you, * yea as a tottering wall shall ye be, and | like a | brok-en | hedge.

4 Their device is only how to put him out whom | God · will ex- | alt :
their delight is in lies, * they give good words with their | mouth, but | curse with · their | heart.

5 Nevertheless my soul, wait thou | still up-on | God :
for my | hope — | is in | him.

6 *He truly is my strength and | my sal- | vation :*
he is my defence, | so that · I | shall not | fall.

7 In God is my | health and · my | glory :
the rock of my | might, and · in | God is · my | trust.

8 O put your trust in him | alway · ye | people :
pour out your hearts be- | fore him · for | God is · our | hope.

9 As for the children of men, | they are · but | vanity :
the children of men are deceitful upon the weights,* they are altogether | lighter · than | vani-ty it- | self.

10 O trust not in wrong and robbery, * give not your- | selves un-to | vanity :
if riches increase, | set not · your | heart up- | on them.

11 God spake once, * and twice I have also | heard the | same :
that power be- | long-eth | un-to | God ;

12 And that thóu | Lord art | merciful :
for thou rewardest évery man ac- | cord-ing | to his | work.

PSALM 63

1 O God, | thou art · my | God :
early | will I | seek — | thee.

2 My soul thirsteth for thee, * my flesh also | long-eth | after thee :
in a barren and dry land, | where no | wa-ter | is.

3 Thus have I look'd for | thee in | holiness :
that I might be- | hold thy | power and | glory.

4 For thy loving-kindness is bétter than the | life it- | self :
my | lips — | shall — | praise thee.

5 As long as I live will I mágnify | thee on · this | manner :
and lift | up my | hands in · thy | Name.

6 My soul shall be satisfi'd, * even as it were with | marrow · and | fatness :
when my mouth | praiseth · thee with | joy-ful | lips.

7 Have I not remémber'd thee | in my | bed :
and thought up- | on thee | when I · was | waking ?

8 Becáuse thou hast | been my | helper :
therefore under the shádow of thy | wings will | I re- | joice.

9 My sóul | hangeth · up- | on thee :
thy | right hand | hath up- | holden me.

10 These also that seek the | hurt of · my | soul :
they shall | go — | under · the | earth.

11 Let them fáll upon the | edge of · the | sword :
that | they may · be a | portion · for | foxes.

12 But the King shall rejoice in God ; * all they also that swéar by | him shall · be com- | mended :
for the mouth of | them that · speak | lies · shall be | stopp'd.

PSALM 64

1 Hear my voice O | God in · my | prayer :
preserve my | life from | fear of · the | enemy.

2 Hide me from the gathering to- | gether · of the | froward :
and from the insur- | rection · of | wick-ed | doers ;

3 Who have whet their | tongue · like a | sword :
and shoot out their arrows, | ev-en | bit-ter | words ;

4 That they may privily shoot at | him that · is | perfect :
súddenly | do they | hit him · and | fear not.

5 They encóurage them- | selves in | mischief :
and commune among themselves how they may lay snares, *
and | say that | no man · shall | see them.

6 They imagine | wickedness · and | practise it :
that they keep secret among themselves, * every man | in
the | deep of · his | heart.

7 But God shall suddenly shoot at them with a | swift — | arrow :
that | they shall | be — | wounded.

8 Yea their own tongues shall | make them | fall :
insomuch that whoso | seeth them · shall | laugh them · to |
scorn.

9 And all men that see it shall say, | This hath | God done :
for they shall per- | ceive that · it is | his — | work.

10 The righteous shall rejoice in the Lord, * and put his | trust in | him:
and all they that are | true of | heart · shall be | glad.

DAY 12. EVENING PRAYER

PSALM 65

Full. 1 Thou O God art | prais'd in | Sion :
and unto thee shall the | vow · be per- | form'd · in Je- |
rusalem.

Full. 2 Thou that | hearest · the | prayer :
unto | thee shall | all flesh | come.

3 My misdeeds pre- | vail a- | gainst me :
O be thou | merci-ful | unto · our | sins.

4 Blessed is the man whom thou choosest, * and re- | ceivest ·
unto | thee :
he shall dwell in thy court, * and shall be satisfi'd with the
pleasures of thy house, | ev'n of · thy | ho-ly | temple.

5 Thou shalt shew us wonderful things in thy righteousness, * O God of | our sal- | vation :
thou that art the hope of all the ends of the earth, * and of thém that re- | main · in the | broad — | sea.

6 Who in his strength setteth | fast the | mountains :
and is | girded · a- | bout with | power.

7 Who stilleth the | raging · of the | sea :
and the noise of his waves, * and the | mad-ness | of the | people.

8 They also that dwell in the uttermost parts of the earth shall be a- | fraid at · thy | tokens
thou that makest the outgoings of the | morning · and | evening · to | praise thee.

9 Thou vísitest the | earth and | blessest it :
thou | makest · it | ve-ry | plenteous.

10 The river of God is | full of | water :
thou preparest their corn, * for só thou pro- | vid-est | for the | earth.

11 Thou waterest her furrows, * thou sendest ráin into the little | valleys · there- | of :
thou makest it soft with the drops of rain, * and | blessest · the | in-crease | of it.

[12] Thou crownest the | year with · thy | good-
ness, * | and thy | clouds drop | fatness.

13 They shall drop upon the | dwellings · of the | wilderness :
and the little hills shall re- | joice on | eve-ry | side.

14 The fólds shall be | full of | sheep :
the valleys also shall stand so thick with corn, that | they shall | laugh and | sing.

PSALM 66

Full. 1 O be joyful in God, | all ye | lands :
sing praises unto the honour of his Name, | make his | praise · to be | glorious.

Full. 2 Say unto God, * O how wonderful art | thou in · thy | works: through the greatness of thy power, * shall thine enemies be | found — | li-ars | unto thee.

3 For áll the | world shall | worship thee : sing of | thee and | praise thy | Name.

4 O come hither, * and behold the | works of | God : how wonderful he is in his doing | toward · the | children · of | men.

5 He turn'd the séa into | dry — | land : so that they went through the water on foot, | there did | we re- | joice thereof.

6 He ruleth with his power for ever ; * his eyes be- | hold the | people : and such as will not believe | shall not · be | able · to ex- | alt themselves.

7 O práise our | God ye | people : and make the | voice of · his | praise · to be | heard ;

8 Who hóldeth our | soul in | life : and suffereth | not our | feet to | slip.

9 For thou O | God hast | prov'd us : thou also hast tri'd us, | like as | silver · is | tri'd.

10 Thou bróughtest us | into · the | snare : and laidest | trouble · up- | on our | loins.

11 Thou sufferedst men to ride | over · our | heads : we went through fire and water, * and thou broughtest us | out in-to a | wealth-y | place.

12 I will go into thine | house with · burnt- | offerings : and will pay thee my vows, * which I promis'd with my lips, and spake with my mouth, | when I | was in | trouble.

13 I will offer unto thee fat burnt-sacrifices, * with the | incense · of | rams : I will | of-fer | bullocks · and | goats.

14 O come hither and hearken, * all | ye that · fear | God :
and I will tell you | what · he hath | done for · my | soul.

15 I cáll'd unto | him with · my | mouth :
and gave him | prais-es | with my | tongue.

16 If I incline unto wickedness | with mine | heart :
the | Lord — | will not | hear me.

Full. 17 But | God hath | heard me :
and con- | sider'd · the | voice of · my | prayer.

Full. 18 Praised be God, who hath not cast | out my | prayer :
nor | turn'd his | mer-cy | from me.

PSALM 67

1 God be mérciful unto | us and | bless us :
and shew us the light of his countenance, | and be | merci-ful | unto us.

2 That thy way may be | known up-on | earth :
thy saving | health a- | mong all | nations.

Unis. 3 *Let the people | praise thee · O | God :*
yea let | all the | peo-ple | praise thee.

4 O let the nations re- | joice and · be | glad:
for thou shalt judge the folk righteously, * and | govern · the | nations up-on | earth.

Unis. 5 *Let the people | praise thee · O | God :*
let | all the | peo-ple | praise thee.

6 Then shall the earth bring | forth her | increase :
and God, even our | own · God shall | give us · his | blessing.

2nd part. 7 God | — shall | bless us :
and áll the | ends of · the | world shall | fear him.

DAY 13. MORNING PRAYER

PSALM 68

Full. 1 Let God arise, * and let his | enemies · be | scatter'd :
let them also that | hate him | flee be- | fore him.

Full. 2 Like as the smoke vanisheth, * só shalt thou | drive · them a- | way :
and like as wax melteth at the fire, * so let the ungodly | perish · at the | presence · of | God.

3 But let the righteous be glád and re- | joice be-fore | God :
let them | also · be | merry · and | joyful.

4 O sing unto God, * and sing praises | unto · his | Name :
magnify him that rideth upon the heav'ns as it were upon an horse, * praise him in his Name | JAH · and re- | joice be- | fore him.

5 He is a Father of the fatherless, * and defendeth the | cause of · the | widows :
even God in his | ho-ly | ha-bi- | tation.

6 He is the God that maketh men to be of one mind in an house, * and bringeth the prisoners | out of · cap- | tivity :
but letteth the | runagates · con- | tinue · in | scarceness.

7 O God, when thou wentest forth be- | fore the | people :
when thou | went-est | through the | wilderness,

8 The earth shook, * and the heavens drópp'd at the | presence · of | God :
even as Sinai also was mov'd at the presence of God, * who | is the | God of | Israel.

9 Thou O God sentest a gracious ráin upon | thine in- | heritance :
and re- | freshedst · it | when it · was | weary.

10 Thy congregation shall | dwell there- | in :
for thou O God hast of thy | goodness · pre- | par'd · for the | poor.

Full. 11 The Lord | gave the | word :
gréat was the | compa-ny | of the | preachers.

Full. 12 Kings with their armies did | flee and · were dis- | comfited :
and they of the | household · di- | vided · the | spoil.

13 Though ye have lien among the pots, * yet shall ye be as the | wings of · a | dove :
that is cover'd with silver | wings · and her | feathers · like | gold.

14 When the Almighty scatter'd | kings for · their | sake :
thén were they as | white as | snow in | Salmon.

15 As the hill of Basan, | so is | God's hill :
even an | high hill · as the | hill of | Basan.

16 Why hop ye so ye high hills ? * this is God's hill in the which it | pleaseth · him to | dwell :
yea the Lórd will a- | bide in | it for | ever.

17 The chariots of God are twenty thousand, * even | thousands · of | angels :
and the Lord is among them, * as in the | ho-ly | place of | Sinai.

18 Thou art gone up on high, * thou hast led captivity captive, and receiv'd | gifts for | men :
yea even for thine enemies, * that the Lórd | God might | dwell a- | mong them.

Full. 19 Praised be the | Lord — | daily :
even the God who helpeth us, and | poureth · his | benefits · up- | on us.

Full. 20 He is our God, * even the God of whom | cometh · sal- | vation :
God is the Lórd by | whom · we es- | cape — | death.

21 God shall wound the | head of · his | enemies :
and the hairy scalp of such a one as | goeth · on | still in · his | wickedness.

22 The Lord hath said, * I will bring my people again, as I | did from | Basan :
mine own will I bring again, * as I did | sometime · from the | deep of · the | sea.

2nd part. 23 That thy foot may be dipp'd in the | blood of · thine | enemies :
and that the tongue of thy | dogs · may be | red · through the | same.

Can. 24 It is well seen O God, | how thou | goest :
how thou my God and King, | go-est | in the | sanctuary.

25 The singers go before, * the | minstrels · follow | after :
in the midst are the | dam-sels | playing · with the | timbrels.

26 Give thanks O Israel unto God the Lord in the | con-gre- | gations :
from the | ground — | of the | heart.

27 There is little Benjamin their ruler, * and the prínces of | Judah · their | counsel :
the princes of Za- | bulon · and the | princes · of | Nephthali.

28 Thy God hath | sent forth | strength for thee :
stablish the thing O | God that | thou hast | wrought in us,

29 For thy témple's | sake · at Je- | rusalem :
so shall kings bring | pres-ents | un-to | thee.

30 When the company of the spear-men, and multitude of the mighty are scatter'd abroad among the beasts of the people, * so that they humbly bring | pieces · of | silver :
and when he hath scatter'd the | people · that de- | light in | war ;

31 Then shall the princes | come · out of | Egypt :
the Morians' land shall soon stretch | out her | hands un-to | God.

Full. 32 Sing unto God, O ye | kingdoms · of the | earth :
O sing | prais-es | unto · the | Lord ;

Full. 33 Who sitteth in the heav'ns over | all · from the be- | ginning :
lo he doth send out his voice, | yea and | that a | mighty voice.

Full. 34 Ascribe ye the power to | God · over | Israel :
his worship and | strength is | in the | clouds.

Full. 35 O God, * wonderful art thou in thy | ho-ly | places :
even the God of Israel, * he will give strength and power unto his | peo-ple, | blessed · be | God.

DAY 13. EVENING PRAYER

PSALM 69

1 Save | me O | God :
for the waters are come in, | ev-en | unto · my | soul.

2 I stick fast in the deep mire where | no — | ground is :
I am come into deep waters, | so that · the | floods run | over me.

3 I am weary of crying, my | throat is | dry :
my sight faileth me for waiting so | long up- | on my | God.

4 They that hate me without a cause, * are more than the | hairs of · my | head :
they that are mine enemies, * and would de- | stroy me | guiltless · are | mighty.

5 I paid them the things that I | nev-er | took :
God thou knowest my simpleness, and my | faults · are not | hid from | thee.

6 Let not them that trust in thee O Lord God of hosts, * be a- | sham'd for · my | cause :
let not those that seek thee be confounded through me, | O Lord | God of | Israel.

7 And why ? * for thy sake have I | suffer'd · re- | proof :
shame | — hath | cover'd · my | face.

8 I am become a stranger | unto · my | brethren :
even an alien | unto · my | mo-ther's | children.

9 For the zeal of thine house hath | ev-en | eaten me :
and the rebukes of them that rebuk'd | thee are | fallen · up- | on me.

10 I wept, and chasten'd my- | self with | fasting :
and that was | turn'd to | my re- | proof.
11 I put on | sack-cloth | also :
and they | jest — | ed up- | on me.
12 They that sit in the gate | speak a- | gainst me :
and the | drunkards · make | songs up- | on me.

13 But Lórd I make my | prayer un-to | thee :
in | an ac- | cepta-ble | time.
14 Hear me O God, * in the multitude | of thy | mercy :
even in the | truth of | thy sal- | vation.
15 Take me out of the | mire · that I | sink not :
O let me be deliver'd from them that hate me, * and | out · of the | deep — | waters.
16 Let not the water-flood drown me, * neither let the deep | swallow · me | up :
and let not the | pit · shut her | mouth up- | on me.
17 Hear me O Lord, * for thy loving- | kindness · is | comfortable :
turn thee unto me, * according to the | multi-tude | of thy | mercies.
18 And hide not thy face from thy servant, for | I am · in | trouble :
O | haste — | thee and | hear me.
19 Draw nígh unto my | soul and | save it :
O de- | liver · me be- | cause of · mine | enemies.
20 Thou hast known my reproof, * my sháme and | my dis- | honour :
mine ádversaries are | all in | thy — | sight.
21 Thy rebuke hath broken my heart, * I am | full of | heaviness .
I look'd for some to have pity on me, * but there was no man, * neither | found I | any · to | comfort me.
22 They gave me | gall to | eat :
and when I was thirsty they | gave me | vinegar · to | drink.

23 Let their table be made a snare to | take them-selves with- | al :
and let the things that should have been for their wealth, * bé unto | them · an oc- | casion · of | falling.

24 Let their eyes be | blinded · that they | see not :
and ever | bow thou | down their | backs.

25 Pour out thine indig- | nation · up- | on them :
and let thy | wrathful · dis- | pleasure · take | hold of them.

26 Lét their habi- | tation · be | void :
ạnd | no · man to | dwell in · their | tents.

27 For they persecute him whom | thou hast | smitten :
and they talk how they may vex | them whom | thou hast | wounded.

28 Let them fall from one wickedness | tọ ạn- | other :
ạnd nọt | come in- | tọ thy | righteousness.

2nd part. 29 Let them be wip'd out of the | book of · the | living :
and not be | written · a- | mong thẹ | righteous.

---

30 As for me, when I am | poor · and in | heaviness :
thy help O | God shall | lift me | up.

31 I will praise the Náme of | God · with a | song :
ạnd | mag-ni- | fy it · with | thanksgiving.

32 This álso shall | please thẹ | Lord :
better than a | bullock · that hath | horns ạnd | hoofs.

33 The humble shall consíder this | ạnd bẹ | glad :
seek yé after | God · and your | soul shall | live.

34 For the Lórd | heareth · the | poor :
and dẹ- | spis-eth | not his | prisoners.

35 Let héav'n and | earth — | praise him :
the séa and | all that | moveth · there- | in.

36 For God will save Sion, * and build the | cities · of | Judah :
that men may dwell there, ạnd | have it | in pọs- | session.

37 The posterity also of his | servants · shall in- | herit it :
ạnd | they that · love his | Name shall | dwell therein.

PSALM 70

1 Haste thee O | God · to de- | liver me :
make | haste to | help me · O | Lord.

2 Let them be asham'd and confounded that seek | after · my | soul :
let them be turn'd backward, * and pút to con- | fusion · that | wish me | evil.

3 Let them for their reward be sóon | brought to | shame :
that cry | over · me, | There — | there.

4 But let all those that séek thee be | joyful · and | glad in thee :
and let all such as delight in thy salvation, say | alway · The | Lord be | prais'd.

5 As for me, I am | poor · and in | misery :
haste thee | un-to | me O | God.

6 Thou art my helper and | my re- | deemer :
O Lord, | make no | long — | tarrying.

DAY 14. MORNING PRAYER

PSALM 71

1 In thee O Lord have I put my trust, * let me never be | put to · con- | fusion :
but rid me, and deliver me in thy righteousness, * incline thine | ear un-to | me and | save me.

2 Be thou my strong hold, * whereuntó I may | alway · re- | sort :
thou hast promis'd to help me, * for thou art my | house of · de- | fence · and my | castle.

3 Deliver me O my God, * out of the | hand of the · un- | godly :
out of the hand of the un- | righteous · and | cru-el | man.

4 For thou O Lord God art the | thing that · I | long for :
thou art my hope, | ev-en | from my | youth.

2nd part. 5 Through thee have I been holden úp ever | since · I was | born :
thou art he that took me out of my mother's womb, * my | praise · shall be | always · of | thee.

6 I am become as it were a | monster · unto | many :
but my | sure — | trust is · in | thee.

7 O let my mouth be | fill'd with · thy | praise :
that I may sing of thy glory and | hon-our | all the · day | long.

8 Cast me not away in the | time of | age :
forsake me | not · when my | strength — | faileth me.

9 For mine enemies speak against me, * and they that lay wait for my soul take their counsel to- | gether, | saying :
God hath forsaken him, * persecute him and take him, | for there · is | none · to de- | liver him.

10 Go not | far from · me O | God :
my | God, — | haste thee · to | help me.

11 Let them be confounded and perish that are a- | gainst my | soul :
let them be cover'd with shame and dishonour that | seek to | do me | evil.

2nd part. 12 As for me, I will patiently a- | bide — | alway :
and will | praise thee | more and | more.

13 My mouth shall daily speak of thy righteousness | and sal- | vation :
for I | know no | end there- | of.

14 I will go forth in the stréngth of the | Lord — | God :
and will make | mention · of thy | righteous-ness | only.

15 Thou O God hast taught me from my | youth up · until | now :
thérefore will I | tell of · thy | won-drous | works.

16 Forsake me not O God in mine old age, * when I am | gray — | headed :
until I have shew'd thy strength unto this generation, * and thy power to all | them that · are | yet · for to | come.

17 Thy righteousness O God is | ve-ry | high :
and great things are they that thou hast done, * O God, | who is | like un-to | thee ?

18 O what great troubles and adversities hast thou shew'd me, *
and yet didst thou | turn and · re- | fresh me :
yea and broughtest me from the | deep of · the | earth a- | gain.

19 Thou hast brought me to | great — | honour :
and cómforted | me on | eve-ry | side.

20 Therefore will I praise thee and thy faithfulness O God, *
pláying upon an | instru-ment of | musick :
unto thee will I sing upon the harp, * O thou | Ho-ly | One of | Israel.

21 My lips will be fain when I | sing un-to | thee :
and só will my | soul, whom | thou hast · de- | liver'd.

22 My tongue also shall talk of thy righteousness | all the · day | long :
for they are confounded and brought unto shame that | seek to | do me | evil.

PSALM 72

Full. 1 Give the King thy | judgements · O | God :
and thy righteousness | unto · the | King's — | son.

Full. 2 Then shall he judge thy people ac- | cording · unto | right :
and de- | fend — | the — | poor.

3 The mountains also shall | bring — | peace :
and the little hills | righteous-ness | unto · the | people.

4 He shall keep the símple | folk by · their | right :
defend the children of the | poor, and | punish · the | wrong doer.

5 They shall fear thee, * as long as the sun and | moon en- | dureth :
from | one · gene- | ration · to an- | other.

6 He shall come down like the rain into a | fleece of | wool :
even as the | drops that | water · the | earth.

2nd part. 7 In his time shall the | right-eous | flourish :
yea and abundance of peace, so | long as · the | moon en- | dureth.

8 His dominion shall be also from the | one · sea to the | other :
and from the | flood un-to the | world's — | end.

9 They that dwell in the wílderness shall | kneel be- | fore him :
his | enemies · shall | lick the | dust.

10 The kings of Tharsis and of the | isles shall · give | presents :
the kings of Arabia and | Saba · shall | bring — | gifts.

11 All kings shall fall | down be- | fore him :
all | nations · shall | do him | service.

12 For he shall delíver the | poor · when he | crieth :
the needy also and | him that | hath no | helper.

13 He shall be fávourable to the | simple · and | needy :
and shall pre- | serve the | souls of · the | poor.

ıd part. 14 He shall deliver their souls from | falsehood · and | wrong :
and dear shall their | blood be | in his | sight.

15 He shall live, * and unto him shall be given of the | gold of · A- | rabia :
prayer shall be made ever unto him, * and | daily · shall | he be | prais'd.

16 There shall be an heap of corn in the earth, | high up-on the | hills :
his fruit shall shake like Libanus, * and shall be green in the | city · like | grass up-on the | earth.

ıd part. 17 His Name shall endure for ever, * his Name shall remain under the sun a- | mong the · pos- | terities :
which shall be blessed through him, * and | all the | heathen · shall | praise him.

18 Blessed be the Lord God, * even the | God of | Israel :
which | only · doeth | won-drous | things ;

19 And blessed be the Name of his | Majesty · for | ever :
and all the earth shall be fill'd with his Majesty, * A- | men, A- | — | men.

DAY 14. EVENING PRAYER

PSALM 73

1 Truly God is | loving · unto | Israel :
even unto súch as | are · of a | clean — | heart.

2 Nevertheless, my feet were | al-most | gone :
my | treadings · had | well-nigh | slipt.

3 And why ? * I was | griev'd · at the | wicked :
I do also see the un- | godly · in | such pros | perity.

4 For they are in no | peril · of | death :
but are | lus-ty | and — | strong.

5 They come in no mis- | fortune · like | other folk :
neither | are they | plagu'd like | other men.

6 And this is the cause that they are so | holden · with | pride :
and | o-ver- | whelm'd with | cruelty.

7 Their eyes | swell with | fatness :
and they do | ev-en | what they | lust.

8 They corrupt other, * and speak of | wick-ed | blasphemy :
their | talking · is a- | gainst the · most | High.

9 For they stretch forth their | mouth un-to the | heav'n :
and their | tongue · goeth | through the | world.

10 Therefore fall the | peo-ple | unto them :
and thereout | suck they · no | small ad- | vantage.

11 Tush say they, * hów should | God per- | ceive it :
is there | know-ledge | in the · most | High ?

12 Lo these are the ungodly, these prosper in the world, * and these have | riches · in pos- | session :
and I said, * Then have I cleans'd my heart in vain and | wash'd mine | hands in | innocency.

13 All the day | long have · I been | punish'd :
and | chas-ten'd | eve-ry | morning.

14 Yea and I had almost said | even · as | they :
but lo, then I should have condemn'd the gene- | ra-tion | of thy | children.

[15] Then | thought I · to | under-
stand | this, · but it | was too | hard for me,

16 Until I wént into the | sanctuary · of | God :
then under- | stood I · the | end of · these | men ;

17 Namely, * how thou dost set them in | slipper-y | places :
and | castest · them | down · and de- | stroyest them.

18 Oh how suddenly | do they · con- | sume :
perish and | come · to a | fear-ful | end !

2nd part. 19 Yea even like as a | dream · when one a- | waketh :
so shalt thou make their image to | van-ish | out of · the |
city.

20 Thus my | heart was | griev'd :
and it went | ev-en | through my | reins.

21 So foolish was | I and | ignorant :
even as it | were a | beast be- | fore thee.

22 Nevertheless, I am | alway · by | thee :
for thou hast holden me | by my | right — | hand.

23 Thou shalt | guide me · with thy | counsel :
and after | that re- | ceive me · with | glory.

24 Whóm have I in | heav'n but | thee :
and there is none upon earth that I de- | sire · in com- |
parison · of | thee.

25 My flésh and my | heart — | faileth :
but God is the strength of my | heart · and my | portion · for |
ever.

26 For lo, they that for- | sake thee · shall | perish :
thou hast destroy'd all thém that com- | mit · forni- |
cation · a- | gainst thee.

Full. 27 But it is good for me to hold me fast by God, * to put my
trust in the | Lord — | God :
and to speak of all thy works in the | gates · of the |
daughter · of | Sion.

PSALM 74

1 O God, wherefore art thou absent | from us · so | long :
why is thy wrath so | hot a-gainst the | sheep of · thy | pasture ?

2 O think upon thy | con-gre- | gation :
whom thou hast | purchas'd · and re- | deem'd of | old.

3 Think upon the tribe of | thine in- | heritance :
and mount | Sion · where- | in · thou hast | dwelt.

4 Lift up thy feet, * that thou mayest utterly destroy | eve-ry | enemy :
which hath done | ev-il | in thy | sanctuary.

5 Thine adversaries roar in the midst of thy | con-gre- | gations :
and set | up their | banners · for | tokens.

6 He that hew'd timber afore out of the | thick — | trees :
was known to | bring it · to an | excel-lent | work.

7 But now they break down all the carved | work there- | of :
with | ax-es | and — | hammers.

8 They have set fire upon thy | ho-ly | places :
and have defil'd the dwelling-place of thy Name, | ev-en | unto · the | ground.

9 Yea they said in their hearts, * Let us make hávock of them | al-to- | gether :
thus have they burnt up all the | houses · of | God · in the | land.

10 We see not our tokens, * there is not | one · prophet | more :
no not one is there among us, * that under- | stand-eth | an-y | more.

11 O God, how long shall the adversary | do · this dis- | honour :
how long shall the enemy blas- | pheme thy | Name, * for | ever ?

12 Why withdrawest | thou thy | hand :
why pluckest thou not thy right hand out of thy | bosom · to con- | sume the | enemy ?

13 For Gód is my | King ọf | old :
the help that is done upon | earth he | doeth it · him- | self.

14 Thou didst divide the | sea · through thy | power :
thou brakest the | heads of · the | dragons · in the | waters.

15 Thou smotest the héads of Le- | viathan · in | pieces :
and gavest him to be | meat · for the | people · in the | wilderness.

16 Thou broughtest out fountains and waters out of the | hard — | rocks :
thọu | driedst · up | migh-ty | waters.

17 The day is thine, and the | night ịs | thine :
thọu hạst prẹ- | par'd thẹ | light and · the | sun.

18 Thou hast set all the | borders · of the | earth :
thọu hạst | made — | summer · and | winter.

19 Remember this O Lord, * how the enemy | hạth rẹ- | buk'd :
and how the foolish | peọple · hath blas- | phem'd thy | Name.

20 O deliver not the soul of thy turtle-dove unto the multitude | ọf thẹ | enemies :
and forget not the cọngrẹ- | gation · of the | poor fọr | ever.

21 Look up- | ọn thẹ | covenant :
for all the earth is full of darkness ạnd | cru-ẹl | hạ-bị- | tations.

22 O let not the símple go a- | way ạ- | sham'd :
but let the poor and | needy · give | praise un-to thy | Name.

23 Arise O God, * mạin- | tain thine · own | cause :
remember how the fóolish | man blas- | phemeth · thee | daily.

24 Forgét not the | voice of · thine | enemies :
the presumption of them that hate thee increaseth | ev-er | more ạnd | more.

DAY 15. MORNING PRAYER

PSALM 75

Full. 1 Unto thee O God dọ | we give | thanks :
yea unto | thee dọ | we give | thanks.

Full. 2 Thy Name also | is so | nigh :
and thát do thy | won-drous | works dẹ- | clare.

3 When I re- | ceive the · congre- | gation :
I shall | judge ạc- | cording · unto | right.

4 The earth is weak, * and all the in- | habiters · there- | of :
I bear | up thẹ | pil-lars | of it.

5 I said unto the fools, | Deal not · so | madly :
and to the ungodly, | Set not | up your | horn.

6 Set not up your | horn on | high :
ạnd | speak not · with a | stiff — | neck.

7 For promotion cometh | neither · from the | east :
nor from the | west, nor | yet · from the | south.

8 And why ? | God · is the | Judge :
he putteth down | one, ạnd | setteth · up an- | other.

9 For in the hand of the Lord there is a cup, ạnd thẹ | wine is | red :
it is full mix'd, * and he | pour-eth | out of · the | same.

10 Ạs | fọr thẹ | dregs thereof :
all the ungodly of the earth shall | drink them · and | suck them | out.

Full. 11 But I will talk ọf thẹ | God ọf | Jacob :
ạnd | praise — | him fọr | ever.

Full. 12 All the horns of the ungodly | also · will I | break :
and the horns ọf thẹ | righteous · shall | be ex- | alted.

PSALM 76

(*Single Chant*)

1 In Jéwry is | God — | known :
hịs | Name is | great in | Israel.

2 Ạt | Salem · is his | tabernacle :
ạnd hịs | dwell-ing | ịn — | Sion.

3 There brake he the | arrows · of the | bow :
the | shield the | sword · and the | battle.

[4] Thou art of | more — | honour
and | might · than the | hills of · the | robbers.

5 The proud are robb'd, * they have | slept their | sleep :
and all the men whose hands were | mighty · have | found — | nothing.

6 At thy rebuke, O | God of | Jacob :
both the | chariot · and | horse are | fallen.

7 Thou, even | thou art · to be | fear'd :
and who may stánd in thy | sight when | thou art | angry.

8 Thou didst cause thy júdgement to be | heard from | heav'n :
the earth | trem-bl'd | and was | still,

9 When God a- | rose to | judgement :
and to | help · all the | meek up-on | earth.

10 The fierceness of man shall | turn to · thy | praise :
and the | fierceness · of them | shalt thou · re- | frain.

11 Promise unto the Lord your God, and keep it, * all yé that are | round a- | bout him :
bring presents unto | him that | ought to · be | fear'd.

12 He shall refrain the | spirit · of | princes :
and is wonderful a- | mong the | kings of · the | earth.

PSALM 77

1 I will cry unto | God with · my | voice :
even unto God will I cry with my voice, * and | he shall | heark-en | unto me.

2 In the time of my trouble I | sought the | Lord :
my sore ran, and ceas'd not in the night-season, * my | soul re- | fus-ed | comfort.

3 When I am in heaviness, I will | think up-on | God :
when my heart is | vex'd I | will com- | plain.

4 Thou hóldest mine | eyes — | waking :
I am so | feeble · that I | can-not | speak.
5 I have consider'd the | days of | old :
and the | years — | that are | past.
6 I call to re- | membrance · my | song :
and in the night I commune with mine own | heart and | search out · my | spirits.
7 Will the Lord ab- | sent him-self for | ever :
and | will he · be no | more in- | treated ?
8 Is his mercy clean | gone for | ever :
and is his promise come útterly to an | end for | ev-er- | more ?

2nd part. 9 Hath God for- | gotten · to be | gracious :
and will he shut up his loving-| kind-ness | in dis- | pleasure ?

10 And I said, It is mine | own in- | firmity :
but I will remember the years of the right | hand · of the | most — | Highest.
11 I will remember the | works of · the | Lord :
and call to | mind thy | wonders · of | old time.

2nd part. 12 I will think also of | all thy | works :
and my | talking · shall | be of · thy | doings.
13 Thy way O | God is | holy :
who is so | great a | God as | our God ?
14 Thou art the | God that · doeth | wonders :
and hast declar'd thy | power a- | mong the | people.
15 Thou hast míghtily de- | liver'd · thy | people :
even the | sons of | Jacob · and | Joseph.
16 The waters saw thee O God, * the waters saw thee and | were a- | fraid :
the | depths — | also · were | troubl'd.
17 The clouds pour'd out water, the | air — | thunder'd :
and thine | ar-rows | went a- | broad.

18 The voice of thy thunder was | heard · round a- | bout :
the lightnings shone upon the ground, * the earth was | mov'd and | shook with- | al.

19 Thy way is in the sea, and thy páths in the | great — | waters :
and thy | foot-steps | are not | known.

20 Thou leddest thy | people · like | sheep :
by the | hand of | Moses · and | Aaron.

DAY 15. EVENING PRAYER

PSALM 78

Full. 1 Hear my law | O my | people :
incline your | ears un-to the | words of · my | mouth.

Full. 2 I will open my | mouth in · a | parable :
I will de- | clare hard | senten-ces of | old ;

Full. 3 Which we have | heard and | known :
and | such as · our | fathers · have | told us ;

Full. 4 That we should not hide them from the chíldren of the gene- | rations · to | come :
but to shew the honour of the Lord, * his mighty and wonderful | works that | he hath | done.

5 He made a covenant with Jacob, and gave | Israel · a | law :
which he commánded our fore- | fathers · to | teach their | children.

6 That their pos- | terity · might | know it :
and the | children · which were | yet un- | born ;

7 To the intént that | when they · came | up :
they might | shew their | children · the | same ;

8 That they might put their | trust in | God :
and not to forget the works of | God · but to | keep his · com- | mandments ;

9 And not to be as their forefathers, a faithless and | stubborn · gene- | ration :
a generation that set not their heart aright, * and whose spirit cleaveth not | steadfast-ly | un-to | God ;

10 Like as the | children · of | Ephraim :
who being harness'd and carrying bows, * túrn'd themselves | back · in the | day of | battle.

11 They kept not the | covenant · of | God :
and | would not | walk in · his | law ;

12 But for- | gat what · he had | done :
and the wonderful | works that · he had | shew-ed | for them.

Full. 13 Marvellous things did he in the sight of our forefathers, * in the | land of | Egypt :
even | in the | field of | Zoan.

Full. 14 He divided the sea and | let them · go | through :
he made the | waters · to | stand on · an | heap.

Full. 15 In the day-time also he | led them · with a | cloud :
and all the night | through · with a | light of | fire.

Full. 16 He clave the hard | rocks · in the | wilderness :
and gave them drink thereof, * as it had been | out of · the | great — | depth.

2nd part. Full. 17 He brought waters out of the | ston-y | rock :
so that it | gush'd out | like the | rivers.

18 Yet for all this they sinn'd | more a- | gainst him :
and provok'd the most | High-est | in the | wilderness.

19 They tempted | God in · their | hearts :
and re- | quir-ed | meat for · their | lust.

20 They spake against God | al-so, | saying :
Shall God prepare a | ta-ble | in the | wilderness ?

21 He smote the stony rock indeed, that the water gush'd out, * and the streams | flow'd with- | al :
but can he give bread also, * or provide | flesh — | for his | people ?

22 When the Lord heard | this · he was | wroth :
so the fire was kindl'd in Jacob, * and there came up heavy dis- | pleasure · a- | gainst — | Israel ;

23 Because they be- | liev'd · not in | God :
and | put not · their | trust in · his | help.

24 So he commanded the | clouds a- | bove :
and | open'd · the | doors of | heav'n.

25 He rain'd down manna also upon them | for to | eat :
and | gave them | food from | heav'n.

26 So man did eat | an-gels' | food :
for he | sent them | meat e- | nough.

27 He caus'd the east-wind to | blow · under | heav'n :
and through his power he brought | in the | south-west | wind.

28 He rain'd flesh upon them as | thick as | dust :
and feather'd fowls | like as · the | sand of · the | sea.

29 He let it fall a- | mong their | tents :
even round a- | bout their | ha-bi- | tation.

2nd part. 30 So they did eat and were well fill'd, for he gave them their | own de- | sire :
they were not disap- | point-ed | of their | lust.

31 But while the meat was yet in their mouths, the heavy wrath of God came upon them, * and slew the | wealthi-est | of them :
yea and smote down the chosen | men that | were in | Israel.

32 But for all this they | sinn'd yet | more :
and be- | liev'd · not his | won-drous | works.

33 Therefore their days did he con- | sume in | vanity :
and their | years — | in — | trouble.

34 When he | slew them · they | sought him :
and turn'd them early, and en- | quir-ed | af-ter | God.

35 And they remember'd that | God was · their | strength :
and that the high | God was | their re- | deemer.

36 Nevertheless, they did but flatter him | with their | mouth :
and dis- | sembl'd · with him | in their | tongue.

37 For their | heart was · not | whole with him :
neither continu'd they | stead-fast | in his | covenant.

38 But he was so merciful, that he for- | gave their · mis- | deeds :
and de- | stroy-ed | them — | not.

39 Yea many a time turn'd he his | wrath a- | way :
and would not suffer his whole dis- | plea-sure | to a- | rise.

40 For he consider'd that they | were but | flesh :
and that they were even a wind that passeth away, * and | com-eth | not a- | gain.

41 Many a time did they pro- | voke him · in the | wilderness :
and | griev'd him | in the | desert.

42 They turn'd back, and | tempt-ed | God :
and mov'd the | Ho-ly | One in | Israel.

43 They thought not | of his | hand :
and of the day when he deliver'd them from the | hand — | of the | enemy ;

44 How he had wrought his | miracles · in | Egypt :
and his | wonders · in the | field of | Zoan.

45 He turn'd their | waters · into | blood :
so that they | might not | drink of · the | rivers.

46 He sent lice among them, and de- | vour'd them | up :
and | frogs — | to de- | stroy them.

47 He gave their | fruit un-to the | caterpillar :
and their | la-bour | unto · the | grasshopper.

48 He destroy'd their | vines with | hail-stones :
and their | mulber-ry- | trees · with the | frost.

49 He smote their cattle | also · with | hail-stones :
and their | flocks with | hot — | thunder-bolts.

50 He cast upon them the furiousness of his wrath, * anger, dis- | pleasure · and | trouble :
and sent | ev-il | angels · a- | mong them.

51 He made a way to his indignation, * and spar'd not their | soul from | death :
but gave their life | ov-er | to the | pestilence ;
52 And smote all the | first-born · in | Egypt :
the most principal and | mightiest · in the | dwellings · of | Ham.

53 But as for his own people, he led them | forth like | sheep :
and carri'd them in the | wilder-ness | like a | flock.
54 He brought them out safely that they | should not | fear :
and overwhelm'd their | ene-mies | with the | sea.
55 And brought them within the | borders · of his | sanctuary :
even to his mountain which he | purchas'd · with his | right — | hand.
56 He cast out the heathen | also · be- | fore them :
caus'd their land to be divided among them for an heritage, *
and made the tribes of | Israel · to | dwell in · their | tents.

57 So they tempted and displeas'd the | most High | God :
and | kept — | not his | testimonies ;
58 But turn'd their backs, and fell a- | way like · their | forefathers :
starting a- | side · like a | brok-en | bow.
d part. 59 For they | griev'd him · with their | hill-altars :
and provok'd him to dis- | plea-sure | with their | images.
60 When God heard this | he was | wroth :
and took | sore dis- | pleasure · at | Israel.
61 So that he forsook the | tabernacle · in | Silo :
even the | tent that · he had | pitch'd a-mong | men.
62 He deliver'd their power | into · cap- | tivity :
and their beauty | into · the | ene-my's | hand.
63 He gave his people over also | unto · the | sword :
and was | wroth with | his in- | heritance.
64 The fire consum'd their | young — | men :
and their | maidens · were not | given · to | marriage.

65 Their priests were | slain with · the | sword :
and there were no | widows · to | make · lamen- | tation.

Full. 66 So the Lord awáked as | one · out of | sleep :
and like a | giant re- | fresh'd with | wine.

Full. 67 He smote his enemies in the | hind-er | parts :
and | put them · to a per- | pet-ual | shame.

Full. 68 He refus'd the | tabernacle · of | Joseph :
and | chose · not the | tribe of | Ephraim ;

Full. 69 But chose the | tribe of | Judah :
even the hill of | Si-on | which he | lov'd.

70 And there he built his | temple · on | high :
and laid the foundation of it, * like the ground which | he hath | made con- | tinually.

71 He chose David | also · his | servant :
and | took him · a- | way from · the | sheep-folds.

72 As he was following the ewes great with | young ones · he | took him :
that he might feed Jacob his people, and | Is-rael | his in- | heritance.

Full. 73 So he fed them with a faithful and | true — | heart :
and rul'd them | prudently · with | all his | power.

DAY 16. MORNING PRAYER

PSALM 79

1 O God, the heathen are cóme into | thine in- | heritance :
thy holy temple have they defil'd, * and made Je- | rusa-lem an | heap of | stones.

2 The dead bodies of thy servants have they given to be meat unto the | fowls of · the | air :
and the flesh of thy | saints un-to the | beasts of · the | land.

3 Their blood have they shed like water on every | side of · Je- | rusalem :
and | there was | no man · to | bury them.

4 We are become an open | shame · to our | enemies :
a very scorn and derision unto | them that · are | round a- | bout us.

5 Lord, how | long wilt · thou be | angry :
shall thy jealousy | burn like | fire for | ever ?

6 Pour out thine indignation upon the heathen that | have not | known thee :
and upon the kingdoms that have not | call'd up- | on thy | Name.

7 Fór they have de- | vour-ed | Jacob :
and | laid — | waste his | dwelling-place.

8 O remember not our old sins, * but have mercy upon us, and | that — | soon :
for we are | come to | great — | misery.

9 Help us O God of our salvation, * for the | glory of · thy | Name :
O deliver us, and be merciful | unto · our | sins · for thy | Name's sake.

[10] Wherefore | do the | heathen
say, | Where is | now their | God ?

11 O let the vengeance of thy servants' | blood that · is | shed :
be openly shew'd upon the | hea-then | in our | sight.

12 O let the sorrowful sighing of the prisoners | come be- | fore thee :
according to the greatness of thy power, * preserve thou | those that · are ap- | pointed · to | die.

13 And for the blasphemy wherewith our neighbours | have blas- | phem'd thee :
reward thou them O Lord | seven-fold | into · their | bosom.

Full. 14 So we that are thy people and sheep of thy pasture, shall give thee | thanks for | ever :
and will alway be shewing forth thy praise from gene- | ration · to | ge-ne- | ration.

Psalm 80

1 Hear O thou Shepherd of Israel, * thou that leadest | Joseph · like a | sheep :
shew thyself also, * thou that | sittest · up- | on the | cherubims.

2 Before Ephraim, Benjamin | and Ma- | nasses :
stir up thy | strength and | come and | help us.

2nd part. Unis. 3 *Turn us a- | gain O | God :*
shew the light of thy | countenance · and | we shall · be | whole.

4 O Lord | God of | hosts :
how long wilt thou be | angry · with thy | people · that | prayeth ?

5 Thou feedest them with the | bread of | tears :
and givest them | plenteousness · of | tears to | drink.

6 Thou hast made us a very | strife un-to our | neighbours :
and our | ene-mies | laugh us · to | scorn.

Unis. 7 *Turn us again thou | God of | Hosts :*
shew the light of thy | countenance · and | we shall · be | whole.

8 Thou hast brought a | vine · out of | Egypt :
thou hast cast | out the | heathen · and | planted it.

9 Thou | mad-est | room for it :
and when it had taken | root it | fill'd the | land.

10 The hills were | cover'd · with the | shadow of it :
and the boughs thereof were | like the | good-ly | cedar-trees.

11 She stretch'd out her branches | unto · the | sea :
and her | boughs un- | to the | river.

12 Why hast thou then broken | down her | hedge :
that all they that go | by pluck | off her | grapes ?

13 The wild boar out of the wood doth | root it | up :
and the wild | beasts of · the | field de- | vour it.

2nd part. Unis. 14 Turn thee again thou God of hosts, * look | down from | heav'n :
be- | hold and | visit · this | vine ;

15 And the place of the vineyard that thy right | hand hath | planted :
and the branch that thou | madest · so | strong for · thy- | self.

16 It is burnt with | fire and · cut | down :
and they shall | perish · at the re- | buke of · thy | countenance.

17 Let thy hand be upon the man of thy | right — | hand :
and upon the son of man, * whom thou madest so | strong for | thine own | self.

18 And so will not | we go | back from thee :
O let us live, * and we shall | call up- | on thy | Name.

2nd part. Unis. 19 *Turn us again O Lord | God of | hosts :*
shew the light of thy | countenance · and | we shall · be | whole.

PSALM 81

(*Single Chant*)

Full. 1 Sing we merrily unto | God our | strength :
make a cheerful | noise un-to the | God of | Jacob.

Full. 2 Take the psalm, bring | hither · the | tabret :
the | mer-ry | harp · with the | lute.

3 Blow up the trúmpet in the | new — | moon :
even in the time appointed, | and up-on our | so-lemn | feast-day.

4 For this was made a | statute · for | Israel :
and a | law of · the | God of | Jacob.

5 This he ordain'd in | Joseph · for a | testimony :
when he came out of the land of Egypt, * and had | heard a | strange — | language.

6 I eas'd his | shoulder · from the | burden :
and his hands were de- | liver'd · from | making · the | pots.

7 Thou calledst upon me in troubles, and | I de- | liver'd thee :
and heard thee what | time as · the | storm · fell up- | on thee.

[8] I | prov'd thee | al-
so | at the | waters · of | strife.

9 Hear O my people, and I will as- | sure thee · O | Israel :
if thou wilt | heark-en | un-to | me,

10 There shall no | strange god | be in thee :
neither shalt thou | worship · any | oth-er | god.

11 I am the Lord thy God, * who brought thee out of the | land of | Egypt :
open thy mouth | wide and | I shall | fill it.

12 But my people would not | hear my | voice :
and | Is-rael | would not · o- | bey me.

13 So I gave them up unto their | own hearts' | lusts :
and let them | follow · their | own im-agi- | nations.

14 O that my people would have | hearken'd · unto | me :
for if | Israel · had | walk'd in · my | ways,

15 I should soon have put | down their | enemies :
and turn'd my | hand a- | gainst their | adversaries.

16 The haters of the Lord should have been | found — | liars :
but their time | should have · en- | dur'd for | ever.

17 He should have fed them also with the | fin-est | wheat-flour :
and with honey out of the stony | rock should | I have | satisfi'd thee.

DAY 16. EVENING PRAYER

PSALM 82

(*Single Chant*)

1 God standeth in the congre- | gation · of | princes :
he | is a | Judge a-mong | gods.

2 How long will ye | give wrong | judgement :
and accept the | per-sons | of the · un- | godly ?

3 Defend the | poor and | fatherless :
see that such as are in | need and · ne- | cessity · have | right.

4 Deliver the | outcast · and | poor :
save them | from the | hand of the · un- | godly.
5 They will not be learned nor understand, * but walk on | still in | darkness :
all the foundations of the | earth are | out of | course.
6 I have said, | Ye are | gods :
and ye are all the | chil-dren | of the · most | Highest.
7 Bút ye shall | die like | men :
and | fall like | one of · the | princes.
Full. 8 Arise O God, and | judge · thou the | earth :
for thou shalt take all | heathen · to | thine in- | heritance.

Psalm 83

1 Hold not thy tongue O God, | keep not · still | silence :
re- | frain not · thy- | self O | God.
2 For lo, thine enemies | make a | murmuring :
and they that | hate thee · have | lift up · their | head.
3 They have imagin'd craftily a- | gainst thy | people :
and taken | counsel · a- | gainst thy | secret ones.
4 They have said, Come and let us root them out, * that they be no | more a | people :
and that the name of Israel may | be no | more · in re- | membrance.
5 For they have cast their heads together with | one con- | sent :
and | are con- | federate · a- | gainst thee ;
6 The tabernacles of the Edomites | and the | Ismaelites :
the | Mo-a- | bites, and | Hagarens ;
7 Gebal, and | Ammon · and | Amalek :
the Philistines, with | them that | dwell at | Tyre.
8 Assur | also · is | join'd with them :
and have | holpen · the | children · of | Lot.
9 But do thou to them as | unto · the | Madianites :
unto Sisera, * and unto | Jabin · at the | brook of | Kison ;

10 Who | perish'd · at | Endor :
and be- | came as · the | dung of · the | earth.

11 Make them and their princes like | Oreb · and | Zeb :
yea make all their princes like as | Ze-ba | and Sal- | mana ;

[12] Who say, Let us | take to · our- | selves
the | houses · of | God in · pos- | session.

13 O my God, * make them | like un-to a | wheel :
and as the | stubble · be- | fore the | wind ;

14 Like as the fire that | burneth · up the | wood :
and as the | flame that · con- | sumeth · the | mountains.

15 Persecute them even | so with · thy | tempest :
and | make them · a- | fraid with · thy | storm.

16 Make their faces a- | sham'd O | Lord :
that | they may | seek thy | Name.

17 Let them be confounded and vex'd ever | more and | more :
let them be | put to | shame and | perish.

Full. 18 And they shall know that thou, whose | Name is · Je- | hovah :
art only the most | Highest · over | all the | earth.

Psalm 84

[1] O how | amia-ble | are
thy | dwellings, · thou | Lord of | hosts !

2 My soul hath a desire and longing to enter into the | courts of · the | Lord :
my heart and my flesh re- | joice · in the | liv-ing | God.

3 Yea the sparrow hath found her an house, * and the swallow a nest, * whére she may | lay her | young :
even thy altars O Lord of | hosts my | King and · my | God.

4 Blessed are they that | dwell in · thy | house :
they | will be | al-way | praising thee.

5 Blessed is the man whose | strength is · in | thee :
in whose | heart — | are thy | ways.

6 Who going through the vale of misery | use it · for a | well :
and the | pools are | fill'd with | water.

2nd part. 7 They will go from | strength to | strength :
and unto the God of gods appeareth | every · one of | them in | Sion.

8 O Lord God of hosts, | hear my | prayer :
heark- | en O | God of | Jacob.

9 Behold O | God · our de- | fender :
and look upon the | face of | thine A- | nointed.

[10]For one | day in · thy | courts
is | bet-ter | than a | thousand.

11 I had rather be a door-keeper in the | house of · my | God :
than to | dwell in · the | tents of · un- | godliness.

12 For the Lord God is a | light and · de- | fence :
the Lord will give grace and worship, * and no good thing shall he withhold from | them that · live a | god-ly | life.

13 O Lord | God of | hosts :
blessed is the man that | putteth · his | trust in | thee.

PSALM 85

1 Lord thou art become gracious | unto · thy | land :
thou hast turn'd a- | way the · cap- | tivity · of | Jacob.

2 Thou hast forgiven the of- | fence of · thy | people :
and | cov-er'd | all their | sins.

2nd part. 3 Thou hast taken away | all · thy dis- | pleasure :
and turn'd thyself from thy | wrath-ful | in-dig- | nation.

4 Turn us then, O | God our | Saviour :
and | let thine | an-ger | cease from us.

5 Wilt thou be dis- | pleas'd at · us for | ever :
and wilt thou stretch out thy wrath from | one · gene- | ration · to an- | other ?

6 Wilt thou not turn a- | gain and | quicken us :
that thy | people · may re- | joice in | thee ?

7 Shew us thy | mercy · O | Lord :
and | grant us | thy sal- | vation.

8 I will hearken what the Lord God will | say con- | cerning me :
for he shall speak peace unto his people and to his | saints ·
that they | turn · not a- | gain.

9 For his salvation is | nigh · them that | fear him :
that | glory · may | dwell in · our | land.

10 Mercy and truth are | met to- | gether :
righteousness and | peace have | kiss'd each | other.

11 Truth shall flourish | out of · the | earth :
and righteousness hath | look-ed | down from | heav'n.

12 Yea the Lord shall shew | lov-ing- | kindness :
and our | land shall | give her | increase.

13 Righteousness shall | go be- | fore him :
and he shall di- | rect his | going · in the | way.

DAY 17. MORNING PRAYER

PSALM 86

1 Bow down thine ear O | Lord and | hear me :
for | I am | poor · and in | misery.

2 Preserve thou my | soul for · I am | holy :
my God save thy | servant · that | putteth · his | trust in thee.

3 Be merciful unto | me O | Lord :
for I will | call — | daily · up- | on thee.

4 Comfort the | soul of · thy | servant :
for unto thee O | Lord, · do I | lift · up my | soul.

5 For thou Lord art | good and | gracious :
and of great | mercy · unto | all · them that | call upon thee.

6 Give ear | Lord un-to my | prayer :
and ponder the | voice of · my | humble · de- | sires.

2nd part. [7] In the | time of · my | trouble
I will | call up-on | thee for · thou | hearest me.

Full. 8 Among the gods there is none like unto | thee O | Lord :
there is not | one that · can | do as | thou doest.

Full. 9 All nations whom thou hast made shall come and | worship · thee O | Lord :
and shall | glo-ri- | fy thy | Name.

2nd part. Full. 10 For thou art great, and doest | won-drous | things :
thou | — art | God a- | lone.

11 Teach me thy way O Lord, * and I will | walk in · thy | truth :
O knit my heart unto | thee that · I may | fear thy | Name.

12 I will thank thee O Lord my God, with | all my | heart :
and will praise thy | Name for | ev-er- | more.

13 For great is thy | mercy · to- | ward me :
and thou hast deliver'd my | soul · from the | nether-most | hell.

14 O God, the proud are | risen · a- | gainst me :
and the congregations of naughty men have sought after my soul, * and have not set | thee be- | fore their | eyes.

15 But thou O Lord God, art full of com- | passion · and | mercy :
long-suffering, | plenteous · in | goodness · and | truth.

16 O turn thee then unto me, and have | mercy · up- | on me :
give thy strength unto thy servant, * and | help the | son of · thine | handmaid.

2nd part. 17 Shew some token upon me for good, * that they who hate me may | see it and · be a- | sham'd :
because thou | Lord hast | holpen · me and | comforted me.

PSALM 87

Full. 1 Her foundations are upon the | ho-ly | hills :
the Lord loveth the gates of Sion | more than · all the | dwellings · of | Jacob.

Full. [2] Very excellent | things are | spoken
of | thee, thou | city · of | God.

3 I will think upon | Rahab · and | Babylon :
with | them that | know — | me.

4 Behold ye the | Philis-tines | also :
and they of Tyre with the | Morians · lo | there was · he | born.
5 And of Sion it shall be reported that | he was | born in her :
and | the most | High shall | stablish her.
6 The Lord shall rehearse it when he | writeth · up the | people :
that | he was | born — | there.
2nd part. 7 The singers also and trumpeters | shall he · re- | hearse :
All my fresh | springs shall | be in | thee.

PSALM 88

1 O Lord God of my salvation, * I have cri'd day and | night be- | fore thee :
O let my prayer enter into thy presence, * in- | cline thine | ear un-to my | calling.
2 For my soul is | full of | trouble :
and my | life · draweth | nigh un-to | hell.
3 I am counted as one of them that go | down in-to the | pit :
and I have been even as a | man that | hath no | strength.
4 Free among the dead, * like unto them that are wounded, and | lie · in the | grave :
who are out of remembrance, * and are | cut a- | way from · thy | hand.
5 Thou hast laid me in the | low-est | pit :
in a place of | darkness · and | in the | deep.
6 Thine indignation | li-eth | hard upon me :
and thou hast | vex'd · me with | all thy | storms.
7 Thou hast put away mine ac- | quain-tance | far from me :
and | made · me to | be ab- | horr'd of them.
[8] I am so | fast in | prison
that I | can-not | get — | forth.
9 My sight faileth for | ve-ry | trouble :
Lord I have call'd daily upon thee, * I have stretch'd | forth my | hands un-to | thee.

10 Dost thou shew wonders a- | mong the | dead :
or shall the dead rise | up a- | gain and | praise thee ?

11 Shall thy loving-kindness be | shew'd · in the | grave :
or thy | faithful-ness | in de- | struction ?

12 Shall thy wondrous works be | known · in the | dark :
and thy righteousness in the land where | all things | are for- | gotten ?

13 Unto thee have I | cri'd O | Lord :
and early shall my | prayer — | come be- | fore thee.

14 Lord why ab- | horrest · thou my | soul :
and | hid-est | thou thy | face from me ?

15 I am in misery, * and like unto him that is at the | point to | die :
even from my youth up, * thy terrors have I | suffer'd · with a | trou-bl'd | mind.

16 Thy wrathful dis- | pleasure · goeth | over me :
and the | fear of · thee | hath un- | done me.

17 They came round about me | daily · like | water :
and compass'd me to- | gether · on | eve-ry | side.

18 My lovers and friends hast thou | put a- | way from me :
and hid mine ac- | quain-tance | out of · my | sight.

DAY 17. EVENING PRAYER

PSALM 89

Full. 1 My song shall be alway of the loving- | kindness · of the | Lord :
with my mouth will I ever be shewing thy truth, * from | one · gene- | ration · to an- | other.

Full. 2 For I have said, * Mercy shall be set | up for | ever :
thy truth shalt thou | stab-lish | in the | heav'ns.

3 I have made a covenant | with my | chosen :
I have | sworn un-to | David · my | servant.

4 Thy seed will I | stablish · for | ever :
and set up thy throne from | one · gene- | ration · to an- | other.

Full. 5 O Lord, the very heav'ns shall praise thy | won-drous | works :
and thy truth in the congre- | ga-tion | of the | saints.

Full. 6 For who is | he a-mong the | clouds :
that shall be com- | par'd un- | to the | Lord ?

Full. 7 And what is | he a-mong the | gods :
that shall be | like un- | to the | Lord ?

8 God is very greatly to be fear'd in the | council · of the | saints :
and to be had in reverence of all | them that · are | round a- | bout him.

9 O Lord God of hosts, * who is | like un-to | thee :
thy truth most mighty | Lord · is on | eve-ry | side.

10 Thou rulest the | raging · of the | sea :
. thou stillest the | waves there-of | when · they a- | rise.

11 Thou hast subdu'd | Egypt · and de- | stroy'd it :
thou hast scatter'd thine enemies a- | broad with · thy | migh-ty | arm.

12 The heavens are thine, the earth | also · is | thine :
thou hast laid the foundation of the round world, and | all that | there-in | is.

13 Thou hast made the | north · and the | south :
Tabor and | Hermon · shall re- | joice in · thy | Name.

14 Thou hast a | migh-ty | arm :
strong is thy | hand and | high is · thy | right hand.

15 Righteousness and equity are the habi- | tation · of thy | seat :
mercy and | truth shall | go be-fore thy | face.

16 Blessed is the people O | Lord that · can re- | joice in thee :
they shall | walk in · the | light of · thy | countenance.

17 Their delight shall be | daily in · thy | Name :
and in thy righteousness | shall they | make their | boast.

18 For thou art the | glory of · their | strength :
and in thy loving-kindness | thou shalt · lift | up our | horns.

2nd part. 19 For the | Lord is · our de- | fence :
the Holy One of | Is-rael | is our | King.

20 Thou spakest sometime in visions unto thy | saints and | saidst :
I have laid help upon one that is mighty, * I have exalted one | cho-sen | out of · the | people.

21 I have found | David · my | servant :
with my holy | oil have | I a- | nointed him.
22 My hand shall | hold him | fast :
and | my — | arm shall | strengthen him.
23 The enemy shall not be able to | do him | violence :
the son of | wicked-ness | shall not | hurt him.
24 I will smite down his foes be- | fore his | face :
and | plague — | them that | hate him.
25 My truth also and my | mercy · shall be | with him :
and in my | Name shall · his | horn · be ex- | alted.
26 I will set his dominion | also · in the | sea :
and his | right hand | in the | floods.
27 He shall call me, | Thou art · my | Father :
my | God · and my | strong sal- | vation.
28 And I will | make him · my | first-born :
higher | than the | kings of · the | earth.
29 My mercy will I keep for him for | ev-er- | more :
and my | covenant · shall | stand — | fast with him.
2nd part. 30 His seed also will I make to en- | dure for | ever :
and his | throne · as the | days of | heaven.
31 But if his children for- | sake my | law :
and | walk not | in my | judgements ;
32 If they break my statutes, * and keep not | my com- | mandments :
I will visit their offences with the | rod · and their | sin with | scourges.
33 Nevertheless, * my loving-kindness will I not | utter-ly | take from him :
nor | suffer · my | truth to | fail.
34 My covenant will I not break, * nor alter the thing that is gone | out of · my | lips :
I have sworn once by my holiness, * that I | will not | fail — | David.
Full. 35 His seed shall en- | dure for | ever :
and his seat is | like as · the | sun be- | fore me.

Full. 36 He shall stand fast for ever- | more · as the | moon :
and as the | faith-ful | witness · in | heav'n.

37 But thou hast abhorr'd and forsaken | thine A- | nointed :
and | art dis- | pleas-ed | at him.

38 Thou hast broken the covenant | of thy | servant :
and | cast his | crown · to the | ground.

39 Thou hast overthrown | all his | hedges :
and | bro-ken | down his | strong holds.

40 All | they that go · by | spoil him :
and he is be- | come a · re- | proach · to his | neighbours.

41 Thou hast set up the right | hand of · his | enemies :
and made all his | adver-saries | to re- | joice.

42 Thou hast taken away the | edge of · his | sword :
and givest him not | victor-y | in the | battle.

43 Thou hast put | out his | glory :
and cast his | throne — | down · to the | ground.

44 The days of his | youth hast · thou | shorten'd :
and | cover'd · him | with dis- | honour.

45 Lord how long wilt thou hide thy- | self, * for | ever :
and shall thy | wrath — | burn like | fire ?

46 O remember how | short my | time is :
wherefore hast thou made | all — | men for | nought ?

47 What man is he that liveth, and | shall not · see | death :
and shall he deliver his | soul · from the | hand of | hell ?

48 Lord where are thy | old · loving- | kindnesses :
which thou swarest unto | Da-vid | in thy | truth ?

49 Remember Lord the re- | buke that · thy | servants have :
and how I do bear in my bosom the re- | bukes of | ma-ny | people ;

50 Wherewith thine enemies | have blas- | phem'd thee :
and slander'd the | footsteps · of | thine A- | nointed ;

2nd part. Full. 51 Praised be the Lord for | ev-er- | more :
A- | men and | A — | men.

DAY 18. MORNING PRAYER

Psalm 90

Full. 1 Lord, thou hast | been our | refuge :
from | one · gene- | ration · to an- | other.

Full. 2 Before the mountains were brought forth, * or ever the earth and the | world were | made :
thou art God from ever- | lasting · and | world with-out | end.

3 Thou turnest | man · to de- | struction :
again thou sayest, * Come a- | gain ye | children · of | men.

4 For a thousand years in thy sight are | but as | yesterday :
seeing that is | past · as a | watch · in the | night.

5 As soon as thou scatterest them they are | even · as a | sleep :
and fade away | sudden-ly | like the | grass.

6 In the morning it is green, and | grow-eth | up :
but in the evening it is cut | down, dri'd | up · and | wither'd.

7 For we consume away in | thy dis- | pleasure :
and are afraid at thy | wrath-ful | in-dig- | nation.

8 Thou hast set our mis- | deeds be- | fore thee :
and our secret | sins · in the | light of · thy | countenance.

9 For when thou art angry, all our | days are | gone :
we bring our years to an end, | as it · were a | tale that · is | told.

10 The days of our age are threescore years and ten, * and though men be so strong that they | come to · fourscore | years :
yet is their strength then but labour and sorrow, * so soon passeth it a- | way and | we are | gone.

11 But who regardeth the | power of · thy | wrath :
for even thereafter as a man feareth, | so is | thy dis- | pleasure.

12 So teach us to | number · our | days :
that we may ap- | ply our | hearts un-to | wisdom.

13 Turn thee again O | Lord · at the | last :
and be | gra-cious | unto · thy | servants.

14 O satisfy us with thy | mercy and · that | soon :
so shall we rejoice and be | glad · all the | days of · our | life.

15 Comfort us again now after the | time that · thou hast | plagu'd us :
and for the years where- | in · we have | suffer'd · ad- | versity.

16 Shew thy | servants · thy | work :
and their | chil-dren | thy — | glory.

2nd part. Full. 17 And the glorious Majesty of the Lord our | God · be up- | on us :
prosper thou the work of our hands upon us, * O | pros-per | thou our | handy-work.

PSALM 91

1 Whoso dwelleth under the de- | fence of the · most | High :
shall abide | under · the | shadow · of the Al- | mighty.

2 I will say unto the Lord, * Thou art my | hope and · my | strong hold :
my | God in | him · will I | trust.

3 For he shall deliver thee from the | snare of · the | hunter :
and | from the | noi-some | pestilence.

4 He shall defend thee under his wings, * and thou shalt be safe | under · his | feathers :
his faithfulness and | truth shall · be thy | shield and | buckler.

5 Thou shalt not be afraid for any | terror · by | night :
nor for the | arrow · that | flieth · by | day;

6 For the pestilence that | walketh · in | darkness :
nor for the sickness that de- | stroy-eth | in the | noon-day.

7 A thousand shall | fall be- | side thee :
and ten thousand at thy right | hand · but it | shall not · come | nigh thee.

8 Yea with thine eyes shalt | thou be- | hold:
and | see · the re- | ward of · the un- | godly.

2nd part. 9 For thou Lord, | art my | hope :
thou hast set thine | house of · de- | fence · very | high.

10 There shall no evil | hap-pen | unto thee :
neither shall any | plague come | nigh thy | dwelling.

11 For he shall give his angels | charge — | over thee :
to | keep · thee in | all thy | ways.

12 They shall | bear thee · in their | hands :
that thou hurt not thy | foot a- | gainst a | stone.

13 Thou shalt go upon the | lion · and | adder :
the young lion and the dragon shalt thou | tread — | under · thy | feet.

Full. 14 Because he hath set his love upon me, * therefore will | I de- | liver him :
I will set him up, be- | cause · he hath | known my | Name.

Full. 15 He shall call upon me, and | I will | hear him :
yea I am with him in trouble, * I will de- | liver him · and | bring him · to | honour.

2nd part. Full. 16 With long | life will · I | satisfy him :
and | shew him | my sal- | vation.

PSALM 92

Full. 1 It is a good thing to give | thanks un-to the | Lord :
and to sing praises unto thy | Name — | O most | Highest ;

Full. 2 To tell of thy loving-kindness | early · in the | morning :
and of thy | truth — | in the | night-season ;

3 Upon an instrument of ten strings, | and up-on the | lute :
upon a loud | instru-ment, | and up-on the | harp.

4 For thou Lord hast made me | glad · through thy | works :
and I will rejoice in giving praise, * for the oper- | a-tions | of thy | hands.

5 O Lord, how glorious | are thy | works :
thy | thoughts are | ve-ry | deep.

6 An unwise man doth not | well con- | sider this :
and a | fool · doth not | un-der- | stand it.

7 When the ungodly are green as the grass, * and when all the workers of | wickedness · do | flourish :
then shall they be destroy'd for ever, * but thou Lord art the most | Highest · for | ev-er- | more.

8 For lo thine enemies O Lord, * lo thine | enemies · shall | perish :
and all the workers of | wickedness · shall | be de- | stroy'd.

9 But mine horn shall be exalted like the | horn of · an | unicorn :
for I am a- | nointed · with | fresh — | oil.

10 Mine eye also shall see his | lust of · mine | enemies :
and mine ear shall hear his desire of the | wicked · that a- | rise · up a- | gainst me.

11 The righteous shall | flourish · like a | palm-tree :
and shall spread a- | broad · like a | cedar · in | Libanus.

12 Such as are planted in the | house of · the | Lord :
shall flourish in the | courts of · the | house of · our | God.

13 They also shall bring forth more | fruit in · their | age :
and | shall be | fat and · well- | liking.

14 That they may shew how true the | Lord my | strength is :
and that there is | no un- | righteous-ness | in him.

DAY 18. EVENING PRAYER

PSALM 93

(*Single Chant*)

Full. 1 The Lord is King, * and hath put on | glorious · ap- | parel :
the Lord hath put on his apparel, and | girded · him- | self with | strength.

Full. [2] He hath | made the · round | world
so | sure · that it | cannot · be | mov'd.

3 Ever since the world began hath thy | seat · been pre- | par'd :
thou | art from | ev-er- | lasting.

4 The floods are risen O Lord, * the floods have lift | up their | voice:
the | floods lift | up their | waves.

5 The waves of the sea are mighty, and | rage — | horribly :
but yet the Lord, who | dwelleth · on | high, is | mightier.

6 Thy testimonies O Lord, are | ve-ry | sure :
holiness be- | cometh · thine | house for | ever.

PSALM 94

1 O Lord God, to whom | vengeance · be- | longeth :
thou God, to whom | vengeance · be- | long-eth, | shew thyself.

2 Arise, thou | Judge of · the | world :
and reward the | proud · after | their de- | serving.

3 Lord how | long · shall the un- | godly :
how | long · shall the un- | god-ly | triumph ?

4 How long shall all wicked doers | speak · so dis- | dainfully :
and | make such | proud — | boasting ?

[5] They smite | down thy | people
O | Lord, and | trouble · thine | heritage.

6 They murder the | widow · and the | stranger :
and | put the | fatherless · to | death.

2nd part. 7 And yet they say, * Tush the | Lord shall · not | see :
neither shall the | God of | Jacob · re- | gard it.

8 Take heed, ye un- | wise a-mong the | people :
O ye fools, | when · will ye | un-der- | stand ?

9 He that planted the ear, | shall he · not | hear :
or he that made the | eye — | shall he · not | see ?

10 Or he that | nurtureth · the | heathen :
it is he that teacheth man | know-ledge | shall not · he | punish ?

[11] The Lord | knoweth · the | thoughts
of | man, that | they are · but | vain.

12 Blessed is the man whom thou | chastenest · O | Lord :
and | teachest · him | in thy | law ;

13 That thou mayest give him patience in | time of · ad- | versity :
until the | pit be · digged | up for · the un- | godly.

14 For the Lord will not | fail his | people :
neither | will he · for- | sake his · in- | heritance ;

15 Until righteousness turn a- | gain un-to | judgement :
all such as are | true in | heart shall | follow it.

16 Who will rise up with me a- | gainst the | wicked :
or who will take my part a- | gainst the | ev-il- | doers ?

17 If the | Lord had · not | help'd me :
it had not fail'd but my | soul had · been | put to | silence.

18 But when I said, My | foot hath | slipt :
thy | mercy · O | Lord · held me | up.

19 In the multitude of the sorrows that I | had in · my | heart :
thy | comforts · have re- | fresh'd my | soul.

20 Wilt thou have any thing to do with the | stool of | wickedness :
which imagineth | mis-chief | as a | law ?

21 They gather them together against the | soul of · the | righteous :
and con- | demn the | inno-cent | blood.

Full. 22 But the | Lord is · my | refuge :
and my | God is · the | strength of · my | confidence.

Full. 23 He shall recompense them their wickedness, * and destroy them in their | own — | malice :
yea the | Lord our | God · shall de- | stroy them.

DAY 19. MORNING PRAYER

PSALM 95

(*Single Chant*)

Full. 1 O come, let us | sing un-to the | Lord :
let us heartily rejoice in the | strength of | our sal- | vation.

Full. 2 Let us come before his | presence · with | thanksgiving :
and shew ourselves | glad in | him with | psalms.

3 For the Lord is a | great — | God :
and a great | King a-bove | all — | gods.

4 In his hand are áll the | corners · of the | earth :
and the | strength of · the | hills is · his | also.

5 The sea is | his and · he | made it :
and his | hands pre- | par'd the · dry | land.

Full. 6 O come, let us worship and | fall — | down :
and | kneel be-fore the | Lord our | Maker.

Full. 7 For he is the | Lord our | God :
and we are the people of his | pasture · and the | sheep of · his | hand.

8 To-day if ye will hear his voice, | harden · not your | hearts :
as in the provocation, * and as in the day of temp- | ta-tion | in the | wilderness ;

9 When your | fa-thers | tempted me :
prov'd | me and | saw my | works.

10 Forty years long was I grieved with this gene- | ration · and | said :
It is a people that do err in their hearts, * for they | have not | known my | ways ;

11 Unto whom I | sware in · my | wrath :
that they should not | en-ter | into · my | rest.

PSALM 96

(*Single or Triple Chant*)

Full. 1 O síng unto the | Lord a · new | song :
síng unto the | Lord —| all the · whole | earth.

Full. 2 Sing unto the Lord and | praise his | Name :
be telling of hís sal- | vation · from | day to | day.

Full. 3 Declare his honour | unto · the | heathen :
and his | wonders · unto | all — | people.

4 For the Lord is great, * and cannot | worthi-ly be | prais'd :
he is | more · to be | fear'd than | all gods.

5 As for all the gods of the heathen, | they are · but | idols ;
but it is the | Lord that | made the | heav'ns.

6 Glory and | worship · are be- | fore him :
power and | honour · are | ịn hịs | sanctuary.

7 Ascribe unto the Lord O ye | kindreds · of the | people :
ascribe unto the | Lord — | worship · and | power.

8 Ascribe unto the Lord the honour | due un-to his | Name :
brịng | presents · and | come in-to his | courts.

9 O worship the Lord in the | beauty · of | holiness :
lẹt thẹ | whole earth | stand ịn | awe of him.

10 Tell it out among the héathen that the | Lord is | King :
and that it is he who hath made the round world so fast that it cannot be mov'd, * and how that he shall | judge thẹ | peo-ple | righteously.

11 Let the heavens rejoice, and lẹt thẹ | earth be | glad :
let the sea make a noise and | all thạt | there-in | is.

12 Let the field be jóyful and | all that · is | in it :
then shall all the trees of the wood rẹ- | joice bẹ- | fore thẹ | Lord.

(*third part.*) 13 For he cometh, * for he cómeth to | judge thẹ | earth :
and with righteousness to judge the world, * ạnd thẹ | peo-ple | wịth hịs | truth.

PSALM 97

(*Single Chant*)

Full. 1 The Lord is King, * thẹ | earth · may be | glad thereof :
yea the | multitude · of the | isles · may be | glad thereof.

Full. 2 Clouds and dárkness are | round ạ- | bout him :
righteousness and júdgement are the habi- | ta-tion | ọf hịs | seat.

3 There shall go a | fire bẹ- | fore him :
and burn up his | enemies · on | eve-ry | side.

4 His lightnings gave | shine un-to the | world :
the earth | saw it · and | wạs ạ- | fraid.

5 The hills melted like wax at the | presence · of the | Lord :
at the presence of the | Lord · of the | whole — | earth.
6 The héav'ns have de- | clar'd his | righteousness :
and all the | people · have | seen his | glory.

7 Confounded be all they that worship carv'd images, * and that de- | light in · vain | gods :
worship | him — | all ye | gods.
8 Sion heard of it | and re- | joic'd :
and the daughters of Judah were glad, * be- | cause of · thy | judgements · O | Lord.

9 For thou Lord art higher than áll that are | in the | earth :
thou art ex- | alt-ed | far a-bove | all gods.
10 O yé that love the Lord, * see that ye hate the | thing which · is | evil :
the Lord preserveth the souls of his saints, * he shall delíver them from the | hand of | the un- | godly.
11 There is sprung up a | light · for the | righteous :
and joyful gládness for | such as · are | true — | hearted.
12 Rejoice in the | Lord ye | righteous :
and give thánks for a re- | mem-brance | of his | holiness.

DAY 19. EVENING PRAYER

PSALM 98

Full. 1 O síng unto the | Lord a · new | song :
for | he hath · done | marvel-lous | things.
Full. 2 With his own right hand, and with his | ho-ly | arm :
hath he | gotten · him- | self the | victory.
3 The Lord de- | clar'd his · sal- | vation :
his righteousness hath he openly | shew'd · in the | sight of · the | heathen.

4 He hath remember'd his mercy and truth toward the | house of | Israel :
and all the ends of the world have séen the sal- | va-tion | of our | God.

5 Shew yourselves jóyful unto the Lord | all ye | lands :
sing, re- | joice and | give — | thanks.

6 Praise the | Lord up-on the | harp :
sing to the | harp · with a | psalm of | thanksgiving.

7 With trumpets | also · and | shawms :
O shew yourselves joyful be- | fore the | Lord the | King.

8 Let the sea make a noise, * and áll that | there-in | is :
the round | world and | they that | dwell therein.

9 Let the floods clap their hands, * and let the hills be joyful togéther be- | fore the | Lord :
for he is | come to | judge the | earth.

[10] With ríghteousness | shall he | judge
the | world, · and the | people · with | equity.

PSALM 99

1 The Lord is King, * be the people | never · so im- | patient :
he sitteth between the cherubims, * be the earth | nev-er | so un- | quiet.

2 The Lord is | great in | Sion :
and | high a- | bove all | people.

3 They shall give | thanks un-to thy | Name :
which is great, | won-der- | ful and | holy.

4 The King's power loveth judgement, * thóu hast pre- | par-ed | equity :
thou hast executed | judgement · and | righteous-ness in | Jacob.

2nd part. 5 *O mágnify the | Lord our | God :*
and fall down before his | footstool · for | he is | holy.

6 Moses and Aaron among his priests, * and Samuel among such as | call up-on his | Name :
these | call'd up-on the | Lord · and he | heard them.

7 He spake unto them out of the | cloud-y | pillar :
for they kept his testimonies, | and the | law that · he | gave them.

8 Thou héardest them O | Lord our | God :
thou forgavest them O God, * and | punishedst · their | own in- | ventions.

9 *O magnify the Lord our God, * and wórship him upon his | ho-ly | hill :*
for the | Lord our | God is | holy.

PSALM 100

Full. 1 O be joyful in the Lord, | all ye | lands :
serve the Lord with gladness, * and cóme before his | pres-ence | with a | song.

Full. 2 Be ye sure that the | Lord · he is | God :
it is he that hath made us and not we ourselves, * we are his | people · and the | sheep of · his | pasture.

3 O go your way into his gates with thánksgiving, * and into his | courts with | praise :
be thankful unto | him and · speak | good of · his | Name.

4 For the Lord is gracious, * his mercy is | ev-er- | lasting :
and his truth endúreth from gene- | ration · to | ge-ne- | ration.

PSALM 101

1 My sóng shall be of | mercy · and | judgement :
unto | thee O | Lord · will I | sing.

[2] O let me have | un-der- | stand-
ing, | in the | way of | godliness.

3 Whén wilt thou | come un-to | me :
I will walk in my | house · with a | per-fect | heart.

4 I will take no wicked thing in hand, * I hate the | sins of · un- | faithfulness :
there shall | no such | cleave un- | to me.

5 A froward | heart · shall de- | part from me :
I will not | know a | wick-ed | person.

[6] Whoso privily | slandereth · his | neigh-
bour, | him will | I de- | stroy.

7 Whoso hath also a proud | look and · high | stomach :
I | will not | suf-fer | him.

8 Mine eyes look upon such as are | faithful · in the | land :
that | they may | dwell — | with me.

9 Whoso leadeth a | god-ly | life :
he | — shall | be my | servant.

10 There shall no deceitful person | dwell in · my | house :
he that telleth líes shall not | tar-ry | in my | sight.

2nd part. 11 I shall soon destroy all the ungódly that are | in the | land :
that I may root out all wicked dóers from the | ci-ty | of
the | Lord.

DAY 20. MORNING PRAYER

PSALM 102

1 Hear my | prayer O | Lord :
and let my | cry-ing | come un-to | thee.

2 Hide not thy face from me in the | time of · my | trouble :
incline thine ear unto me when I call, * O | hear me · and |
that right | soon.

3 For my days are consum'd a- | way like | smoke :
and my bones are burnt | up · as it | were a | fire-brand.

4 My heart is smitten dówn and | wither'd · like | grass :
só that I for- | get to | eat my | bread.

5 For the | voice of · my | groaning :
my | bones will · scarce | cleave to · my | flesh.

6 I am become like a pélican | in the | wilderness :
and like an | owl · that is | in the | desert.

2nd part. 7 I have watch'd, * and am éven as it | were a | sparrow :
that | sitteth · a- | lone up-on the | house-top.

8 Mine enemies revile me | all the · day | long :
and they that are mad upon me are | sworn to- | gether · a- | gainst me.

9 For I have eaten ashes | as it · were | bread :
and | mingl'd · my | drink with | weeping ;

10 And that because of thine indig- | nation · and | wrath :
for thou hast taken me | up and | cast me | down.

11 My days are | gone · like a | shadow :
and | I am | wither'd · like | grass.

Full. 12 But thou O Lord shalt en- | dure for | ever :
and thy re- | membrance · throughout | all · gene- | rations.

Full. 13 Thou shalt arise and have | mercy up-on | Sion :
for it is time that thou have mercy upon her, | yea the | time is | come.

2nd part. 14 And why ? * thy servants | think up-on her | stones :
and it pítieth them to | see her | in the | dust.

15 The heathen shall fear thy | Name O | Lord :
and áll the | kings of · the | earth thy | Majesty ;

16 When the Lord shall | build up | Sion :
and when his | glo-ry | shall ap- | pear ;

17 When he turneth him unto the práyer of the | poor — | destitute :
and de- | spiseth · not | their de- | sire.

18 This shall be written for | those that · come | after :
and the péople which shall be | born shall | praise the | Lord.

19 For he hath look'd | down · from his | sanctuary :
out of the héav'n did the | Lord be- | hold the | earth ;

20 That he might hear the mournings of súch as are | in cap- | tivity :
and deliver the children ap- | point-ed | un-to | death ;

21 That they may declare the Name of the | Lord in | Sion :
and his | wor-ship | at Je- | rusalem ;

22 When the péople are | gather'd · to- | gether :
and the kingdoms | also · to | serve the | Lord.

23 He brought down my | strength · in my | journey :
and | short-en'd | my — | days.

24 But I said, O my God, * take me not awáy in the | midst of · mine | age :
as for thý years, * they en- | dure through-out | all · gene- | rations.

25 Thou Lord in the beginning hast laid the foun- | dation · of the | earth :
and the | heav'ns · are the | work of · thy | hands.

26 They shall perish, but | thou shalt · en- | dure :
they all shall wax | old as | doth a | garment ;

27 And as a vesture shalt thou change them, * and | they shall · be | chang'd :
but thou art the | same and · thy | years · shall not | fail.

28 The children of thy | servants · shall con- | tinue :
and their | seed shall · stand | fast in · thy | sight.

PSALM 103

Full. 1 Praise the Lord | O my | soul :
and all that is within me | praise his | ho-ly | Name.

Full. 2 Praise the Lord | O my | soul :
and for- | get not | all his | benefits ;

3 Who forgiveth | all thy | sin :
and | heal-eth | all · thine in- | firmities ;

4 Who sáveth thy | life from · de- | struction :
and crówneth thee with | mercy · and | lov-ing- | kindness ;

2nd part. 5 Who satisfieth thy mouth with | good — | things :
making thee young and | lus-ty | as an | eagle.

6 The Lord executeth | righteousness · and | judgement :
for all | them that · are op- | press'd with | wrong.

7 He shewed his | ways un-to | Moses :
his | works un-to the | children · of | Israel.

8 The Lord is fúll of com- | passion · and | mercy :
long-súffering | and of | great — | goodness.

9 He will not | alway · be | chiding :
neither | keepeth · he his | anger · for | ever.

2nd part. 10 He hath not deált with us | after · our | sins :
nor re- | warded · us ac- | cording · to our | wickednesses.

11 For look how high the héav'n is in com- | parison · of the | earth :
so great is his mercy | also · toward | them that | fear him.

12 Look how wide also the | east is · from the | west :
so fár hath he | set our | sins — | from us.

13 Yea like as a father pítieth his | own — | children:
even só is the Lord | merciful · unto | them that | fear him.

14 For he knóweth where- | of · we are | made :
he re- | memb'reth · that | we are · but | dust.

15 The days of mán are | but as | grass :
for he flóurisheth as a | flow-er | of the | field.

16 For as soon as the wind goeth óver it, | it is | gone :
and the | place there-of shall | know it · no | more.

17 But the merciful goodness of the Lord, * endureth for ever and ever upon | them that | fear him :
and his | righteous-ness upon | chil-dren's | children ;

18 Even upon such as | keep his | covenant :
and thínk upon | his com- | mandments · to | do them.

19 The Lord hath prepar'd his | seat in | heav'n :
and his kingdom | rul-eth | ov-er | all.

20 O praise the Lord ye angels of his, * yé that ex- | cel in | strength :
ye that fulfil his commandment, * and hearken | unto · the | voice of · his | words.

21 O praise the Lord, all | ye his | hosts :
ye servants of | his that | do his | pleasure.

22 O speak good of the Lord all ye works of his, * in all pláces of | his dọ- | minion :
praise thou the | Lord — | O my | soul.

DAY 20. EVENING PRAYER

PSALM 104

Full. 1 Praise the Lord | O my | soul :
O Lord my God, thou art become exceeding glorious, * thou art | cloth'd with | majesty · ạnd | honour.

Full. 2 Thou deckest thyself with líght as it | were · with a | garment :
and spreadest | out thẹ | heav'ns · like a | curtain.

3 Who layeth the beams of his | chambers · in the | waters :
and maketh the clouds his chariot, * ạnd | walketh up-on the | wings of · the | wind.

4 He maketh his | an-gels | spirits :
ạnd hịs | minis-ters a | flam-ing | fire.

5 He laid the foun- | dations · of the | earth :
thạt ịt | never · should | move ạt | any time.

6 Thou coveredst it with the deep, | like as · with a | garment :
thẹ | wa-ters | stand · in the | hills.

7 At thy re- | buke they | flee :
at the voice of thy | thun-der | they are · a- | fraid.

8 They go up as high as the hills, * and dówn to the | valleys · be- | neath :
even unto the place which | thou · hast ap- | point-ed | for them.

9 Thou hast set them their bounds whịch thẹy | shall not | pass :
neither turn ạ- | gain tọ | cover · the | earth.

10 He sendeth the | springs in-to the | rivers :
whịch | run ạ- | mọng thẹ | hills.

11 All beasts of the | field — | drink thereof :
and the wild | ass-es | quench their | thirst.

12 Beside them shall the fowls of thẹ áir have their | ha-bi-* | tation :
ạnd | sing ạ- | mọng thẹ | branches.

13 He wátereth the | hills · from a- | bove :
the earth is | fill'd · with the | fruit of · thy | works.

14 He bringeth fórth | grass · for the | cattle :
and green | herb · for the | service · of | men ;

15 That he may bring food out of the earth, * and wíne that maketh | glad the · heart of | man :
and oil to make him a cheerful countenance, * and | bread to | strengthen · man's | heart.

16 The trees of the Lord also are | full of | sap :
even the cedars of | Liban-us | which he · hath | planted;

17 Wherein the birds | make their | nests :
and the fír-trees are a | dwell-ing | for the | stork.

18 The high hills are a réfuge for the | wild — | goats :
and só are the | ston-y | rocks · for the | conies.

19 He appointed the | moon for · certain | seasons :
and the sun | knoweth · his | go-ing | down.

20 Thou makest dárkness that it | may be | night :
wherein all the | beasts · of the | forest · do | move.

21 The lions roaring | after · their | prey :
do | seek their | meat from | God.

22 The sun ariseth, and they gét them a- | way to- | gether :
and | lay them | down · in their | dens.

nd part. [23] Man goeth | forth · to his | work
and to his | labour, · un- | til the | evening.

24 O Lord, how mánifold | are thy | works :
in wisdom hast thou made them all, * the | earth is | full of · thy | riches.

25 So is the great and wide | sea — | also :
wherein are things creeping innumerable, * both | small and | great — | beasts.

26 There go the ships, and | there is · that Le- | viathan :
whom thou hast | made to · take his | pastime · there- | in.

27 These wait | all up-on | thee :
that thou mayest | give them | meat in · due | season.

28 When thou gívest it | them they | gather it :
and when thou openest thy | hand · they are | fill'd with | good.

29 When thou hídest thy | face · they are | troubl'd :
when thou takest away their breath they die, * ạnd ạre. | turn'd ạ- | gain to · their | dust.

30 When thou lettest thy breath go | forth they · shall be | made :
and thou shalt rẹ- | new thẹ | face of · the | earth.

31 The glorious Majesty of the Lórd shall en- | dure fọr | ever :
thẹ | Lord · shall re- | joice in · his | works.

32 The éarth shall | tremble · at the | look of him :
if he do but | touch thẹ | hills · they shall | smoke.

33 I will sing unto the Lórd as | long as · I | live :
I will praise my | God · while I | have my | being.

34 And só shall my | words — | please him :
mỵ | joy shall | be in · the | Lord.

35 As for sinners, they shall be consum'd out of the earth, * and the ungódly shall | come · to an | end :
praise thou the Lórd O my | soul, * praise | — thẹ | Lord.

DAY 21. MORNING PRAYER

PSALM 105

Full. 1 O give thanks unto the Lord, * ạnd | call up-on his | Name :
tell the | people · what | things · he hath | done.

Full. 2 O let your songs be of | him ạnd | praise him :
and let your tálking be of | all his | won-drous | works.

3 Rejóice in his | ho-ly | Name :
let the heart of them rẹ- | joice that | seek thẹ | Lord.

4 Seek the | Lord and · his | strength :
seek his | face — | ẹv-ẹr- | more.

5 Remember the marvellous | works that · he hath | done :
his wónders and the | judge-ments | ọf hịs | mouth,

6 O ye seed of | Abraham · his | servant :
yẹ | children · of | Jacob · his | chosen.

7 He is the | Lord our | God :
his | judgements · are in | all the | world.

8 He hath been alway mindful of his | covenant · and | promise :
that he made to a | thou-sand | ge-ne- | rations ;

9 Even the cóvenant that he | made with | Abraham :
and the | oath that · he | sware · unto | Isaac ;

10 And appointed the same unto | Jacob · for a | law :
and to Israel for an | ev-er- | last-ing | testament ;

11 Saying, Unto thee will I give the | land of | Canaan :
the | lot of | your in- | heritance ;

12 When there were | yet · but a | few of them :
and they | stran-gers | in the | land ;

13 What time as they went from óne | nation · to an- | other :
from óne | kingdom · to an- | oth-er | people ;

14 He suffer'd nó man to | do them | wrong :
but re- | próv'd · even | kings for · their | sakes ;

2nd part. 15 Touch not | mine A- | nointed :
and | do my | prophets · no | harm.

16 Moreover, he call'd for a | dearth up-on the | land :
and destroy'd | all the · pro- | vision · of | bread.

17 But he had sent a | man be- | fore them :
even Jóseph who was | sold to | be a | bond-servant ;

18 Whose feet they | hurt · in the | stocks :
the iron | en-ter'd | into · his | soul ;

19 Until the time cáme that his | cause was | known :
the | word of · the | Lord — | tri'd him.

20 The king | sent · and de- | liver'd him :
the prince of the | peo-ple | let him · go | free.

21 He made him lord | also · of his | house :
and | ruler · of | all his | substance ;

2nd part. 22 That he might inform his princes | after · his | will :
and | teach his | sena-tors | wisdom.

23 Israel also | came · into | Egypt :
and Jacob was a | stranger · in the | land of | Ham.

24 And he increas'd his | people · ex- | ceedingly :
and made them | strong-er | than their | enemies ;

25 Whose heart turn'd só that they | hated · his | people :
and | dealt un- | tru-ly · with his | servants.

26 Then sent he | Moses · his | servant :
and | Aa-ron | whom he · had | chosen.

27 And these shew'd his | tokens · a- | mong them :
and | wonders · in the | land of | Ham.

28 He sent darkness, | and it · was | dark :
and they were not o- | be-dient | unto · his | word.

[29] He | turn'd · their | waters
into | blood, and | slew their | fish.

30 Their land | brought forth | frogs :
yea | even · in their | kings' — | chambers.

31 He spake the word, * and there came all | manner · of | flies :
and | lice in | all their | quarters.

32 He gave them | hailstones · for | rain :
and | flames of | fire in · their | land.

33 He smote their vines | also · and | fig-trees :
and destroy'd the | trees that · were | in their | coasts.

34 He spake the word, and the grasshoppers came, * and | caterpillars · in- | numerable :
and did eat up all the grass in their land, * and de- | vour'd the | fruit of · their | ground.

35 He smote all the first-born | in their | land :
even the | chief of | all their | strength.

36 He brought them forth álso with | silver · and | gold :
there was not óne féeble | person · a- | mong their | tribes.

[37] Egypt was | glad at · their de- | part-
ing, | for they | were a- | fraid of them.

38 He spread out a | cloud to · be a | covering :
and | fire to · give | light · in the | night-season.

39 At their de- | sire he · brought | quails :
and he | fill'd them · with the | bread of | heaven.

40 He open'd the rock of stone, * and the | waters · flow'd | out :
so that rivers | ran · in the | dry — | places.

41 For why ? * he remember'd his | ho-ly | promise :
and | A-bra- | ham his | servant.

[42] And he brought | forth his | people
with | joy, · and his | chosen · with | gladness ;

43 And gáve them the | lands of · the | heathen :
and they took the lábours of the | peo-ple | in pos- | session ;

44 That they might | keep his | statutes :
and ob- | serve — | his — | laws.

DAY 21. EVENING PRAYER

PSALM 106

1 O give thanks unto the Lord, for | he is | gracious :
and his | mercy · en- | dureth · for | ever.

2 Who can express the noble | acts of · the | Lord :
or | shew forth | all his | praise ?

[3] Blessed are | they that | alway
keep | judge-ment | and do | righteousness.

4 Remember me O Lord, * according to the favour that thou bearest | unto · thy | people :
O | visit · me with | thy sal- | vation.

2nd part. 5 That I may see the felicity | of thy | chosen :
and rejoice in the gladness of thy people, * and give | thanks with | thine in- | heritance.

6 We have | sinn'd · with our | fathers :
we have | done a- | miss and · dealt | wickedly.

7 Our fathers regarded not thy wonders in Egypt, * neither kept they thy great | goodness · in re- | membrance :
but were disobedient at the sea, | even · at the | Red — | sea.

8 Nevertheless, * he | help'd them · for his | Name's sake :
that he might | make his | power · to be | known.

9 He rebuk'd the Red sea also, * and it was | dri-ed | up :
so he léd them through the | deep ạs | thrọugh ạ | wilderness.

10 And he sáv'd them from the | adver-sary's | hand :
and delíver'd them | frọm thẹ | hand of · the | enemy.

11 As for those that troubl'd them, * the | wa-ters · over- | whelm'd them :
thẹre | was not | one of · them | left.

2nd part. 12 Then believ'd | they his | words :
and sang | praise — | ụn-tọ | him.

13 But within a while they for- | gat his | works :
ạnd | would not · a- | bide his | counsel.

14 But lust came up- | on them · in the | wilderness :
ạnd thẹy | tempt-ed | God · in the | desert.

15 Ạnd hẹ | gave them · their de- | sire :
and sent léanness with- | al ịn- | tọ thẹir | soul.

16 They anger'd Moses | also · in the | tents :
ạnd | Aaron · the | saint of · the | Lord.

17 So the earth ópen'd and | swallow'd · up | Dathan :
and cover'd the congre- | ga-tion | ọf Ạ- | biram.

18 And the fire was | kindl'd · in their | company :
thẹ | flame burnt | up · the un- | godly.

19 They made ạ | calf in | Horeb :
ạnd | worshipp'd · the | mol-ten | image.

[20] Thus they | turn'd their | glory
into the similitude ọf ạ | calf thạt | eat-eth | hay.

21 And they forgat | God their | Saviour :
who had done so | great — | things ịn | Egypt.

22 Wondrous works in the | land ọf | Ham :
and fearful | things · by the | Red — | sea.

23 So he said he would have destroy'd them, * had not Moses his chosen stood be- | fore him · in the | gap :
to turn away his wrathful indignation, | lest he | should dẹ- | stroy them.

24 Yea they thought scorn of that | plea-sant | land :
and gave no | cre-dence | unto · his | word ;

2nd part. 25 But | murmur'd · in their | tents :
and hearken'd not | unto · the | voice of · the | Lord.

26 Then líft he up his | hand a- | gainst them :
to over- | throw them | in the | wilderness ;

27 To cast out their seed a- | mong the | nations :
and to | scatter · them | in the | lands.

28 They join'd themselves unto | Baal — | peor :
and ate the | offer-ings | of the | dead.

29 Thus they provok'd him to ánger with their | own in- | ventions :
and the | plague was | great a- | mong them.

30 Then stood up | Phinees · and | pray'd :
and | so the | plague — | ceas'd.

31 And that was cóunted unto | him for | righteousness :
among all pos- | terities · for | ev-er- | more.

32 They anger'd him álso at the | waters · of | strife :
so that he punish'd | Moses · for | their — | sakes ;

33 Becáuse they pro- | vok'd his | spirit :
so that he spáke unad- | vised-ly | with his | lips.

34 Neither de- | stroy'd · they the | heathen :
as the | Lord com- | mand-ed | them ;

35 But were míngl'd a- | mong the | heathen :
and | learn-ed | their — | works.

36 Insomuch that they worshipp'd their idols, * which túrn'd to their | own de- | cay :
yea they offer'd their sóns and their | daugh-ters | un-to | devils ;

37 And shed innocent blood, * even the blood of their | sons and · of their | daughters :
whom they offer'd unto the idols of Canaan, * and the | land · was de- | fil'd with | blood.

2nd part. 38 Thus were they stáin'd with their | own — | works :
and went a | whoring · with their | own in- | ventions.

39 Therefore was the wrath of the Lord kindl'd a- | gainst his | people :
insomuch that he ab- | horr'd his | own in- | heritance.

40 And he gave them over into the | hand of · the | heathen :
and they that | hated them · were | lords — | over them.

41 Their | enemies · op- | press'd them :
and | had them | in sub- | jection.

42 Many a time did | he de- | liver them :
but they rebell'd against him with their own inventions, *
| and were · brought | down in · their | wickedness.

43 Nevertheless, when he | saw · their ad- | versity :
he | heard — | their com- | plaint.

44 He thought upon his covenant and pitied them, * according unto the múltitude | of his | mercies :
yea he made all those that | led them a-way | captive · to | pity them.

Full. 45 Deliver us, O Lord our God, * and gáther us from a- | mong the | heathen :
that we may give thanks unto thy holy Name, * and | make our | boast of · thy | praise.

Full. Unis. 46 Blessed be the Lord God of Israel from everlasting * and | world with-out | end :
and let áll the | peo-ple | say, A- | men.

DAY 22. MORNING PRAYER

PSALM 107

Full. 1 O give thanks unto the Lord, for | he is | gracious :
and his | mercy · en- | dureth · for | ever.

Full. 2 Let them give thánks whom the | Lord · hath re- | deem'd :
and de- | liver'd · from the | hand of · the | enemy ;

Full. 2nd part. 3 And gather'd them out of the lands, * from the east and | from the | west :
from the | north and | from the | south.

4 They went astray in the wilderness | out of · the | way :
and | found no | city · to | dwell in ;

5 Hun- | gry and | thirsty :
their | soul — | faint-ed | in them.

6 So they cri'd unto the | Lord in · their | trouble :
and he de- | liver'd · them | from their · dis- | tress.

7 He led them forth by the | right — | way :
that they might go to the | ci-ty | where they | dwelt.

Unis. 8 *O that men would therefore praise the | Lord for · his | goodness :*
and declare the wonders that he | doeth · for the | children · of | men !

Unis. 9 For he satisfieth the | emp-ty | soul :
and filleth the | hun-gry | soul with | goodness.

10 Such as sit in darkness, * and in the | shadow · of | death :
being fast | bound in | misery · and | iron ;

11 Because they rebell'd against the | words of · the | Lord :
and lightly regarded the | coun-sel | of the · most | Highest ;

2nd part. 12 He also brought down their | heart through | heaviness :
they fell down, and | there was | none to | help them.

13 So when they cri'd unto the | Lord in · their | trouble :
he delíver'd them | out of | their dis- | tress.

14 For he brought them out of darkness, * and out of the | shadow · of | death :
and | brake their | bonds in | sunder.

Unis. 15 *O that men would therefore praise the | Lord for · his | goodness :*
and declare the wonders that he | doeth · for the | children · of | men !

Unis. 16 For he hath broken the | gates of | brass :
and smítten the | bars of | iron · in | sunder.

17 Foolish men are plagu'd for | their of- | fence :
and be- | cause of | their — | wickedness.

18 Their soul abhorr'd all | manner · of | meat :
and they were even | hard at | death's — | door.

19 So when they cri'd unto the | Lord in · their | trouble :
he deliver'd them | out of | their dis- | tress.

20 He sent his | word and | heal'd them :
and they were | sav'd from | their de- | struction.

Unis. 21 *O that men would therefore praise the | Lord for · his | goodness :*
and declare the wonders that he | doeth · for the | children · of | men!

Unis. 22 That they would offer unto him the | sacrifice · of | thanksgiving :
and tell | out his | works with | gladness !

23 They that go down to the | sea in | ships :
and occupy their | business · in | great — | waters ;

24 These men see the | works of · the | Lord :
and his | won-ders | in the | deep.

25 For at his word the stormy | wind a- | riseth :
which | lift-eth | up the | waves thereof.

26 They are carri'd up to the heav'n, * and down a- | gain · to the | deep :
their soul mélteth a- | way be- | cause of · the | trouble.

27 They reel to and fro, * and stágger like a | drunk-en | man :
and are | at their | wit's — | end.

28 So when they cry unto the | Lord in · their | trouble :
he delívereth them | out of | their dis- | tress.

29 For he maketh the | storm to | cease :
so that the | waves there- | of are | still.

30 Then are they glad, be- | cause they · are at | rest :
and so he bringeth them unto the | hav-en | where they · would | be.

Unis. 31 *O that men would therefore praise the | Lord for · his | goodness :*
and declare the wonders that he | doeth · for the | children · of | men!

Unis. 32 That they would exalt him also in the congre- | gation · of the | people :
and | praise him · in the | seat of · the | elders !

33 Who turneth the | floods in-to a | wilderness :
and | dri-eth | up the | water-springs.

34 A fruitful land | maketh · he | barren :
for the | wickedness · of | them that | dwell therein.

35 Again, he maketh the wilderness a | stand-ing | water :
and water- | springs · of a | dry — | ground.

36 And thére he | setteth · the | hungry :
that they may | build them · a | city · to | dwell in ;

37 That they may sow their land and | plant — | vineyards :
to | yield them | fruits of | increase.

38 He blesseth them, só that they | multiply · ex- | ceedingly :
and súffereth not their | cat-tle | to de- | crease.

39 And again, * when they are mínish'd and | brought — | low :
through oppréssion, * through | an-y | plague or | trouble ;

40 Though he suffer them to be evil in- | treated · through | tyrants :
and let them wander | out of · the | way in · the | wilderness ;

2nd part. 41 Yet helpeth he the | poor · out of | misery :
and maketh him households | like a | flock of | sheep.

Full. 42 The righteous will consíder | this · and re- | joice :
and the mouth of all | wicked-ness | shall be | stopp'd.

Full. 43 Whoso is wise will | ponder · these | things :
and they shall understánd the loving- | kind-ness | of the | Lord.

DAY 22. EVENING PRAYER

PSALM 108

(*Single Chant*)

Full. 1 O God my heart is ready, * my | heart is | ready :
I will sing and give praise with the best | mem-ber | that I | have.

Full. 2 Awake, thou | lute ạnd | harp :
I my- | self · will a- | wake right | early.
3 I will give thanks unto thee O Lord, ạ- | mong thẹ | people :
I will sing praises unto | thee ạ- | mong thẹ | nations.
4 For thy mercy is | greater · than the | heav'ns :
and thy truth | reach-eth | unto · the | clouds.
Unis. 5 Set up thyself O God ạ- | bove thẹ | heav'ns :
ạnd thỵ | glory a-bove | all thẹ | earth.
6 That thy belóved may | bẹ dẹ- | liver'd :
let thy right hand | save them · and | hear thou | me.
Unis. 7 God hath | spoken · in his | holiness :
I will rejoice therefore and divide Sichem, * and mete | out thẹ | valley · of | Succoth.
Unis. 8 Gilead is míne, and Ma- | nasses · is | mine :
Ephraim | also · is the | strength of · my | head.
Unis. 9 Judah is my law-giver, | Moab · is my | wash-pot :
over Edom will I cast out my shoe ; * upon Phị- | lis-tia | will I | triumph.
10 Who will lẹad me into the | strong — | city :
and whó will | bring me | in-to | Edom ?
11 Hast not thou for- | saken us · O | God :
and wilt not thou O | God go | forth with · our | hosts?
12 O hélp us a- | gainst thẹ | enemy :
fọr | vain · is the | help ọf | man.
Full. 13 Through God we shall | do great | acts :
and it is | he that · shall | tread · down our | enemies.

PSALM 109

1 Hold not thy tongue, O | God of · my | praise :
for the mouth of the ungodly, * yea the móuth of the de- | ceitful · is | open'd · up- | on me.
2 And they have spoken agáinst me with | fạlse — | tongues :
they compass'd me about also with words of hatred, * and fought ạ- | gainst · me with- | out ạ | cause.

3 For the love that I had unto them, * lo they take now my | contra-ry | part :
but I | give my-self | un-to | prayer.

4 Thus have they rewárded me | evil · for | good:
and | hatred · for | my good- | will.

5 Set thou an ungodly man to be | ru-ler | over him :
And let Satan | stand at · his | right — | hand.

6 When sentence is given upon him, | let him · be con- | demn'd:
and let his | prayer be | turn'd · into | sin.

7 Let his | days be | few :
and let an- | oth-er | take his | office.

[8] Let his | children · be | father-less, | and his | wife a | widow.

9 Let his children be vágabonds, and | beg their | bread :
let them seek it also | out of | deso-late | places.

10 Let the extortioner consume | all that · he | hath :
and let the | strang-er | spoil his | labour.

11 Let there be | no man · to | pity him :
nor to have com- | passion up-on his | father-less | children.

12 Let his postérity | be de- | stroy'd :
and in the next generátion let his | name be | clean put | out.

13 Let the wickedness of his fathers be had in remémbrance * in the | sight of · the | Lord :
and let not the sín of his | mother · be | done a | way.

14 Let them álway be be- | fore the | Lord :
that he may root out the memorial | of them · from | off the | earth ;

15 And that because his mind was | not to · do | good :
but persecuted the poor helpless man, * that he might slay | him that · was | vex'd · at the | heart.

16 His delight was in cursing, * and it shall | hap-pen | unto him:
he lov'd not blessing, * therefore | shall it · be | far — | from him.

17 He cloth'd himself with cursing, | like as · with a | raiment :
and it shall come into his bowels like water, * and like | oil in- | to his | bones.

18 Let it be unto him as the cloke that he | hath up- | on him :
and as the gírdle that he is | al-way | girded · with- | al.

2nd part. 19 Let it thus happen from the | Lord un-to mine | enemies :
and to those that speak | evil · a- | gainst my | soul.

20 But deal thou with me O Lord God, according | unto · thy | Name :
for | sweet — | is thy | mercy.

21 O deliver me, * for I am | helpless · and | poor :
and my | heart is | wounded · with- | in me.

22 I go hence like the | shadow · that de- | parteth :
and am | driven · a- | way · as the | grasshopper.

23 My knees are | weak through | fasting :
my flesh is dri'd | up for | want of | fatness.

2nd part. 24 I became | also · a re- | proach unto them :
they that | look'd up-on me | shaked · their | heads.

25 Hélp me O | Lord my | God :
O sáve me ac- | cord-ing | to thy | mercy ;

26 And they shall know, how that this is | thy — | hand :
and that | thou — | Lord hast | done it.

27 Though they curse, yet | bless — | thou :
and let them be confounded that rise up against me ; * but | let thy | servant · re- | joice.

28 Let mine ádversaries be | cloth'd with | shame :
and let them cover themselves with their own con- | fu-sion, | as · with a | cloke.

Full. 29 As for me, * I will give great thánks unto the | Lord with · my | mouth :
and | praise · him a- | mong the | multitude ;

Full. 30 For he shall stand at the right | hand of · the | poor :
to save his | soul from · un- | right-eous | judges.

DAY 23. MORNING PRAYER

PSALM 110

Full. 1 The Lord sáid unto | my — | Lord :
Sit thou on my right hand,* until I | make thine | enemies · thy | footstool.

Full. 2 The Lord shall send the rod of thy | power · out of | Sion :
be thou ruler, * éven in the | midst ạ- | mong thine | enemies.

2nd part. 3 In the day of thy power shall the people offer thee free-will offerings, * wịth ạn | ho-ly | worship :
the dew of thy | birth is · of the | womb of · the | morning.

4 The Lord sware, ạnd | will not · re- | pent :
Thou art a Priest for ever * after the | or-der | ọf Mẹl- | chisedech.

5 The Lórd upon | thy right | hand :
shall wound even | kings · in the | day of · his | wrath.

6 He shall judge among the heathen, * he shall fill the pláces with the | dead — | bodies :
and smite in sunder the | heads · over | di-vers | countries.

7 He shall drink of the | brook · in the | way :
therefore | shall he · lift | up his | head.

PSALM 111

1 I will give thanks unto the Lord with my | whole — | heart :
secretly among the | faithful · and | in the · congre- | gation.

2 The works of the | Lord are | great :
sought out of all | them that · have | pleasure · there- | in.

3 His work is worthy to be prais'd, ạnd | hạd ịn | honour :
ạnd his | righteousness · ẹn- | dureth · for | ever.

4 The merciful and gracious Lord hath so done his | marvel-lous | works :
that they | ought to · be | had in · re- | membrance.

5 He hath given meat unto | them that | fear him :
he shall éver be | mind-ful | of his | covenant.

6 He hath shew'd his people the | power of · his | works :
that he may gíve them the | heri-tage | of the | heathen.

7 The works of his hands are | verity · and | judgement :
all | his com- | mandments · are | true.

8 They stand fast for | ever · and | ever :
and are | done in | truth and | equity.

9 He sent redemption | unto · his | people :
he hath commanded his covenant for ever, * hóly and | rever-end | is his | Name.

10 The fear of the Lord is the be- | ginning · of | wisdom :
a good understanding have all they that do thereafter, * the | praise of it · en- | dureth · for | ever.

PSALM 112

1 Blessed is the man that | feareth · the | Lord :
he hath great de- | light in | his com- | mandments.

2 His seed shall be | mighty up-on | earth :
the generátion of the | faith-ful | shall be | bless'd.

3 Riches and plenteousness shall | be in · his | house :
and his | righteousness · en- | dureth · for | ever.

4 Unto the godly there ariseth up | light · in the | darkness :
he is | merci-ful, | loving · and | righteous.

5 A good man is | merciful · and | lendeth :
and will | guide his | words · with dis- | cretion.

6 For he shall | never · be | mov'd :
and the righteous shall be had in | ev-er- | lasting · re- | membrance.

7 He will not be afraid of any | ev-il | tidings :
for his heart standeth fást and be- | liev-eth | in the | Lord.

8 His heart is estáblish'd, and | will not | shrink :
until he see his de- | sire up- | on his | enemies.

9 He hath dispers'd abroad, and | given · to the | poor :
and his righteousness remaineth for ever, * his | horn shall · be ex- | alted · with | honour.

10 The ungodly shall see it, and | it shall | grieve him :
he shall gnash with his teeth and consume away, * the de- | sire of · the un- | godly · shall | perish.

PSALM 113
(*Single Chant*)

1 Praise the | Lord ye | servants :
O | praise the | Name of · the | Lord.

2 Blessed be the | Name of · the | Lord :
from this time | forth for | ev-er- | more.

3 The Lord's | Name is | prais'd :
from the rising up of the sún unto the | go-ing | down of · the | same.

4 The Lord is high a- | bove all | heathen :
and his | glory · a- | bove the | heav'ns.

5 Who is like unto the Lord our God, * that hath his | dwelling · so | high :
and yet humbleth himself to behold the | things that · are in | heav'n and | earth ?

6 He taketh up the simple | out of · the | dust :
and lifteth the | poor — | out of · the | mire ;

7 That he may | set him · with the | princes :
even with the | prin-ces | of his | people.

8 He maketh the barren | woman to · keep | house :
and to be a | joy-ful | mother · of | children.

DAY 23. EVENING PRAYER

PSALM 114

1 When Israel | came · out of | Egypt :
and the house of Jácob from a- | mong the | strange — | people,

[2] Judah | was his | sanctuary
and | Is-rael | his do- | minion.
3 The sea | saw that · and | fled :
Jor- | dan was | driv-en | back.
4 The mountains | skipp'd like | rams :
and the little | hills like | young — | sheep.
5 What aileth thee O thou | sea that · thou | fleddest :
and thou Jordan, that | thou wast | driv-en | back ?
6 Ye mountains that ye | skipp'd like | rams :
and ye little | hills like | young — | sheep ?
7 Tremble thou earth at the | presence · of the | Lord :
at the | presence · of the | God of | Jacob ;
8 Who turn'd the hárd róck into a | stand-ing | water :
and the flint-stone | into · a | spring-ing | well.

PSALM 115

1 Not unto us O Lord, not unto us, * but unto thý | Name · give the | praise :
for thy loving | mer-cy | and for · thy | truth's sake.
2 Whérefore shall the | hea-then | say :
Where | — is | now their | God ?
3 As for óur God, | he is · in | heav'n :
he hath | done · whatso- | ev-er | pleas'd him.
4 Their ídols are | silver · and | gold :
even the | work of | men's — | hands.
5 They have | mouths and | speak not :
eyes | — have | they and | see not.
6 They have | ears and | hear not :
no- | ses have | they and | smell not.
7 They have hands and handle not, * feet have | they and | walk not :
neither | speak they | through their | throat.
8 They that | make them · are | like unto them :
and so are | all · such as | put their | trust in them.

9 But thou, house of Israel, | trust thou · in the | Lord :
Full. hé is their | suc-cour | and de- | fence.
10 Ye house of Aaron, * put your | trust · in the | Lord :
Full. hé is their | help-er | and de- | fender.
11 Ye that fear the Lord, put your | trust · in the | Lord :
Full. hé is their | help-er | and de- | fender.
12 The Lord hath been mindful of us, and | he shall | bless us :
even he shall bless the house of Israel, * he shall | bless the | house of | Aaron.
[13] He shall bless | them that | fear
the | Lord, * both | small and | great.
[14] The Lord shall in- | crease you | more
and | more, — * | you and · your | children.
15 Ye are the | blessed · of the | Lord :
who | made — | heav'n and | earth.
16 All the whole | heav'ns · are the | Lord's :
the earth hath he | given · to the | children · of | men.
17 The dead praise not | thee O | Lord :
neither all | they that · go | down in-to | silence.
Full. 18 But wé will | praise the | Lord :
from this time forth for evermore, | Praise — | — the | Lord.

DAY 24. MORNING PRAYER

PSALM 116

[1] I am | well — | pleas'd
that the Lord hath | heard the | voice of · my | prayer ;
2 That he hath in- | clin'd his | ear unto me :
therefore will I cáll upon | him as | long as · I | live.
3 The snares of death cómpass'd me | round a- | bout :
and the pains of | hell gat | hold up- | on me.
4 I shall find trouble and heaviness, * and I will call upon the Name of · the | Lord :
O Lord I be- | seech · thee de- | liver · my | soul.

5 Grácious is the | Lord and | righteous :
yea | our — | God is | merciful.

6 The Lord pre- | serveth · the | simple :
I was in | miser-y | and he | help'd me.

7 Turn again then unto thy rest, | O my | soul :
for the | Lord — | hath re- | warded thee.

8 And why ? * thou hast delíver'd my | soul from | death :
mine eyes from | tears · and my | feet from | falling.

[9] I will | walk be- | fore
the | Lord · in the | land of · the | living.

10 I believ'd and therefore will I speak ; * but I was | sore — | troubl'd :
I said in my haste, | All — | men are | liars.

11 What rewárd shall I | give un-to the | Lord :
for all the | bene-fits that | he hath · done un- | to me ?

12 I will receive the | cup of · sal- | vation :
and | call up-on the | Name of · the | Lord.

13 I will pay my vows now in the presence of | all his | people :
right dear in the sight of the | Lord · is the | death of · his | saints.

14 Behold O Lord, how that | I am · thy | servant :
I am thy servant and the son of thine handmaid, * thou hast | broken · my | bonds in | sunder.

15 I will offer to thee the | sacrifice · of | thanksgiving :
and will | call up-on the | Name of · the | Lord.

16 I will pay my vows unto the Lord, * in the sight of | all his | people :
in the courts of the Lord's house, * even in the midst of thee, O Jerusalem, (*Full*) | Praise — | — the | Lord.

PSALM 117

Full. 1 O praise the Lord, | all ye | heathen :
praise | — him, | all ye | nations.

Full. 2 For his merciful kindness is ever more and | more to- | wards us :
and the truth of the Lord endureth for ever, | Praise — | — the | Lord.

PSALM 118

Full. 1 O give thanks unto the Lord, for | he is | gracious :
because his | mercy · en- | dureth · for | ever.
Full. 2 Let Israel now conféss that | he is | gracious :
and that his | mercy · en- | dureth · for | ever.
Full. [3] Let the house of Aaron | now con- | fess
that his | mercy · en- | dureth · for | ever.
Full. [4] Yea let them now that fear the | Lord con- | fess
that his | mercy · en- | dureth · for | ever.
5 I call'd upon the | Lord in | trouble :
and the | Lord — | heard me · at | large.
6 The Lord is | on my | side :
I will not | fear what | man · doeth | unto me.
2nd part. 7 The Lord taketh my part with | them that | help me :
therefore shall I see my de- | sire up- | on mine | enemies.
8 It is better to | trust · in the | Lord :
than to | put · any | confidence · in | man.
9 It is better to | trust · in the | Lord :
than to | put · any | confidence · in | princes.
Full. 10 All nations cómpass'd me | round a- | bout :
but in the Name of the | Lord will | I de- | stroy them.
Full. 11 They kept me in on every side, * they kept me in I say on | eve-ry | side :
but in the Name of the | Lord will | I de- | stroy them.
Full. 2nd part. 12 They came about me like bees, * and are extinct even as the | fire a-mong the | thorns :
for in the Name of the | Lord I | will de- | stroy them.
13 Thou hast thrust sore at me, that | I might | fall :
but the | Lord — | was my | help.

14 The Lord is my | strength and · my | song :
and | is be- | come · my sal- | vation.

Full. 15 The voice of joy and health is in the | dwellings · of the | righteous :
the right hand of the Lord bringeth | migh-ty | things to | pass.

Full. 16 The right hand of the Lord | hath the · pre- | eminence :
the right hand of the Lord bringeth | migh-ty | things to | pass.

17 I shall not | die but | live :
and de- | clare the | works of · the | Lord.

18 The Lord hath | chasten'd · and cor- | rected me :
but he hath not | given · me | over · unto | death.

19 Open me the | gates of | righteousness :
that I may go into them, * and give | thanks un- | to the | Lord.

20 Thís is the | gate of · the | Lord :
the | righteous · shall | en-ter | into it.

21 I will thank thee, for | thou hast | heard me :
and art be- | come — | my sal- | vation.

22 The same stone which the | builders · re- | fus'd :
is become the | head-stone | in the | corner.

Full. 23 Thís is the | Lord's — | doing :
and it is | marvel-lous | in our | eyes.

Full. 24 This is the day which the | Lord hath | made :
we will re- | joice · and be | glad in | it.

25 Hélp me | now O | Lord :
O Lord, | send us | now pros- | perity.

26 Blessed be he that cómeth in the | Name of · the | Lord :
we have wish'd you good luck, * yé that | are of · the | house of · the | Lord.

2nd part. 27 God is the Lord who hath | shew'd us | light :
bind the sacrifice with cords, * yea even | unto · the | horns of · the | altar.

Full. 28 Thou art my God, and | I will | thank thee :
thou art my | God and | I will | praise thee.

Full. 29 O give thanks unto the Lord, for | he is | gracious :
and his | mercy · en- | dureth · for | ever.

DAY 24. EVENING PRAYER

PSALM 119

1 Blessed are thóse that are unde- | fil'd · in the | way:
and | walk in · the | law of · the | Lord.

2 Blessed are they that | keep his | testimonies :
and | seek him · with their | whole — | heart.

[3] For | they who | do
no | wicked-ness | walk in · his | ways.

[4] Thou | — hast | charg'd
that we shall | dili-gently | keep · thy com- | mandments.

5 O that my ways were made | so di- | rect :
that | I might | keep thy | statutes !

6 Só shall I | not · be con- | founded :
whíle I have re- | spect · unto | all · thy com- | mandments.

7 I will thánk thee with an un- | feign-ed | heart :
when I shall have learn'd the | judge-ments | of thy | righteousness.

8 I will | keep thy | ceremonies :
O for- | sake me | not — | utterly.

9 Wherewithal shall a young man | cleanse his | way :
even by | ruling him-self | after · thy | word.

10 With my whole | heart · have I | sought thee :
O let me not go | wrong · out of | thy com- | mandments.

11 Thy words have I | hid with-in my | heart :
that I | should not | sin a- | gainst thee.

12 Bléssed art | thou O | Lord :
O | teach — | me thy | statutes.

[13] With my lips have | I been | telling
of áll the | judge-ments | of thy | mouth.
14 I have had as great delight in the | way of · thy | testimonies :
as | in all | manner · of | riches.
15 I will tálk of | thy com- | mandments :
and have re- | spect un- | to thy | ways.
16 My delight shall | be in · thy | statutes :
and I | will not · for- | get thy | word.

17 O do | well un-to thy | servant :
that I may | live and | keep thy | word.
18 Open | thou mine | eyes :
that I may see the | won-drous | things of · thy | law.
19 I am a | stranger up-on | earth :
O hide not | thy com- | mand-ments | from me.
20 My soul breaketh óut for the very | fervent · de- | sire :
that it hath | al-way | unto · thy | judgements.
21 Thou hast re- | buk'd the | proud :
and cursed are they that do | err from | thy com- | mand-ments.
22 O túrn from me | shame · and re- | buke :
for | I have | kept thy | testimonies.
23 Princes also did sit and | speak a- | gainst me :
but thy sérvant is | occu-pi'd | in thy | statutes.
[24] For thy | testi-monies | are
my de- | light, — | and my | counsellors.

25 My soul | cleaveth · to the | dust:
O quicken thou me ac- | cord-ing | to thy | word.
26 I have acknowledg'd my | ways and · thou | heardest me :
O | teach — | me thy | statutes.
27 Make me to understand the way of | thy com- | mandments :
and só shall I | talk of · thy | won-drous | works.

28 My soul melteth awáy for | ve-ry | heaviness :
comfort thou me ac- | cord-ing | unto · thy | word.
29 Take from me the | way of | lying :
and cause thou | me to · make | much of · thy | law.
30 I have chósen the | way of | truth :
and thy | judgements · have I | laid be- | fore me.
31 I have | stuck un-to thy | testimonies :
O | Lord con- | found me | not.
32 I will run the way of | thy com- | mandments :
whén thou hast | set my | heart at | liberty.

DAY 25. MORNING PRAYER

33 Teach me O Lord, the | way of · thy | statutes :
and I shall | keep it | unto · the | end.
34 Give me understanding, and I shall | keep thy | law :
yea I shall | keep it · with my | whole — | heart.
35 Make me to go in the path of | thy com- | mandments :
for there- | in is | my de- | sire.
36 Incline my | heart un-to thy | testimonies :
and | not to | cove-tous- | ness.
37 O turn away mine eyes, lest they be- | hold — | vanity :
and | quicken · thou | me in · thy | way.
[38] O | stablish · thy | word
in thy | servant, · that | I may | fear thee.
39 Take away the rebuke that | I am · a- | fraid of :
for thy | judge-ments | are — | good.
40 Behold, my delight is in | thy com- | mandments :
O | quicken · me | in thy | righteousness.

41 Let thy loving mercy come also unto | me, O | Lord :
even thy salvation, ac- | cord-ing | unto · thy | word.
42 So shall I make ánswer unto | my blas- | phemers :
for my | trust is | in thy | word.

43 O take not the word of thy truth utterly | out of · my | mouth :
for my | hope is | in thy | judgements.

[44] So shall I | al-way | keep
thy | law, · yea for | ever · and | ever.

45 And I will | walk at | liberty :
for I | seek — | thy com- | mandments.

46 I will speak of thy testimonies also, | even be-fore | kings :
and | will not | be a- | sham'd.

[47] And my de- | light shall · be in | thy
com- | mand-ments, | which · I have | lov'd.

48 My hands also will I lift up unto thy commándments | which · I have | lov'd :
and my | study · shall | be in · thy | statutes.

49 O think upon thy sérvant as con- | cerning · thy | word :
wherein thou hast | caus'd · me to | put my | trust.

50 The same is my | comfort · in my | trouble :
for | thy — | word hath | quicken'd me.

51 The proud have had me exceedingly | in de- | rision :
yet have I not | shrink-ed | from thy | law.

[52] For I remember'd thine ever- | last-ing | judgements
O | Lord, · and re- | ceiv-ed | comfort.

[53] I am | horribly · a- | fraid
for the un- | godly · that for- | sake thy | law.

[54] Thy | statutes · have | been
my | songs, · in the | house of · my | pilgrimage.

[55] I have thought upon thy Name, O | Lord · in the | night-season, * | and have | kept thy | law.

[56] This I | had, be- | cause
I | kept — | thy com- | mandments.

57 Thou art my | portion O | Lord :
I have | promis'd · to | keep thy | law.

58 I made my humble petition in thy presence, * with my | whole — | heart :
O be merciful unto me, ac- | cord-ing | to thy | word.
59 I call'd mine own | ways · to re- | membrance :
and turn'd my | feet un- | to thy | testimonies.
[60] I made haste, and pro- | long'd · not the | time
to | keep — | thy com- | mandments.
61 The congregátions of the un- | godly · have | robb'd me :
but I | have not · for- | gotten · thy | law.
62 At midnight I will rise to give | thanks un-to | thee :
be- | cause of · thy | right-eous | judgements.
63 I am a companion of | all · them that | fear thee :
and | keep — | thy com- | mandments.
64 The earth O Lord is | full of · thy | mercy :
O | teach — | me thy | statutes.

65 O Lord, thou hast dealt graciously | with thy | servant :
ac- | cord-ing | unto · thy | word.
66 O learn me true under- | standing · and | knowledge :
for I have be- | liev-ed | thy com- | mandments.
67 Before I was troubl'd, I | went — | wrong :
but | now · have I | kept thy | word.
68 Thou art | good and | gracious :
O | teach — | me thy | statutes.
69 The proud have imagin'd a | lie a- | gainst me :
but I will keep thy com- | mandments · with my | whole — | heart.
70 Their heart is as | fat as | brawn :
but my de- | light hath | been in · thy | law.
71 It is good for me that I have | been in | trouble :
that | I may | learn thy | statutes.
72 The law of thy mouth is | dear-er | unto me :
than | thousands · of | gold and | silver.

DAY 25. EVENING PRAYER

73 Thy hands have | made me · and | fashion'd me :
O give me understanding, * that I may | learn — | thy com- | mandments.

74 They that fear thee will be | glad · when they | see me :
because I have | put my | trust in · thy | word.

75 I know O Lord, that thy | judgements · are | right :
and that thou of very faithfulness hast | caus'd me | to be | troubled.

76 O let thy merciful | kindness · be my | comfort :
according to thy | word un- | to thy | servant.

77 O let thy loving mercies come unto me, that | I may | live :
for thy | law is | my de- | light.

78 Let the proud be confounded, * for they go wickedly a- | bout · to de- | stroy me :
but I will be | occupi'd · in | thy com- | mandments.

79 Let such as fear thee and have | known thy | testimonies :
be | turn-ed | un-to | me.

80 O let my heart be | sound in · thy | statutes :
that | I be | not a- | sham'd.

81 My soul hath lóng'd for | thy sal- | vation :
and I have a good | hope be- | cause of · thy | word.

82 Mine eyes long | sore for · thy | word :
say- | ing O | when wilt · thou | comfort me ?

83 For I am becóme like a | bottle · in the | smoke :
yét do I | not for- | get thy | statutes.

84 How mány are the | days of · thy | servant :
when wilt thou be a- | veng'd of | them that | persecute me ?

85 The proud have | dig-ged | pits for me :
which | are not | after · thy | law.

86 All thy com- | mandments · are | true :
they persecute me falsely, | O be | thou my | help.

87 They had almost made an énd of | me up-on | earth :
but I for- | sook not | thy com- | mandments.
88 O quicken me áfter thy | lov-ing- | kindness :
and so shall I keep the | testi-monies | of thy | mouth.

[89] O | Lord, thy | word
en- | dureth · for | ever · in | heav'n.
90 Thy truth also remaineth from one gene- | ration · to an- | other:
thou hast laid the foundátion of the | earth and | it a- | bideth.
91 They continue this day ac- | cording · to thine | ordinance :
for | all things | serve — | thee.
92 If my delíght had not | been in · thy | law :
I should have | per-ish'd | in my | trouble.
93 I will never for- | get · thy com- | mandments :
for with | them — | thou hast | quicken'd me.
94 I am | thine, O | save me :
for | I have | sought thy · com- | mandments.
95 The ungodly laid wáit for me | to de- | stroy me :
but | I will · con- | sider · thy | testimonies.
96 I see that all things | come · to an | end :
but thy com- | mandment · is ex- | ceed-ing | broad.

97 Lord, what lóve have I | unto · thy | law :
all the day | long is · my | stud-y | in it.
98 Thou through thy commandments hast made me | wiser · than mine | enemies :
for | they are | ev-er | with me.
99 I have more under- | standing · than my | teachers :
for thy | testi-monies | are my | study.
100 I am | wiser · than the | aged :
be- | cause I | keep · thy com- | mandments.
101 I have refrain'd my feet from every | ev-il | way :
that | I may | keep thy | word.

[102] I | have not | shrunk
from thy | judgements · for | thou — | teachest me.
103 O how sweet are thy | words un-to my | throat :
yea sweeter than | hon-ey | unto · my | mouth.
104 Through thy commándments I | get un-der- | standing :
thérefore I | hate all | ev-il | ways.

DAY 26. MORNING PRAYER

105 Thy word is a lantern | unto · my | feet :
and a | light un- | to my | paths.
[106] I have sworn, and am | stedfast-ly | purpos'd
to | keep thy | right-eous | judgements.
107 I am | troubl'd a-bove | measure :
quicken me O Lord, ac- | cord-ing | to thy | word.
108 Let the free-will offerings of my mouth | please thee, O | Lord:
and | teach — | me thy | judgements.
109 My soul is | alway · in my | hand :
yét do I | not for- | get thy | law.
110 The ungodly have | laid a | snare for me :
but yet I | swerv'd not · from | thy com- | mandments.
111 Thy testimonies have I claim'd as mine | heritage · for | ever :
and why ? * they are the | ve-ry | joy of · my | heart.
[112] I have appli'd my heart to fulfil thy | sta-tutes | al-
way, | ev-en | unto · the | end.

113 I hate them that imagine | ev-il | things :
but | thy law | do I | love.
114 Thou art my de- | fence and | shield :
and my | trust is | in thy | word.
115 Away from | me ye | wicked :
I will keep the com- | mand-ments | of my | God.
116 O stablish me according to thy word, that | I may | live :
and let me nót be disap- | point-ed | of my | hope.

117 Hold thou me up, and | I shall · be | safe :
yea my delight shall be | ev-ẹr | ịn thỵ | statutes.

118 Thou hast trodden down all thém that de- | part from · thy | statutes :
for they ịm- | a-gine | bụt dẹ- | ceit.

119 Thou puttest away all the ungódly of the | earth like | dross :
there- | fọre Ị | love thy | testimonies.

120 My flesh | trembleth · for | fear of thee :
ạnd | I am · a- | fraid of · thy | judgements.

121 I deal with the thíng that is | lawful · and | right :
O give me not | over · unto | mine ọp- | pressors.

122 Make thou thy servant to delight in | that · which is | good :
thạt thẹ | proud — | do me · no | wrong.

123 Mine eyes are wasted away with | looking for · thy | health :
ạnd | fọr thẹ | word of · thy | righteousness.

124 O deal with thy servant according unto thy | lov-ing | mercy :
ạnd | teach — | me thy | statutes.

125 I am thy servant, Ọ | grant me · under- | standing :
thạt | I may | know thy | testimonies.

126 It is time for thee Lord to lay | to thine | hand :
fọr | they have · de- | stroy'd thy | law.

127 Fọr Ị | love · thy com- | mandments :
above | gold ạnd | pre-cious | stone.

128 Therefore hold I straight | all · thy com- | mandments :
and all false | ways I | utter-ly ab- | hor.

129 Thỵ | testimonies · are | wonderful :
thẹrefọre | doth my | soul — | keep them.

130 When thy | word · goeth | forth :
it giveth light and under- | stand-ing | unto · the | simple.

131 I open'd my mouth, and drew | in my | breath :
fọr mỵ dẹ- | light · was in | thy cọm- | mandments.

132 O look thou upon me, and be | merci-ful | unto me :
as thou usest to do unto | those that | love thy | Name.
133 Order my | steps in · thy | word :
and so shall no wíckedness | have do- | min-ion | over me.
134 O deliver me from the wrongful | dealings · of | men :
and | so shall · I | keep · thy com- | mandments.
135 Shew the light of thy countenance up- | on thy | servant :
and | teach — | me thy | statutes.
136 Mine eyes gush | out with | water :
be- | cause men | keep not · thy | law.

137 Righteous art | thou O | Lord :
and | true — | is thy | judgement.
[138] The testimonies that | thou · hast com- | manded
are ex- | ceed-ing | righteous · and | true.
139 My zeal hath | even · con- | sum'd me :
because mine énemies | have for- | gotten · thy | words.
140 Thy word is | tri'd · to the | uttermost :
and | thy — | ser-vant | loveth it.
141 I am small, and of | no · repu- | tation :
yét do I | not for- | get · thy com- | mandments.
142 Thy righteousness is an ever- | last-ing | righteousness :
and | thy — | law is · the | truth.
143 Trouble and heaviness have taken | hold up- | on me :
yét is my de- | light in | thy com- | mandments.
144 The righteousness of thy téstimonies is | ev-er- | lasting :
O grant me under- | standing · and | I shall | live.

DAY 26. EVENING PRAYER

145 I call with my | whole — | heart :
hear me O | Lord · I will | keep thy | statutes.
146 Yea even unto | thee · do I | call :
help me and | I shall | keep thy | testimonies.

147 Early in the mórning do I | cry un-to | thee :
for | in thy | word is · my | trust.

148 Mine eyes pre- | vent the | night-watches :
that I might be | occu-pi'd | in thy | words.

149 Hear my voice O Lord, * according unto thy | lov-ing- | kindness :
quicken me, ac- | cording · as | thou art | wont.

150 They draw nigh that of | ma-lice | persecute me :
and are | far — | from thy | law.

151 Be thou nigh at | hand O | Lord :
for | all · thy com- | mandments · are | true.

152 As concerning thy testimonies, I have | known long | since :
that thou hast | ground-ed | them for | ever.

153 O consider mine adversity, | and de- | liver me :
for I | do not · for- | get thy | law.

154 Avenge thou my | cause · and de- | liver me :
quicken me ac- | cord-ing | to thy | word.

155 Health is | far · from the un- | godly :
for | they re- | gard not · thy | statutes.

156 Great is thy | mercy · O | Lord :
quicken | me as | thou art | wont.

157 Many there are that | trouble me · and | persecute me :
yet | do I · not | swerve · from thy | testimonies.

158 It grieveth me when I | see the · trans- | gressors :
be- | cause they | keep not · thy | law.

159 Consider O Lord how I | love · thy com- | mandments :
O quicken me ac- | cording · to thy | lov-ing- | kindness.

160 Thy word is true from | ev-er- | lasting :
all the judgements of thy ríghteousness en- | dure for | ev-er- | more.

161 Princes have pérsecuted me with- | out a | cause :
but my heart | standeth · in | awe of · thy | word.

162 I am as | glad of · thy | word :
as | one that | findeth · great | spoils.

163 As for lies, I | hate · and ab- | hor them :
but | thy law | do I | love.

164 Seven times a | day · do I | praise thee :
be- | cause of · thy | right-eous | judgements.

165 Great is the peace that they have who | love thy | law :
and they | are not · of- | fend-ed | at it.

166 Lord I have lóok'd for thy | sav-ing | health :
and | done · after | thy com- | mandments.

167 My soul hath | kept thy | testimonies :
and | lov-ed | them ex- | ceedingly.

168 I have képt thy com- | mandments · and | testimonies :
for | all my | ways · are be- | fore thee.

169 Let my complaint come be- | fore thee · O | Lord :
give me understánding, ac- | cord-ing | to thy | word.

170 Let my supplication | come be- | fore thee :
delíver me, ac- | cord-ing | to thy | word.

171 My lips shall | speak of · thy | praise :
when | thou hast | taught me · thy | statutes.

172 Yea my tongue shall | sing of · thy | word :
for | all · thy com- | mandments · are | righteous.

173 Lét thine | hand — | help me :
for I have | chos-en | thy com- | mandments.

174 I have long'd for thy saving | health O | Lord :
and in thy | law is | my de- | light.

175 O let my soul | live and · it shall | praise thee :
and thy | judge-ments | shall — | help me.

176 I have gone astray like a | sheep · that is | lost :
O seek thy servant, for I | do not · for- | get · thy com- | mandments.

DAY 27. MORNING PRAYER

PSALM 120

[1] When I was in trouble I | call'd up- | on
the | Lord, — | and he | heard me.

2 Deliver my soul O Lord from | ly-ing | lips :
and | from a · de- | ceit-ful | tongue.

3 What reward shall be given or done unto thee thou | false — | tongue :
even mighty and sharp | arrows · with | hot · burning | coals.

4 Wo is me, * that I am constrain'd to | dwell with | Mesech :
and to have my habitation a- | mong the | tents of | Kedar.

[5] My soul hath long | dwelt a-mong | them
that are | ene-mies | un-to | peace.

6 I labour for peace, but when I speak unto | them there- | of :
they | make them | ready · to | battle.

PSALM 121

1 I will lift up mine | eyes un-to the | hills :
from | whence — | cometh · my | help.

2 My help cometh | even · from the | Lord :
who | hath made | heav'n and | earth.

3 He will not suffer thy | foot to · be | mov'd :
and he that | keepeth · thee | will not | sleep.

[4] Behold, he that | keep-eth | Israel
shall | nei-ther | slumber · nor | sleep.

5 The Lord him- | self is · thy | keeper :
the Lord is thy de- | fence up-on thy | right — | hand ;

[6] So that the | sun shall · not | burn thee by
day, | neither · the | moon by | night.

7 The Lord shall preserve thee from | all — | evil :
yea it is even | he that · shall | keep thy | soul.

8 The Lord shall preserve thy going out, and thy | com-ing | in :
from this time | forth for | ev-er- | more.

PSALM 122

1 I was glád when they | said un-to | me :
We will | go in-to the | house of · the | Lord.
[2] Our | feet shall | stand
in thy | gates, — | O Je- | rusalem.
3 Jerusalem is | built · as a | city :
that is at | uni-ty | in it- | self.
4 For thither the tribes go up, * éven the | tribes of · the | Lord :
to testify unto Israel, * to give | thanks un-to the | Name of · the | Lord.
2nd part. 5 For thére is the | seat of | judgement :
even the | seat of · the | house of | David.
6 O pray for the | peace of · Je- | rusalem :
they shall | pros — | per that | love thee.
7 Peace be with- | in thy | walls :
and | plenteous-ness with- | in thy | palaces.
8 For my bréthren and com- | pan-ions' | sakes :
I will | wish — | thee pros- | perity.
9 Yea because of the house of the | Lord our | God :
I will | seek to | do thee | good.

PSALM 123

1 Unto thee lift I | up mine | eyes :
O thou that | dwell-est | in the | heav'ns.
2 Behold, even as the eyes of servants look unto the hand of their masters, * and as the eyes of a maiden unto the | hand of · her | mistress :
even so our eyes wait upon the Lord our God, * un- | til he · have | mercy · up- | on us.
3 Have mercy upon us O Lord, have | mercy · up- | on us :
for | we are | utter-ly de- | spis'd.
4 Our soul is fill'd with the scornful re- | proof of · the | wealthy :
and with the de- | spiteful-ness | of the | proud.

PSALM 124

Full. 1 If the Lord himself had not been on óur side, * now may | Is-rael | say :
if the Lord himself had not been on óur side, * when | men rose | up a- | gainst us ;

Full. 2 They had | swallow'd us · up | quick :
when they were so | wrathfully · dis- | pleas-ed | at us.

3 Yea the | waters · had | drown'd us :
and the | stream had · gone | over · our | soul.

4 The deep | waters · of the | proud :
had gone | ev-en | over · our | soul.

5 But | prais'd · be the | Lord :
who hath not given us óver for a | prey un- | to their | teeth.

6 Our soul is escap'd, * even as a bird out of the | snare of · the | fowler :
the snare is | broken · and | we are · de- | liver'd.

2nd part. 7 Our hélp stándeth in the | Name of · the | Lord :
who | hath made | heav'n and | earth.

PSALM 125

Full. 1 They that put their trust in the Lord shall be éven as the | mount — | Sion :
which may not be remov'd, but | stand-eth | fast for | ever.

Full. 2 The hills | stand a-bout Je- | rusalem :
even so standeth the Lord round about his people, * from this time | forth for | ev-er- | more.

2nd part. 3 For the rod of the ungodly cometh not into the | lot of · the | righteous :
lest the | righteous · put their | hand un-to | wickedness.

[4] Do | well, O | Lord
unto those that are | good and | true of | heart.

5 As for such as turn báck unto their | own — | wickedness :
the Lord shall lead them forth with the evil-doers ; * but | peace shall | be up-on | Israel.

DAY 27. EVENING PRAYER

PSALM 126

1 When the Lord turn'd agáin the cap- | tivi-ty of | Sion :
thén were we | like · unto | them that | dream.

2 Then was our mouth | fill'd with | laughter :
ạnd | ọur — | tongue with | joy.

3 Then said they a- | mong thẹ | heathen :
Thẹ | Lord hath · done | great things | for them.

4 Yea the Lord hath done great things | for us · al- | ready :
whẹre- | of — | we rẹ- | joice.

5 Turn our cap- | tivi-ty O | Lord :
ạs thẹ | riv-ẹrs | ịn thẹ | south.

6 They that | sow in | tears :
shạll | reap — | ịn — | joy.

2nd part. 7 He that now goeth on his way weeping, * and beareth | forth good | seed :
shall doubtless come again with joy, ạnd | bring his | sheaves — | with him.

PSALM 127

1 Except the | Lord · build the | house :
their labour | is but | lost that | build it.

2 Except the | Lord · keep the | city :
the watchman | wak-eth | but in | vain.

3 It is but lost labour that ye haste to rise up early and so late take rest, * and eat the | bread ọf | carefulness :
for so he | giveth · his be- | lov-ed | sleep.

4 Lo chíldren and the | fruit of · the | womb :
are an heritage and | gift that | cometh · of the | Lord.

5 Like as the árrows in the | hand of · the | giant :
ẹvẹn | so · are the | young — | children.

6 Happy is the man that hath his | quiv-er | full of them :
they shall not be asham'd when they speak with their | ene-mies | in the | gate.

PSALM 128

[1] Blessed are | all they · that | fear
the | Lord, and | walk in · his | ways.
2 For thou shalt eat the | labours · of thine | hands :
O well is thee, and | hap-py | shalt thou | be.
3 Thy wife shall be as the | fruit-ful | vine :
up- | on the | walls of · thine | house.
[4] Thy children like the | o-live | branch-
es, | round a- | bout thy | table.
2nd part. 5 Lo thús shall the | man be | bless'd :
that | fear — | eth the | Lord.
6 The Lord from out of Sion shall | so — | bless thee :
that thou shalt see Jerusalem in pros- | peri-ty | all thy · life | long.
7 Yea that thou shalt see thy | chil-dren's | children :
and | peace up- | on — | Israel.

PSALM 129

1 Many a time have they fought against me from my | youth — | up :
may | Is-rael | now — | say.
2 Yea many a time have they vex'd me from my | youth — | up :
but they | have not · pre- | vail'd a- | gainst me.
3 The plowers | plow'd up-on my | back :
and | made — | long — | furrows.
4 But the | right-eous | Lord :
hath hewn the | snares of · the un- | godly · in | pieces.
5 Let them be confóunded and | turn-ed | backward :
as mány as have | ev-il | will at | Sion.
6 Let them be even as the grass grówing up- | on the | house-tops :
which wíthereth a- | fore · it be | pluck-ed | up ;
7 Whereof the mower | filleth · not his | hand :
neither he that | bindeth · up the | sheaves his | bosom.

8 So that they who go by say not so much as, The | Lord — | prosper you :
we wish you good | luck · in the | Name of · the | Lord.

PSALM 130

1 Out of the deep have I cáll'd unto | thee, O | Lord :
Lord, | hear — | my — | voice.
[2] O let thine ears con- | si-der | well
the | voice of | my com- | plaint.
3 If thou Lord wilt be extreme to márk what is | done a- | miss :
O | Lord — | who · may a- | bide it?
4 For there is | mercy · with | thee :
there- | fore shalt | thou be | fear'd.
5 I look for the Lord, my | soul doth | wait for him :
in his | word — | is my | trust.
6 My soul fleeth | unto · the | Lord :
before the morning watch I say, be- | fore the | morning | watch.
7 O Israel trust in the Lord, * for with the | Lord · there is | mercy :
and with | him is | plenteous · re- | demption.
[8] And he shall re- | deem — | Israel
from | all — | his — | sins.

PSALM 131

1 Lord I am | not high- | minded :
I | have no | proud — | looks.
[2] I do not | exer-cise my- | self in
great | matters, · which | are too | high for me.
3 But I refrain my soul and keep it low, * like as a child that is | wean'd · from his | mother :
yea my soul is | even · as a | wean-ed | child.
Full. [4] O Israel, | trust · in the | Lord
from this time | forth for | ev-er- | more.

DAY 28. MORNING PRAYER

PSALM 132

1 Lord re- | mem-ber | David :
and | all — | his — | trouble ;
2 How he | sware un-to the | Lord :
and vow'd a vów unto the Al- | migh-ty | God of | Jacob ;
3 I will not come within the tábernacle | of mine | house :
nor | climb up | into · my | bed ;
4 I will not suffer mine eyes to sleep, nor mine | eye-lids · to | slumber :
neither the témples of my | head to | take · any | rest ;

2nd part. 5 Until I find out a place for the | temple · of the | Lord :
an habitátion for the | migh-ty | God of | Jacob.
6 Lo we heard of the | same at · Eph- | rata :
and | found it | in the | wood.
7 We will | go in-to his | tabernacle :
and fall low on our | knees be- | fore his | footstool.

Full. 8 Arise O | Lord in-to thy | resting-place :
thou | and the | ark of · thy | strength.

Full. 9 Let thy priests be | cloth'd with | righteousness :
and let thy | saints — | sing with | joyfulness.
10 For thy | ser-vant | David's sake :
turn not away the | presence · of | thine A- | nointed.
11 The Lord hath made a faithful | oath un-to | David :
and he | shall not | shrink — | from it ;
12 Of the | fruit of · thy | body :
shall I | set up- | on thy | seat.
13 If thy children will keep my covenant, * and my téstimonies that | I shall | learn them :
their children also shall sít upon thy | seat for | ev-er- | more.
14 For the Lord hath chosen Síon to be an habi- | tation · for him- | self :
he hath | long-ed | for — | her.

15 This shall be my | rest for | ever :
here will I dwell, * for I | have a · de- | light there- | in.

16 I will bless her | victuals · with | increase :
and will | satisfy · her | poor with | bread.

17 I will deck her | priests with | health :
and her | saints · shall re- | joice and | sing.

18 There shall I make the horn of | David · to | flourish :
I have ordain'd a | lantern · for | mine A- | nointed.

19 As for his enemies, * I shall | clothe them · with | shame :
but upon him- | self · shall his | crown — | flourish.

PSALM 133

1 Behold how good and joyful a | thing it | is :
brethren to | dwell to- | gether · in | unity !

2 It is like the precious ointment upon the head, * that ran | down un-to the | beard :
even unto Aaron's beard, * and went | down · to the | skirts of · his | clothing.

[3] Like as the | dew of | Hermon
which | fell up-on the | hill of | Sion.

4 For there the Lord | promis'd · his | blessing :
and | life for | ev-er- | more.

PSALM 134

1 Behold now | praise the | Lord :
all ye | ser-vants | of the | Lord ;

2 Ye that by night stand in the | house of · the | Lord :
éven in the | courts of · the | house of · our | God.

3 Lift up your | hands · in the | sanctuary :
and | praise — | — the | Lord.

4 The Lord that made | heav'n and | earth :
give thee | bless-ing | out of | Sion.

PSALM 135

Full. 1 O praise the Lord, * laud ye the | Name of · the | Lord :
praise it O ye | ser-vants | of the | Lord ;

Full. 2 Ye that stand in the | house of · the | Lord :
in the | courts of · the | house of · our | God.

3 O praise the Lord for the | Lord is | gracious :
O sing praises unto his | Name for | it is | lovely.

4 For why ? * the Lord hath chosen Jacob | unto · him- | self :
and | Israel · for his | own pos- | session.

5 For I knów that the | Lord is | great :
and that our | Lord · is a- | bove — | all gods.

6 Whatsoever the Lord pleas'd, * that did he in | heav'n · and in | earth :
and in the | sea · and in | all deep | places.

7 He bringeth forth the clouds from the | ends of · the | world :
and sendeth forth lightnings with the rain, * bringing the | winds — | out of · his | treasures.

[8] He smote the | first-born · of | E-
gypt, | both of | man and | beast.

9 He hath sent tokens and wonders into the midst of thee, * O thou | land of | Egypt :
upon | Pharaoh · and | all his | servants.

10 He smote | di-vers | nations :
and | slew — | migh-ty | kings ;

11 Sehon king of the Amorites, * and Og the | king of | Basan :
and | all the | kingdoms · of | Canaan ;

12 And gave their | land to · be an | heritage :
even an héritage unto | Is-ra- | el his | people.

13 Thy Name O Lord, en- | dureth · for | ever :
so doth thy memorial O Lord, * from | one · gene- | ra-tion · to an- | other.

14 For the Lord will a- | venge his | people :
and be | gra-cious | unto · his | servants.

15 As for the images of the heathen, * théy are but | silver · and | gold :
the | work of | men's — | hands.

16 They have | mouths and | speak not :
eyes | have they | but they | see not.

17 They have ears, and | yet they | hear not :
neither is there | an-y | breath in · their | mouths.

18 They that | make them · are | like unto them :
and so are all | they that | put their | trust in them.

Unis. 19 Praise the Lord ye | house of | Israel :
praise the | Lord ye | house of | Aaron.

Unis. 20 Praise the Lord ye | house of | Levi :
ye that | fear the · Lord | praise the | Lord.

Unis. 2nd part. 21 Praised be the | Lord · out of | Sion :
who | dwell-eth | at Je- | rusalem.

DAY 28. EVENING PRAYER

PSALM 136

Full. 1 O give thanks unto the Lord for | he is | gracious :
and his | mercy · en- | dureth · for | ever.

Full. 2 O give thanks unto the God of | all — | gods :
for his | mercy · en- | dureth · for | ever.

2nd part. Full. 3 O thank the Lord of | all — | lords :
for his | mercy · en- | dureth · for | ever.

4 Who only | doeth · great | wonders :
for his | mercy · en- | dureth · for | ever.

5 Who by his excellent wisdom | made the | heavens :
for his | mercy · en- | dureth · for | ever.

6 Who laid out the | earth a-bove the | waters :
for his | mercy · en- | dureth · for | ever.

7 Who hath | made great | lights :
for his | mercy · en- | dureth · for | ever.

8 The sun to | rule the | day :
for his | mercy · en- | dureth · for | ever.
9 The moon and the stars to | govern · the | night :
for his | mercy · en- | dureth · for | ever.
10 Who smote | Egypt · with their | first-born :
for his | mercy · en- | dureth · for | ever.
11 And brought out | Israel · from a- | mong them :
for his | mercy · en- | dureth · for | ever.
nd part. 12 With a mighty hánd, and | stretch'd out | arm :
for his | mercy · en- | dureth · for | ever.
13 Who divided the Red | sea in · two | parts :
for his | mercy · en- | dureth · for | ever.
14 And made Israel to | go · through the | midst of it :
for his | mercy · en- | dureth · for | ever.
15 But as for Pharaoh and his host, * he overthréw them in the | Red — | sea :
for his | mercy · en- | dureth · for | ever.
16 Who led his | people · through the | wilderness :
for his | mercy · en- | dureth · for | ever.
17 Who | smote great | kings :
for his | mercy · en- | dureth · for | ever ;
18 Yea and slew | migh-ty | kings :
for his | mercy · en- | dureth · for | ever ;
19 Sehon | king of · the | Amorites :
for his | mercy · en- | dureth · for | ever ;
20 And Og the | king of | Basan :
for his | mercy · en- | dureth · for | ever ;
21 And gave away their | land · for an | heritage :
for his | mercy · en- | dureth · for | ever ;
22 Even for an heritage unto | Israel · his | servant :
for his | mercy · en- | dureth · for | ever.
23 Who remember'd us | when we · were in | trouble :
for his | mercy · en- | dureth · for | ever ;

24 And hath delíver'd us | from our | enemies :
for his | mercy · en- | dureth · for | ever.

2nd part. 25 Who giveth | food to · all | flesh :
for his | mercy · en- | dureth · for | ever.

Full. 26 O give thánks unto the | God of | heav'n :
for his | mercy · en- | dureth · for | ever.

Full. 27 O give thánks unto the | Lord of | lords :
for his | mercy · en- | dureth · for | ever.

PSALM 137

(*Single or Triple Chant*)

1 By the waters of Babylon we sat | down and | wept :
when we re- | mem-ber'd | thee O | Sion.

2 As for our harps we | hanged · them | up :
upon the | trees that | are there- | in.

3 For they that led us away captive requir'd of us then a song, * and mélody | in our | heaviness :
Sing us | one of · the | songs of | Sion.

[4] How shall we | sing the | Lord's
— | song · in a | strange — | land ?

5 If I forget thee | O Je- | rusalem :
let my right | hand for- | get her | cunning.

6 If I do not remember thee, * let my tongue cléave to the | roof of · my | mouth :
yea if I prefér not Je- | rusa-lem | in my | mirth.

7 Remember the children of Edom O Lord, * in the | day of · Je- | rusalem:
how they said, * Down with it, | down with · it | even · to the | ground.

8 O daughter of Babylon, | wasted · with | misery :
yea happy shall he be that rewardeth thee, as | thou hast | serv-ed | us.

9 Blessed shall he be that | taketh · thy | children :
and | throweth · them a- | gainst the | stones.

PSALM 138

Full. 1 I will give thanks unto thee O Lord with my | whole — | heart :
even before the gods will I sing | praise — | un-to | thee.

Full. 2 I will worship toward thy holy temple and praise thy Name, *
because of thy loving- | kindness · and | truth :
for thou hast mágnifi'd thy | Name and · thy | Word a-bove | all things.

3 When I call'd upon | thee thou | heardest me :
and en- | duedst · my | soul with · much | strength.

4 All the kings of the earth shall | praise · thee O | Lord :
for they have | heard the | words of · thy | mouth.

5 Yea they shall sing in the | ways of · the | Lord :
that | great · is the | glory of · the | Lord.

6 For though the Lord be high, * yet hath he re- | spect un-to the | lowly :
as for the proud, * he be- | holdeth · them a- | far — | off.

7 Though I walk in the midst of trouble, * yet shalt | thou re- | fresh me :
thou shalt stretch forth thy hand upon the furiousness of mine enemies, * and | thy right | hand shall | save me.

8 The Lord shall make good his loving- | kindness · to- | ward me :
yea thy mercy O Lord endureth for ever ; * despise not then the | works of · thine | own — | hands.

DAY 29. MORNING PRAYER

PSALM 139

1 O Lord, thou hast search'd me | out and | known me :
thou knowest my down-sitting and mine up-rising, * thou under- | standest · my | thoughts · long be- | fore.

2 Thou art about my path, and a- | bout my | bed :
and | spiest · out | all my | ways.

3 For lo, there is not a | word in · my | tongue :
but thou O Lord | knowest · it | al-to- | gether.

4 Thou hast fáshion'd me be- | hind · and be- | fore :
and | laid thine | hand up- | on me.

2nd part. 5 Such knowledge is too wónderful and | excel-lent | for me :
I | cannot · at- | tain un- | to it.

6 Whither shall I go then | from thy | Spirit :
or whither shall I | go then | from thy | presence ?

7 If I climb up into heav'n, | thou art | there :
if I go down to | hell · thou art | there — | also.

8 If I take the | wings of · the | morning :
and remain in the | utter-most | parts of · the | sea ;

9 Even there also shall | thy hand | lead me :
and | thy right | hand shall | hold me.

10 If I say, * Peradventure the | darkness · shall | cover me :
thén shall my | night be | turn'd to | day.

11 Yea the darkness is no darkness with thee, * but the night is as | clear as · the | day :
the darkness and light to | thee are | both a- | like.

12 For my | reins are | thine :
thou hast cóver'd me | in my | mo-ther's | womb.

13 I will give thanks unto thee, * for I am fearfully and | wonder-fully | made :
marvellous are thy works, * and that my | soul — | knoweth · right | well.

14 My bones | are not | hid from thee :
though I be made secretly, * and | fashion'd · be- | neath · in the | earth.

15 Thine eyes did see my substance, yet | being · im- | perfect :
and in thy book were | all my | mem-bers | written ;

2nd part. 16 Which day by | day were | fashion'd :
when as | yet — | there was | none of them.

17 How dear are thy counsels unto | me, O | God :
Ọ họw | great — | is the | sum of them !

18 If I tell them, * they are more in | number · than the | sand :
when I wake | up · I am | present · with | thee.

19 Wilt thou not slay the | wicked · O | God :
dẹ- | part from · me ye | blood-thirsty | men.

20 For they speak un- | righteously · a- | gainst thee :
and thine enemies | take thy | Name ịn | vain.

21 Do not I hate them O | Lord that · hate | thee :
and am not I griev'd with | those that · rise | up ạ- | gainst thee ?

22 Yea I | hate them · right | sore :
ẹven ạs | though they | were mine | enemies.

23 Try me O God, * and seek thẹ | ground of · my | heart :
prove me, | ạnd ẹx- | amine · my | thoughts.

24 Look well if there be any wáy of | wicked-ness | in me :
ạnd | lead me · in the | way · ever- | lasting.

Psalm 140

1 Deliver me O | Lord · from the | evil man :
ạnd prẹ- | serve me | frọm thẹ | wicked man.

2 Who imagine | mischief · in their | hearts :
and stir up | strife — | all the · day | long.

3 They have sharpen'd their | tongues · like a | serpent :
adder's | poison · is | under · their | lips.

4 Keep me O Lord, from the | hands of · the un- | godly :
preserve me from the wicked men, * who are purpos'd to | o-ver- | throw my | goings.

nd part. 5 The proud have laid a snare for me, * and spread a net a- | broad with | cords :
yea | ạnd sẹt | traps in · my | way.

6 I said unto the Lord, | Thou art · my | God :
hear the | voice of · my | prayers O | Lord.

7 O Lord God, thou | strength of · my | health :
thou hast cover'd my | head · in the | day of | battle.

8 Let not the ungodly have his de- | sire O | Lord :
let not his mischievous imagination prosper, | lest they | be too | proud.

9 Let the mischief of their own lips fall upon the | head of | them :
that | com-pass | me a- | bout.

10 Let hot burning | coals · fall up- | on them :
let them be cast into the fire and into the pit, * that they | never · rise | up a- | gain.

11 A man full of words shall not prosper up- | on the | earth :
evil shall húnt the wicked | person · to | ov-er- | throw him.

12 Sure I am that the Lórd will a- | venge the | poor :
and main- | tain the | cause of · the | helpless.

13 The righteous also shall give | thanks un-to thy | Name :
and the júst shall con- | tin-ue | in thy | sight.

PSALM 141

1 Lord I call upon thee, | haste thee | unto me :
and consider my | voice · when I | cry un- | to thee.

2 Let my prayer be set forth in thy | sight as · the | incense :
and let the lifting up of my | hands · be an | eve-ning | sacrifice.

3 Set a watch O Lord be- | fore my | mouth :
and | keep the | door of · my | lips.

4 O let not mine heart be inclín'd to | an-y | evil thing :
let me not be occupi'd in ungodly works with the men that work wickedness, * lest I | eat of · such | things as | please them.

[5] Let the righteous | ra-ther | smite
me | friend-ly, | and re- | prove me.

6 But let not their precious balms | break my | head :
yea I will pray | yet a- | gainst their | wickedness.

7 Let their judges be overthrown in | ston-y | places:
that they may hear my | words for | they are | sweet.
8 Our bones lie scátter'd be- | fore the | pit:
like as when one breaketh and heweth | wood up- | on the | earth.

9 But mine eyes look unto thee O | Lord — | God :
in thee is my trust, O | cast not | out my | soul.
10 Keep me from the snáre that | they have | laid for me :
and from the | traps of · the | wick-ed | doers.
2nd part. 11 Let the ungodly fall into their own | nets to- | gether :
and | let me | ever · es- | cape them.

DAY 29. EVENING PRAYER

PSALM 142

1 I cri'd unto the | Lord with · my | voice :
yea even unto the Lord did I | make my | sup-pli- | cation.
2 I póured out my com- | plaints be- | fore him :
and | shew'd him | of my | trouble.
3 When my spirit was in heaviness, * thou | knewest · my | path :
in the way wherein I walk'd have they | privi-ly | laid a | snare for me.
4 I look'd also upon my | right — | hand :
and saw there was | no man | that would | know me.
2nd part. 5 I had no | place to | flee unto :
and | no man | car'd for · my | soul.
6 I cri'd unto thee O | Lord, and | said :
Thou art my hope, * and my | portion · in the | land of · the | living.
7 Consider | my com- | plaint :
for I am | brought — | ve-ry | low.
8 O deliver me | from my | persecutors :
for | they are | too — | strong for me.

9 Bring my soul out of prison, * that I may give | thanks un-to thy | Name :
which thing if thou wilt grant me, * then shall the | righteous · re- | sort un-to my | company.

PSALM 143

1 Hear my prayer O Lord,* and con- | sider · my de- | sire :
hearken unto me for thy | truth and | righteous-ness' | sake.

2 And enter not into | judgement · with thy | servant :
for in thy sight shall | no man | living · be | justifi'd.

3 For the enemy hath persecuted my soul ; * he hath smitten my life | down · to the | ground :
he hath laid me in the darkness, * as the | men that · have been | long — | dead.

4 Therefore is my spirit | vex'd with- | in me :
and my | heart with- | in me · is | desolate.

5 Yet do I remember the time past ; * I muse upon | all thy | works :
yea I exercise my- | self · in the | works of · thy | hands.

6 I stretch forth my | hands · unto | thee :
my soul gaspeth unto | thee · as a | thirs-ty | land.

7 Hear me O Lord and that soon, * for my spirit | wax-eth | faint :
hide not thy face from me,* lest I be like unto | them that · go | down in-to the | pit.

8 O let me hear thy loving-kindness betimes in the morning, * for in | thee is · my | trust :
shew thou me the way that I should walk in, * for I lift | up my | soul un-to | thee.

9 Deliver me O | Lord · from mine | enemies :
for I | flee un-to | thee to | hide me.

10 Teach me to do the thing that pleaseth thee, for | thou art · my | God :
let thy loving Spirit lead me | forth in-to the | land of | righteousness.

11 Quicken me O | Lord · for thy | Name's sake :
and for thy righteousness' sake | bring my | soul · out of | trouble.

12 And of thy goodness | slay mine | enemies :
and destroy all them that vex my | soul for | I am · thy | servant.

DAY 30. MORNING PRAYER

PSALM 144

Full. 1 Blessed be the | Lord my | strength :
who teacheth my hands to | war · and my | fingers · to | fight;

Full. 2 My hope and my fortress, my castle and deliverer, * my defender in | whom I | trust :
who subdueth my | peo-ple | that is | under me.

3 Lord what is man * that thou hast such re- | spect un- | to him :
or the son of | man that · thou | so re- | gardest him?

4 Man is like a | thing of | nought :
his time | passeth · a- | way · like a | shadow.

5 Bow thy heav'ns O | Lord and · come | down :
touch the | mountains · and | they shall | smoke.

6 Cast forth thy | lightning · and | tear them :
shoot out thine | ar-rows | and con- | sume them.

7 Send down thine | hand · from a- | bove :
deliver me and take me out of the great waters, * from the | hand of | strange — | children ;

8 Whose mouth | talketh · of | vanity :
and their right | hand is a · right | hand of | wickedness.

9 I will sing a new sóng unto | thee O | God :
and sing praises unto | thee up-on a | ten-string'd | lute.

10 Thou hast given víctory | un-to | kings :
and hast deliver'd David thy sérvant from the | pe-ril | of the | sword.

2nd part. 11 Save me and deliver me from the | hand of · strange | children :
whose mouth talketh of vanity, * and their right | hand is a · right | hand of · in- | iquity.

12 That our sons may grow | up as the · young | plants :
and that our daughters may be as the | pol-ish'd | corners · of the | temple.

13 That our garners may be full and plenteous with all | manner · of | store :
that our sheep may bring forth thousands, * and | ten · thousands | in our | streets.

14 That our oxen may be strong to labour, * that there be | no de- | cay :
no leading into captivity, * and no com- | plain-ing | in our | streets.

Full. 15 Happy are the people that are in | such a | case :
yea blessed are the people who have the | Lord — | for their | God.

PSALM 145

Full. 1 I will magnify thee, O | God my | King :
and I will praise thy | Name for | ever · and | ever.

Full. 2 Every day will I give | thanks · un- | to thee :
and praise thy | Name for | ever · and | ever.

3 Great is the Lord, * and marvellous | worthy · to be | prais'd :
there | is no | end of · his | greatness.

4 One generation shall praise thy | works un-to an- | other :
and de- | clare — | thy — | power.

5 As for me, I will be | talking of · thy | worship :
thy glory, thy | praise and | won-drous | works ;

6 So that men shall speak of the might of thy | marvel-lous | acts :
and I will | al-so | tell of · thy | greatness.

2nd part. 7 The memorial of thine abundant | kindness · shall be | shew'd :
and | men shall | sing of · thy | righteousness.

8 The Lord is | gracious · and | merciful :
long-súffering, | and of | great — | goodness.

9 The Lord is | loving · unto | every man :
and his mercy is | ov-er | all his | works.

10 All thy works | praise thee · O | Lord :
and thy | saints give | thanks un- | to thee.

11 They shew the | glory of · thy | kingdom :
and | talk — | of thy | power ;

12 That thy power, thy glory and míghtiness | of thy | kingdom :
might be | known — | un-to | men.

13 Thy kingdom is an ever- | last-ing | kingdom :
and thy domínion en- | dureth · through- | out all | ages.

14 The Lord upholdeth | all · such as | fall :
and lifteth | up all | those that · are | down.

15 The eyes of all wait upon | thee O | Lord :
and thou | givest · them their | meat in · due | season.

16 Thou | openest · thine | hand :
and fillest | all things | living · with | plenteousness.

17 The Lord is ríghteous in | all his | ways :
and | holy · in | all his | works.

18 The Lord is nigh unto all | them that | call upon him :
yea all such as | call up- | on him | faithfully.

19 He will fulfil the desire of | them that | fear him :
he also will | hear their | cry and · will | help them.

20 The Lord preserveth all | them that | love him :
but scattereth a- | broad — | all the · un- | godly.

Full. 21 My mouth shall speak the | praise of · the | Lord :
and let all flesh give thanks unto his holy | Name for | ever · and | ever.

PSALM 146

(*Single or Triple Chant*)

Full. 1 Praise the Lord O my soul, * while I líve will I | praise the | Lord :
yea as long as I have any being, * I will sing | prais-es | unto · my | God.

Full. 2 O put not your trust in princes, * nor in any | child of | man :
for there | is no | help in | them.

Full. 3 For when the breath of man goeth forth, he shall turn a- | gain to · his | earth :
and | then · all his | thoughts — | perish.

4 Blessed is he that hath the God of | Jacob · for his | help :
and whose | hope is · in the | Lord his | God ;

5 Who made heaven and earth, * the sea and | all that · therein | is :
who | keepeth · his | promise · for | ever ;

6 Who helpeth them to right that | suf-fer | wrong :
who | feed — | eth the | hungry.

7 The Lord lóoseth | men · out of | prison :
the | Lord · giveth | sight · to the | blind.

8 The Lord hélpeth | them that · are | fallen :
the Lord | car-eth | for the | righteous.

9 The Lord careth for the strangers ; * he defendeth the | fatherless · and | widow :
as for the way of the ungodly, * he | turneth · it | up-side | down.

(*third part.*) 10 The Lord thy God O Sion, shall be Kíng for | ev-er- | more :
and throughout | all — | ge-ne- | rations.

DAY 30. EVENING PRAYER

PSALM 147

Full. 1 O praise the Lord, * for it is a good thing to sing praises | unto · our | God :
yea a joyful and pleasant | thing it | is · to be | thankful.

Full. 2 The Lord doth build | up Je- | rusalem :
and gather to- | gether · the | outcasts · of | Israel.

3 He healeth those that are | broken · in | heart :
and giveth | medicine · to | heal their | sickness.

4 He telleth the | number · of the | stars :
and | calleth · them | all by · their | names.

5 Great is our Lord, and | great is · his | power :
yea | and his | wisdom · is | infinite.

6 The Lord setteth | up the | meek :
and bríngeth the un- | god-ly | down · to the | ground.

7 O sing unto the | Lord with | thanksgiving :
sing praises upon the | harp un- | to our | God ;

8 Who covereth the heav'n with clouds, * and prepareth | rain · for the | earth :
and maketh the grass to grow upon the mountains, * and | herb · for the | use of | men ;

9 Who giveth fodder | unto · the | cattle :
and feedeth the young | ravens · that | call up- | on him.

10 He hath no pléasure in the | strength of · an | horse :
neither de- | lighteth · he in | any · man's | legs.

11 But the Lord's delight is in | them that | fear him :
and | put their | trust in · his | mercy.

12 Praise the Lord, | O Je- | rusalem :
praise | — thy | God, O | Sion.

13 For he hath made fast the | bars of · thy | gates :
and hath | bless'd thy | children · with- | in thee.

14 He maketh | peace in · thy | borders :
and filleth thee | with the | flour of | wheat.

15 He sendeth forth his com- | mandment up-on | earth :
and his word | run-neth | ve-ry | swiftly.

16 He giveth | snow like | wool :
and | scattereth · the | hoarfrost · like | ashes.

17 He casteth forth his | ice like | morsels :
who is | able · to a- | bide his | frost ?

18 He sendeth out his | word and | melteth them :
He bloweth with his | wind · and the | wa-ters | flow.

19 He sheweth his | word · unto | Jacob :
his státutes and | ordi-nances | un-to | Israel.

Unis. 20 He hath not dealt só with | an-y | nation :
neither have the heathen | know-ledge | of his | laws.

PSALM 148

Full. 1 O praise the | Lord of | heav'n :
praise | — him | in the | height.

Full. 2 Praise him, all ye | angels · of | his :
praise | — him | all his | host.

Full. 3 Praise him, | sun and | moon :
praise him, | all ye | stars and | light.

Full. 4 Praise him, | all ye | heav'ns :
and ye wáters that | are a- | bove the | heav'ns.

5 Let them praise the | Name of · the | Lord :
for he spake the word and they were made, * he com- | manded · and | they were · cre- | ated.

6 He hath made them fást for | ever · and | ever :
he hath given them a | law which | shall not · be | broken.

7 Praise the | Lord up-on | earth :
ye | dragons · and | all — | deeps ;

8 Fire and hail, | snow and | vapours :
wind and | storm ful- | filling · his | word ;

9 Mountains and | all — | hills :
fruitful | trees and | all — | cedars ;

10 Beasts and | all — | cattle :
worms | — and | feath-er'd | fowls ;

11 Kings of the earth and | all — | people :
princes and all | judg-es | of the | world ;

12 Young men and maidens, old men and children, * praise the | Name of · the | Lord :
for his Name only is excellent, * and his | praise a-bove | heav'n and | earth.

2nd part. 13 He shall exalt the horn of his people, * all his | saints shall | praise him :
even the children of Israel, | even · the | people · that | serveth him.

PSALM 149

Full. 1 O síng unto the | Lord a · new | song :
let the congre- | gation · of | saints — | praise him.

Full. 2 Let Israel rejoice in | him that | made him :
and let the children of Sion be | joy-ful | in their | King.

3 Let them praise his | Name in · the | dance :
let them sing praises unto | him with | tabret · and | harp.

4 For the Lord hath | pleasure · in his | people :
and | helpeth · the | meek — | hearted.

5 Let the saints be | joyful · with | glory :
let | them re- | joice in · their | beds.

6 Let the praises of | God be in · their | mouth :
and a | two-edg'd | sword in · their | hands ;

7 To be a- | veng'd · of the | heathen :
and | to re- | buke the | people ;

8 To bind their | kings in | chains :
and their | nobles · with | links of | iron.

2nd part. 9 That they may be avéng'd of them, | as it · is | written :
Such | honour · have | all his | saints.

PSALM 150

Full. 1 O praise | God in · his | holiness :
praise him in the | firma-ment | of his | power.

Full. 2 Praise him in his | no-ble | acts :
praise him ac- | cording · to his | excel-lent | greatness.

3 Praise him in the | sound of · the | trumpet :
praise him up- | on the | lute and | harp.

4 Praise him in the | cymbals · and | dances :
praise him up- | on the | strings and | pipe.

5 Praise him upon the | well-tun'd | cymbals :
praise him up- | on the | loud — | cymbals.

Full. Unis. 6 Let every | thing that · hath | breath :
praise | — | — the | Lord.

Psalm 149.

1 O sing unto the | Lord a | new | song: let the congregation of | saints | praise him.

2 Let Israel rejoice in | him that | made him: and let the children of Sion be | joyful | in their | King.

3 Let them praise his | Name in | the | dance: let them sing praises unto him with | tabret | and | harp.

4 For the Lord hath | pleasure | in his | people: and | helpeth | the | meek-hearted.

5 Let the saints be | joyful | with | glory: let them re- | joice in | their | beds.

6 Let the praises of | God be | in their | mouth: and a | two-edged | sword | in their | hands;

7 To be avenged | of the | heathen: and | to re- | buke the | people;

8 To bind their | kings in | chains: and their | nobles with | links of | iron.

9 That they may be avenged of them, | as it is | written: Such | honour | have all his | saints.

Psalm 150.

1 O praise God in his | holiness: praise him in the firmament | of his | power.

2 Praise him in his | noble | acts: praise him according to his | excellent | greatness.

3 Praise him in the | sound of | the | trumpet: praise him up- | on the | lute and | harp.

4 Praise him in the | cymbals | and | dances: praise him up- | on the | strings and | pipe.

5 Praise him upon the | well-tuned | cymbals: praise him up- | on the | loud | cymbals.

6 Let every | thing that | hath | breath: praise | the | Lord.

PROPER PSALMS

CHRISTMAS DAY

MORNING PRAYER

PSALM 19

Full. 1 The heav'ns declare the | glory · of | God :
and the | firma-ment | sheweth · his | handy-work.

Full. 2 One day | telleth · an- | other :
and one night | cer-ti- | fieth · an- | other.

3 There is neither | speech nor | language :
but their | voices · are | heard a- | mong them.

4 Their sound is gone óut into | all — | lands :
and their | words in-to the | ends of · the | world.

Full. 5 In them hath he set a tabernacle | for the | sun :
which cometh forth as a bridegroom out of his chamber, *
and rejóiceth as a | giant · to | run his | course.

Full. 6 It goeth forth from the uttermost part of the heaven, * and runneth about unto the | end of it · a- | gain :
and there is nothing | hid · from the | heat there- | of.

7 The law of the Lord is an undefil'd law, con- | verting · the | soul :
the testimony of the Lord is sure, * and giveth | wis-dom | unto · the | simple.

8 The statutes of the Lord are ríght, and re- | joice the | heart :
the commandment of the Lord is pure, * and giveth | light un- | to the | eyes.

9 The fear of the Lord is cléan, and en- | dureth · for | ever :
the judgements of the Lord are true, and | right-eous | al-to- | gether.

10 More to be desir'd are they than gold, * yéa than | much fine | gold :
sweeter also than | hon-ey, | and the | honey-comb.

11 Moreover by thém is thy | ser-vant | taught :
and in kéeping of them | there is | great re- | ward.

12 Who can tell how | oft · he of- | fendeth :
O cléanse thou | me from · my | se-cret | faults.

13 Keep thy servant also from presumptuous sins, * lest they get the do- | min-ion | over me :
so shall I be undefil'd, * and innocent | from thẹ | great of- | fence.

14 Let the words of my mouth, * and the meditation of my heart, * be alway acceptable | in thy | sight :
O Lórd my | strength ạnd | my̡ rẹ- | deemer.

PSALM 45

Full. 1 My heart is indíting of a | good — | matter :
I speak of the things which I have | made ụn- | tọ thẹ | King.

Full. [2]My | tongue — | is
thẹ | pen of · a | read-y | writer.

3 Thou art fáirer than the | children · of | men :
full of grace are thy lips, * bẹcạuse | God hath | blessed · thee for | ever.

4 Gird thee with thy sword upon thy thigh O | thou most | Mighty :
accórding to thy | wor-ship | ạnd rẹ- | nown.

5 Good luck have thou | with thine | honour :
ride on because of the word of truth, * of meekness and righteousness, * and thy right hand shạll | teach thee | terri-ble | things.

6 Thy arrows are very sharp, * and the people shall be sub- | du'd un-to | thee :
even in the | midst a-mong the | King's — | enemies.

7 Thy seat O God en- | dureth · for | ever :
the sceptre of thy | kingdom · is a | right — | sceptre.

8 Thou hast lov'd ríghteousness and | hated · in- | iquity :
wherefore God, even thý God, * hath anointed thee with the oil of | gladness · a- | bove thy | fellows.

9 All thy garments smell of myrrh, | aloes · and | cassia :
out of the ivory pálaces, where- | by · they have | made thee | glad.

10 King's daughters were among thy | honour-able | women :
upon thy right hand did stand the queen in a vesture of gold, * wrought a- | bout with | di-vers | colours.

11 Hearken O daughter and consider, in- | cline thine | ear :
forget also thine own | people · and thy | fa-ther's | house.

12 So shall the King have | pleasure · in thy | beauty :
for he is thy Lord | God, and | worship · thou | him.

13 And the daughter of Tyre shall be | there · with a | gift :
like as the rich also among the people, * shall | make their · suppli- | cation · be- | fore thee.

14 The King's daughter is all | glorious · with- | in :
her | clothing · is of | wrought — | gold.

15 She shall be brought unto the King in | raiment · of | needle-work :
the virgins that be her fellows shall bear her company, * and | shall be | brought · unto | thee.

16 With joy and gládness shall | they be | brought :
and shall enter | into · the | King's — | palace.

17 Instead of thy fathers | thou shalt · have | children :
whom thou mayest make | princes · in | all — | lands.

18 I will remember thy Name from one gene- | ration · to an- | other :
therefore shall the people give thánks unto thee, | world with- | out — | end.

PSALM 85

1 Lord thou art become gracious | unto · thy | land :
thou hast turn'd a- | way the · cap- | tivity · of | Jacob.

2 Thou hast forgiven the of- | fence of · thy | people :
and | cov-er'd | all their | sins.

2nd part. 3 Thou hast taken away | all · thy dis- | pleasure :
and turn'd thyself from thy | wrath-ful | in-dig- | nation.

4 Turn us then, O | God our | Saviour :
and | let thine | an-ger | cease from us.

5 Wilt thou be dis- | pleas'd at · us for | ever :
and wilt thou stretch out thy wrath from | one · gene- | ration · to an- | other ?

6 Wilt thou not turn a- | gain and | quicken us :
that thy | people · may re- | joice in | thee ?

7 Shew us thy | mercy · O | Lord :
and | grant us | thy sal- | vation.

8 I will hearken what the Lord God will | say con- | cerning me :
for he shall speak peace unto his people and to his | saints · that they | turn · not a- | gain.

9 For his salvation is | nigh · them that | fear him :
that | glory · may | dwell in · our | land.

10 Mercy and truth are | met to- | gether :
righteousness and | peace have | kiss'd each | other.

11 Truth shall flourish | out of · the | earth :
and righteousness hath | look-ed | down from | heav'n.

12 Yea the Lord shall shew | lov-ing- | kindness :
and our | land shall | give her | increase.

13 Righteousness shall | go be- | fore him :
and he shall di- | rect his | going · in the | way.

EVENING PRAYER

PSALM 89

Full. 1 My song shall be alway of the loving- | kindness · of the | Lord :
with my mouth will I ever be shewing thy truth, * from | one · gene- | ration · to an- | other.

Full. 2 For I have said, * Mercy shall be set | up for | ever :
thy truth shalt thou | stab-lish | in the | heav'ns.

3 I have made a covenant | with my | chosen :
I have | sworn un-to | David · my | servant.

4 Thy seed will I | stablish · for | ever :
and set up thy throne from | one · gene- | ration · to an- | other.

Full. 5 O Lord, the very heav'ns shall praise thy | won-drous | works :
and thy truth in the congre- | ga-tion | of the | saints.

Full. 6 For who is | he a-mong the | clouds :
that shall be com- | par'd un- | to the | Lord ?

Full. 7 And what is | he a-mong the | gods :
that shall be | like un- | to the | Lord ?

8 God is very greatly to be fear'd in the | council · of the | saints :
and to be had in reverence of all | them that · are | round a- | bout him.

9 O Lord God of hosts, * who is | like un-to | thee :
thy truth most mighty | Lord · is on | ev-ery | side.

10 Thou rulest the | raging · of the | sea :
thou stillest the | waves there-of | when · they a- | rise.

11 Thou hast subdu'd | Egypt · and de- | stroy'd it :
thou hast scatter'd thine enemies a- | broad with · thy | migh-ty | arm.

12 The heavens are thine, the earth | also · is | thine :
thou hast laid the foundation of the round world, and | all that | there-in | is.

13 Thou hast made the | north · and the | south :
Tabor and | Hermon · shall re- | joice in · thy | Name.

14 Thou hast a | migh-ty | arm :
strong is thy | hand and | high is · thy | right hand.

15 Righteousness and equity are the habi- | tation · of thy | seat :
mercy and | truth shall | go be-fore thy | face.

16 Blessed is the people O | Lord that · can re- | joice in thee :
they shall | walk in · the | light of · thy | countenance.

17 Their delight shall be | daily in · thy | Name :
and in thy righteousness | shall they | make their | boast.

18 For thou art the | glory of · their | strength :
and in thy loving-kindness | thou shalt · lift | up our | horns.

2nd part. 19 For the | Lord is · our de- | fence :
the Holy One of | Is-rael | is our | King.

20 Thou spakest sometime in visions unto thy | saints and | saidst :
I have laid help upon one that is mighty, * I have exalted one | cho-sen | out of · the | people.

21 I have found | David · my | servant :
with my holy | oil have | I a- | nointed him.

22 My hand shall | hold him | fast :
and | my — | arm shall | strengthen him.

23 The enemy shall not be able to | do him | violence :
the son of | wicked-ness | shall not | hurt him.

24 I will smite down his foes be- | fore his | face :
and | plague — | them that | hate him.

25 My truth also and my | mercy · shall be | with him :
and in my | Name shall · his | horn · be ex- | alted.

26 I will set his dominion | also · in the | sea :
and his | right hand | in the | floods.

27 He shall call me, | Thou art · my | Father :
my | God · and my | strong sal- | vation.

28 And I will | make him · my | first-born :
higher | than the | kings of · the | earth.

29 My mercy will I keep for him for | ev-er- | more :
and my | covenant · shall | stand — | fast with him.

2nd part. 30 His seed also will I make to en- | dure for | ever :
and his | throne · as the | days of | heaven.

31 But if his children for- | sake my | law :
and | walk not | in my | judgements ;

32 If they break my statutes, * and keep not | my com- | mandments :
I will visit their offences with the | rod · and their | sin with | scourges.

33 Nevertheless, * my loving-kindness will I not | utter-ly | take from him :
nor | suffer · my | truth to | fail.

34 My covenant will I not break, * nor alter the thing that is gone | out of · my | lips :
I have sworn once by my holiness, * that I | will not | fail — | David.

Full. 35 His seed shall en- | dure for | ever :
and his seat is | like as · the | sun be- | fore me.

Full. 36 He shall stand fast for ever- | more · as the | moon :
and as the | faith-ful | witness · in | heav'n.

37 But thou hast abhorr'd and forsaken | thine A- | nointed :
and | art dis- | pleas-ed | at him.

38 Thou hast broken the covenant | of thy | servant :
and | cast his | crown · to the | ground.

39 Thou hast overthrown | all his | hedges :
and | bro-ken | down his | strong holds.

40 All | they that go · by | spoil him :
and he is be- | come a · re- | proach · to his | neighbours.

41 Thou hast set up the right | hand of · his | enemies :
and made all his | adver-saries | to re- | joice.

42 Thou hast taken away the | edge of · his | sword :
and givest him not | victor-y | in the | battle.

43 Thou hast put | out his | glory :
and cast his | throne — | down · to the | ground.

44 The days of his | youth hast · thou | shorten'd :
and | cover'd · him | with dis- | honour.

45 Lord how long wilt thou hide thy- | self, * for | ever :
and shall thy | wrath — | burn like | fire ?

46 O remember how | short my | time is :
wherefore hast thou made | all — | men for | nought ?

47 What man is he that liveth, and | shall not · see | death :
and shall he deliver his | soul · from the | hand of | hell ?

48 Lord where are thy | old · loving- | kindnesses :
which thou swarest unto | Da-vid | in thy | truth ?

49 Remember Lord the re- | buke that · thy | servants have :
and how I do bear in my bosom the re- | bukes of | ma-ny | people ;

50 Wherewith thine enemies | have blas- | phem'd thee :
and slander'd the | footsteps · of | thine A- | nointed ;

2nd part. Full. 51 Praised be the Lord for | ev-er- | more :
A- | men and | A — | men.

PSALM 110

Full. 1 The Lord sáid unto | my — | Lord :
Sit thou on my right hand,* until I | make thine | enemies · thy | footstool.

Full. 2 The Lord shall send the rod of thy | power · out of | Sion :
be thou ruler, * éven in the | midst a- | mong thine | enemies.

2nd part. 3 In the day of thy power shall the people offer thee free-will offerings, * with an | ho-ly | worship :
the dew of thy | birth is · of the | womb of · the | morning.

4 The Lord sware, and | will not · re- | pent :
Thou art a Priest for ever * after the | or-der | of Mel- | chisedech.

5 The Lórd upon | thy right | hand :
shall wound even | kings · in the | day of · his | wrath.

6 He shall judge among the heathen, * he shall fill the pláces with the | dead — | bodies :
and smite in sunder the | heads · over | di-vers | countries.

7 He shall drink of the | brook · in the | way :
therefore | shall he · lift | up his | head.

PSALM 132

1 Lord re- | mem-ber | David :
and | all — | his — | trouble ;
2 How he | sware un-to the | Lord :
and vow'd a vów unto the Al- | migh-ty | God of | Jacob ;
3 I will not come within the tábernacle | of mine | house :
nor | climb up | into · my | bed ;
4 I will not suffer mine eyes to sleep, nor mine | eye-lids · to | slumber :
neither the témples of my | head to | take · any | rest ;

2nd part. 5 Until I find out a place for the | temple · of the | Lord :
an habitátion for the | migh-ty | God of | Jacob.
6 Lo we heard of the | same at · Eph- | rata :
and | found it | in the | wood.
7 We will | go in-to his | tabernacle :
and fall low on our | knees be- | fore his | footstool.

Full. 8 Arise O | Lord in-to thy | resting-place :
thou | and the | ark of · thy | strength.

Full. 9 Let thy priests be | cloth'd with | righteousness :
and let thy | saints — | sing with | joyfulness.
10 For thy | ser-vant | David's sake :
turn not away the | presence · of | thine A- | nointed.
11 The Lord hath made a faithful | oath un-to | David :
and he | shall not | shrink — | from it ;
12 Of the | fruit of · thy | body :
shall I | set up- | on thy | seat.
13 If thy children will keep my covenant, * and my téstimonies that | I shall | learn them :
their children also shall sít upon thy | seat for | ev-er- | more.
14 For the Lord hath chosen Síon to be an habi- | tation · for him- | self :
he hath | long-ed | for — | her.

15 This shall be my | rest for | ever :
here will I dwell, * for I | have a · de- | light there- | in.
16 I will bless her | victuals · with | increase :
and will | satisfy · her | poor with | bread.
17 I will deck her | priests with | health :
and her | saints · shall re- | joice and | sing.
18 There shall I make the horn of | David · to | flourish :
I have ordain'd a | lantern · for | mine A- | nointed.
19 As for his enemies, * I shall | clothe them · with | shame :
but upon him- | self · shall his | crown — | flourish.

ASH WEDNESDAY

MORNING PRAYER

PSALM 6

(*Single Chant*)

1 O Lord rebúke me not in thine | in-dig- | nation :
neither | chasten · me in | thy dis- | pleasure.
2 Have mercy upon me O Lord for | I am | weak :
O Lord | heal me · for my | bones are | vex'd.
3 My soul álso is | sore — | troubl'd :
but | Lord how | long wilt · thou | punish me ?
4 Turn thee O Lórd and de- | liver · my | soul :
O | save me · for thy | mer-cy's | sake.
5 For in death | no man · re- | membereth thee :
and who will | give thee | thanks · in the | pit ?
6 I am weary of my groaning, * every night | wash I · my | bed :
and | water · my | couch with · my | tears.
7 My beauty is gone for | ve-ry | trouble :
and worn away be- | cause of | all mine | enemies.

Full. 8 Away from me all | ye that · work | vanity :
for the Lord hath | heard the | voice of · my | weeping.

9 The Lord hath | heard · my pe- | tition :
the | Lord · will re- | ceive my | prayer.

10 All mine enemies shall be confounded and | sore — | vex'd :
they shall be turned báck and | put to | shame — | suddenly.

PSALM 32

1 Blessed is he whose unríghteousness | is for- | giv'n :
and | whose — | sin is | cover'd.

2 Blessed is the man unto whom the Lord im- | puteth · no | sin :
and in whose | spirit · there | is no | guile.

3 For while I | held my | tongue :
my bones consum'd a- | way · through my | daily · com- | plaining.

4 For thy hand is heavy upon me | day and | night :
and my móisture is | like the | drought in | summer.

5 I will acknowledge my | sin · unto | thee :
and mine un- | righteous-ness | have I · not | hid.

6 I said, I will confess my | sins un-to the | Lord :
and so thou forgavest the | wicked-ness | of my | sin.

7 For this shall every one that is godly make his prayer unto thee, * in a tíme when thou | mayest · be | found :
but in the great water-floods | they shall | not come | nigh him.

8 Thou art a place to hide me in, * thou shalt pre- | serve me · from | trouble :
thou shalt cómpass me a- | bout with | songs of · de- | liverance.

9 I will inform thee, * and teach thee in the wáy where- | in thou · shalt | go :
and I will | guide thee | with mine | eye.

10 Be ye not like to horse and mule, which have | no · under- | standing
whose mouths must be held with bit and | bri-dle, | lest they | fall upon thee.

11 Great plagues re- | main · for the un- | godly :
but whoso putteth his trust in the Lord, * mércy em- | braceth · him on | eve-ry | side.

Full. 12 Be glad O ye righteous and re- | joice · in the | Lord :
and be joyful, áll | ye that · are | true of | heart.

Psalm 38

1 Put me not to rebuke O | Lord in · thine | anger :
neither chásten me | in thy | heavy · dis- | pleasure :

2 For thine árrows stick | fast in | me :
and thy | hand — | presseth · me | sore.

3 There is no health in my flesh, be- | cause of · thy dis- | pleasure :
neither is there any rest in my bones, by | rea-son | of my | sin.

4 For my wickednesses are gone | over · my | head :
and are like a sore búrden too | heavy · for | me to | bear.

[5] My | wounds — | stink
and are cor- | rupt — | through my | foolishness.

6 I am brought into so great | trouble · and | misery :
that I go | mourn-ing | all the · day | long.

7 For my loins are fill'd with a | sore dis- | ease :
and there is nó | whole part | in my | body.

8 I am feeble and | sore — | smitten :
I have roar'd for the very dis- | quiet-ness | of my | heart

9 Lord thou knówest | all · my de- | sire :
and my | groan-ing | is not | hid from thee.

10 My heart panteth, my | strength hath | fail'd me :
and the | sight of · mine | eyes is | gone from me.

11 My lovers and my neighbours did stand lóoking up- | on my | trouble :
and my | kins-men | stood a-far | off.

12 They also that sought after my | life laid | snares for me :
and they that went about to do me evil talk'd of wickedness, * and imagin'd de- | ceit — | all the · day | long.

13 As for me, I was like a | deaf · man and | heard not :
and as one that is dumb, * who | doth not | open · his | mouth.

14 I became even as a | man that | heareth not :
and in whose | mouth are | no re- | proofs.

15 For in thee O Lord have I | put my | trust :
thou shalt answer | for me · O | Lord my | God.

16 I have requir'd that they, even mine enemies, * should not | tri-umph | over me :
for when my foot slipp'd, they re- | joic-ed | greatly · a- | gainst me.

17 And I truly am | set in · the | plague :
and my heaviness is | ev-er | in my | sight.

18 Fór I will con- | fess my | wickedness :
and be | sor-ry | for my | sin.

19 But mine enemies | live and · are | mighty :
and they that hate me | wrongfully · are | many · in | number.

20 They also that reward evil for | good · are a- | gainst me :
because I follow the | thing that | good — | is.

21 Forsake me not O | Lord my | God :
be not | thou — | far — | from me.

22 Haste | thee to | help me :
O Lord | God of | my sal- | vation

EVENING PRAYER

PSALM 102

1 Hear my | prayer O | Lord :
and let my | cry-ing | come un-to | thee.

2 Hide not thy face from me in the | time of · my | trouble :
incline thine ear unto me when I call, * O | hear me · and | that right | soon.

3 For my days are consum'd a- | way like | smoke :
and my bones are burnt | up · as it | were a | fire-brand.

4 My heart is smitten dówn and | wither'd · like | grass :
só that I for- | get to | eat my | bread.

5 For the | voice of · my | groaning :
my | bones will · scarce | cleave to · my | flesh.

6 I am become like a pélican | in the | wilderness :
and like an | owl · that is | in the | desert.

2nd part. 7 I have watch'd, * and am éven as it | were a | sparrow :
that | sitteth · a- | lone up-on the | house-top.

8 Mine enemies revile me | all the · day | long :
and they that are mad upon me are | sworn to- | gether · a- | gainst me.

9 For I have eaten ashes | as it · were | bread :
and | mingl'd · my | drink with | weeping ;

10 And that because of thine indig- | nation · and | wrath :
for thou hast taken me | up and | cast me | down.

11 My days are | gone · like a | shadow :
and | I am | wither'd · like | grass.

Full. 12 But thou O Lord shalt en- | dure for | ever :
and thy re- | membrance · throughout | all · gene- | rations.

Full. 13 Thou shalt arise and have | mercy up-on | Sion :
for it is time that thou have mercy upon her, | yea the | time is | come.

2nd part. 14 And why ? * thy servants | think up-on her | stones :
and it pítieth them to | see her | ịn thẹ | dust.

15 The heathen shall fear thy | Name Ọ | Lord :
and áll the | kings of · the | earth thy | Majesty ;

16 When the Lord shall | build up | Sion :
ạnd whẹn hịs | glo-ry | shạll ạp- | pear ;

17 When he turneth him unto thẹ práyer of the | poor — | destitute :
ạnd dẹ- | spiseth · not | their dẹ- | sire.

18 This shall be written for | those that · come | after :
and the péople which shall be | born shall | praise thẹ | Lord.

19 For he hath look'd | down · from his | sanctuary :
out of the héav'n did the | Lord bẹ- | hold thẹ | earth ;

20 That he might hear the mournings of súch as are | ịn cạp- | tivity :
and delịver the children ap- | point-ed | ụn-tọ | death ;

21 That they may declare the Name of the | Lord ịn | Sion :
ạnd hịs | wor-ship | ạt Jẹ- | rusalem ;

22 When the péople are | gather'd · to- | gether :
and the kingdoms | also · to | serve thẹ | Lord.

23 He brought down my | strength · in my | journey :
ạnd | short-en'd | mỵ — | days.

24 But I said, O my God, * take me not awáy in the | midst of · mine | age :
as for thý years, * they en- | dure through-out | all · gene- | rations.

25 Thou Lòrd in the beginning hast laid the foun- | dation · of the | earth :
ạnd thẹ | heav'ns · are the | work of · thy | hands.

26 They shall perish, bụt | thou shalt · en- | dure :
they all shall wax | old ạs | dọth ạ | garment ;

27 And as a vesture shalt thou change them, * and | they shall · be | chang'd :
but thou art the | same and · thy | years · shall not | fail.
28 The children of thy | servants · shall con- | tinue :
and their | seed shall · stand | fast in · thy | sight.

PSALM 130

1 Out of the deep have I cáll'd unto | thee, O | Lord :
Lord, | hear — | my — | voice.
[2] O let thine ears con- | si-der | well
the | voice of | my com- | plaint.
3 If thou Lord wilt be extreme to márk what is | done a- | miss :
O | Lord — | who · may a- | bide it ?
4 For there is | mercy · with | thee :
there- | fore shalt | thou be | fear'd.
5 I look for the Lord, my | soul doth | wait for him :
in his | word — | is my | trust.
6 My soul fleeth | unto · the | Lord :
before the morning watch I say, be- | fore the | morning | watch.
7 O Israel trust in the Lord, * for with the | Lord · there is | mercy :
and with | him is | plenteous · re- | demption.
[8] And he shall re- | deem — | Israel
from | all — | his — | sins.

PSALM 143

1 Hear my prayer O Lord,* and con- | sider · my de- | sire :
hearken unto me for thy | truth and | righteous-ness' | sake.
2 And enter not into | judgement · with thy | servant :
for in thy sight shall | no man | living · be | justifi'd.

3 For the enemy hath persecuted my soul ; * he hath smitten my life | down · to the | ground :
he hath laid me in the darkness, * as the | men that · have been | long — | dead.

4 Therefore is my spirit | vex'd with- | in me :
and my | heart with- | in me · is | desolate.

5 Yet do I remember the time past ; * I muse upon | all thy | works :
yea I exercise my- | self · in the | works of · thy | hands.

6 I stretch forth my | hands · unto | thee :
my soul gaspeth unto | thee · as a | thirs-ty | land.

7 Hear me O Lord and that soon, * for my spirit | wax-eth | faint :
hide not thy face from me,* lest I be like unto | them that · go | down in-to the | pit.

8 O let me hear thy loving-kindness betimes in the morning, * for in | thee is · my | trust :
shew thou me the way that I should walk in, * for I lift | up my | soul un-to | thee.

9 Deliver me O | Lord · from mine | enemies :
for I | flee un-to | thee to | hide me.

10 Teach me to do the thing that pleaseth thee, for | thou art · my | God :
let thy loving Spirit lead me | forth in-to the | land of | righteousness.

11 Quicken me O | Lord · for thy | Name's sake :
and for thy righteousness' sake | bring my | soul · out of | trouble.

12 And of thy goodness | slay mine | enemies :
and destroy all them that vex my | soul, for | I am · thy | servant.

GOOD FRIDAY

MORNING PRAYER

PSALM 22

1 My God, my God look upon me, * why hast | thou for- | saken me :
and art so far from my health, * and from the | words of | my com- | plaint ?

2 O my God I cry in the daytime, | but thou | hearest not :
and in the night-season | also · I | take no | rest.

3 And thou con- | tin-uest | holy :
O | thou — | worship · of | Israel.

4 Our fathers | hoped · in | thee :
they trusted in | thee, and | thou · didst de- | liver them.

5 They call'd upon | thee and · were | holpen :
they put their trust in | thee and | were not · con- | founded.

6 But as for me, I am a | worm and · no | man :
a very scorn of men, and the | out-cast | of the | people.

7 All they that see me | laugh me · to | scorn :
they shoot out their lips and | shake their | heads — | saying,

Full. 8 He trusted in God that | he would · de- | liver him :
lét him de- | liver · him | if he · will | have him.

9 But thou art he that took me out of my | mo-ther's | womb :
thou wast my hope, * when I hánged | yet up-on my | mo-ther's | breasts.

10 I have been left unto thée ever | since · I was | born :
thou art my God | even · from my | mo-ther's | womb.

11 O go not from me, for trouble is | hard at | hand :
and | there is | none to | help me.

12 Many oxen are | come a- | bout me :
fat bulls of Basan close me | in on | eve-ry | side.

13 They gápe upon me | with their | mouths :
as it were a | ramping · and a | roar-ing | lion.

14 I am poured out like water, * and all my bones are | out of | joint :
my heart also in the midst of my body is | even · like | melt-ing | wax.

15 My strength is dried up like a potsherd, * and my tongue | cleaveth · to my | gums :
and thou shalt bring me | into · the | dust of | death.

16 For many dogs are | come a- | bout me :
and the council of the wicked | lay-eth | siege a- | gainst me.

17 They pierced my hands and my feet, * I may tell | all my | bones :
they stand | staring · and | looking · up- | on me.

18 They part my | garments · a- | mong them :
and cast | lots up- | on my | vesture.

2nd part. 19 But be not thou fár | from me · O | Lord :
thou art my | suc-cour | haste · thee to | help me.

20 Deliver my | soul · from the | sword :
my | darling · from the | power · of the | dog.

21 Sáve me from the | li-on's | mouth :
thou hast heard me also from a- | mong the | horns of · the | unicorns.

Full. 22 I will declare thy | Name un-to my | brethren :
in the midst of the congre- | ga-tion | will I | praise thee.

Full. 23 O praise the Lórd | ye that | fear him :
magnify him all ye of the seed of Jacob, * and féar him | all ye | seed of | Israel ;

24 For he hath not despis'd nor abhórr'd the low es- | tate of · the | poor :
he hath not hid his face from him, * but when he | call'd un-to | him he | heard him.

25 My praise is of thée in the | great · congre- | gation :
my vows will I perform in the | sight of | them that | fear him.

2nd part. 26 The poor shall | eat · and be | satisfi'd :
they that seek after the Lord shall praise him, * your | heart shall | live for | ever.

Full. 27 All the ends of the world shall remember themselves, * and be | turn'd un-to the | Lord :
and all the kíndreds of the | nations · shall | worship · be- | fore him.

Full. 28 For the | kingdom · is the | Lord's :
and he is the | Governor · a- | mong the | people.

29 All such as be | fat up-on | earth :
have | eat-en | and — | worshipp'd.

30 All they that go down into the dust shall | kneel be- | fore him :
and nó man hath | quicken'd · his | own — | soul.

31 My | seed shall | serve him :
they shall be cóunted unto the | Lord · for a | ge-ne- | ration.

32 They shall come, * and the héav'ns shall de- | clare his | righteousness :
unto a people that shall be | born · whom the | Lord hath | made.

Psalm 40

Full. 1 I waited | patiently · for the | Lord :
and he inclín'd unto | me and | heard my | calling.

Full. 2 He brought me also out of the horrible pit, * out of the | mire and | clay :
and set my feet upon the | rock and | order'd · my | goings.

3 And he hath put a new | song in · my | mouth :
even a | thanks-giving | unto · our | God.

4 Many shall | see it · and | fear :
and shall | put their | trust in · the | Lord.

5 Blessed is the man that hath set his | hope in · the | Lord :
and turn'd not unto the proud, * and to | such as · go a- | bout with | lies.

6 O Lord my God, great are the wondrous works which thou hast done, * like as be also thy thoughts which | are to | us-ward :
and yet there is | no man · that | ordereth · them | unto thee.

7 If I should de- | clare them · and | speak of them :
they should be more than I am | ab-le | to ex- | press.

8 Sacrifice and meat- | off'ring · thou | wouldest not :
but mine | ears — | hast thou | open'd.

9 Burnt-offerings and sacrifice for sin, hast thou | not re- | quir'd :
then | said I, | Lo I | come,

10 In the volume of the book it is written of me, * that I should fulfil thy will | O my | God :
I am content to do it, * yea thy | law · is with- | in my | heart.

Full. 11 I have declar'd thy righteousness in the | great · congre- | gation :
lo I will not refrain my lips O | Lord, and | that thou | knowest.

Full. 12 I have not hid thy righteousness with- | in my | heart :
my talk hath been of thy | truth · and of | thy sal- | vation.

2nd part. 13 I have not kept back thy loving | mercy · and | truth :
from the | great — | con-gre- | gation.

14 Withdraw not thou thy mercy | from me · O | Lord :
let thy loving-kindness and thy | truth — | alway · pre- | serve me.

15 For innumerable troubles are come about me, * my sins have taken such hold upon me, * that I am not | able to · look | up :
yea they are more in number than the hairs of my | head, · and my | heart hath | fail'd me.

16 O Lord, let it be thy | pleasure · to de- | liver me :
make | haste O | Lord to | help me.

17 Let them be asham'd and confounded together, * that seek after my | soul · to de- | stroy it :
let them be driven backward, and put to re- | buke that | wish me | evil.

18 Let them be desolate and re- | warded · with | shame :
that say unto me, Fie up- | on thee, | fie up- | on thee.

19 Let all those that seek thee be joyful and | glad in | thee :
and let such as love thy salvation say | alway · The | Lord be | prais'd.

20 As for me, I am | poor and | needy :
but the | Lord — | car-eth | for me.

21 Thou art my | helper · and re- | deemer :
make no long | tarry-ing, | O my | God.

PSALM 54

1 Save me O | God · for thy | Name's sake :
and a- | venge me | in thy | strength.

2 Hear my | prayer O | God :
and hearken | unto · the | words of · my | mouth.

2nd part. 3 For strangers are risen | up a- | gainst me :
and tyrants, which have not God before their | eyes, seek | after · my | soul.

4 Behold, | God is · my | helper :
the Lord is with | them that · up- | hold my | soul.

5 He shall reward evil | unto · mine | enemies :
de- | stroy thou | them in · thy | truth.

6 An offering of a free heart will I give thee, * and praise thy | Name O | Lord :
be- | cause it | is so | comfortable.

7 For he hath deliver'd me out of | all my | trouble :
and mine eye hath seen his de- | sire up- | on mine | enemies.

EVENING PRAYER

PSALM 69

1 Save | me O | God :
for the waters are come in, | ev-en | unto · my | soul.

2 I stick fast in the deep mire where | no — | ground is :
I am come into deep waters, | so that · the | floods run | over me.

3 I am weary of crying, my | throat is | dry :
my sight faileth me for waiting so | long up- | on my | God.

4 They that hate me without a cause, * are more than the | hairs of · my | head :
they that are mine enemies, * and would de- | stroy me | guiltless · are | mighty.

5 I paid them the things that I | nev-er | took :
God thou knowest my simpleness, and my | faults · are not | hid from | thee.

6 Let not them that trust in thee O Lord God of hosts, * be a- | sham'd for · my | cause :
let not those that seek thee be confounded through me, | O Lord | God of | Israel.

7 And why ? * for thy sake have I | suffer'd · re- | proof :
shame | — hath | cover'd · my | face.

8 I am become a stranger | unto · my | brethren :
even an alien | unto · my | mo-ther's | children.

9 For the zeal of thine house hath | ev-en | eaten me :
and the rebukes of them that rebuk'd | thee are | fallen · up- | on me.

10 I wept, and chasten'd my- | self with | fasting :
and that was | turn'd to | my re- | proof.

11 I put on | sack-cloth | also :
    and they | jest — | ed up- | on me.
12 They that sit in the gate | speak a- | gainst me :
    and the | drunkards · make | songs up- | on me.
13 But Lórd I make my | prayer un-to | thee :
    in | an ac- | cepta-ble | time.
14 Hear me O God, * in the multitude | of thy | mercy :
    even in the | truth of | thy sal- | vation.
15 Take me out of the | mire · that I | sink not :
    O let me be deliver'd from them that hate me, * and | out · of the | deep — | waters.
16 Let not the water-flood drown me, * neither let the deep | swallow · me | up :
    and let not the | pit · shut her | mouth up- | on me.
17 Hear me O Lord, * for thy loving- | kindness · is | comfortable :
    turn thee unto me, * according to the | multi-tude | of thy | mercies.
18 And hide not thy face from thy servant, for | I am · in | trouble :
    O | haste — | thee and | hear me.
19 Draw ních unto my | soul and | save it :
    O de- | liver · me be- | cause of · mine | enemies.
20 Thou hast known my reproof, * my sháme and | my dis- | honour :
    mine ádversaries are | all in | thy — | sight.
21 Thy rebuke hath broken my heart, * I am | full of | heaviness :
    I look'd for some to have pity on me, * but there was no man, * neither | found I | any · to | comfort me.
22 They gave me | gall to | eat :
    and when I was thirsty they | gave me | vinegar · to | drink.
23 Let their table be made a snare to | take them-selves with- | al :
    and let the things that should have been for their wealth, * bé unto | them · an oc- | casion · of | falling.
24 Let their eyes be | blinded · that they | see not :
    and ever | bow thou | down their | backs.

25 Pour out thine indig- | nation · up- | on them :
and let thy | wrathful · dis- | pleasure · take | hold of them.

26 Lét their habi- | tation · be | void :
and | no · man to | dwell in · their | tents.

27 For they persecute him whom | thou hast | smitten :
and they talk how they may vex | them whom | thou hast | wounded.

28 Let them fall from one wickedness | to an- | other :
and not | come in- | to thy | righteousness.

2nd part. 29 Let them be wip'd out of the | book of · the | living :
and not be | written · a- | mong the | righteous.

30 As for me, when I am | poor · and in | heaviness :
thy help O | God shall | lift me | up.

31 I will praise the Náme of | God · with a | song :
and | mag-ni- | fy it · with | thanksgiving.

32 This álso shall | please the | Lord :
better than a | bullock · that hath | horns and | hoofs.

33 The humble shall consíder this | and be | glad :
seek yé after | God · and your | soul shall | live.

34 For the Lórd | heareth · the | poor :
and de- | spis-eth | not his | prisoners.

35 Let héav'n and | earth — | praise him :
the séa and | all that | moveth · there- | in.

36 For God will save Sion, * and build the | cities · of | Judah :
that men may dwell there, and | have it | in pos- | session.

37 The posterity also of his | servants · shall in- | herit it :
and | they that · love his | Name shall | dwell therein.

PSALM 88

1 O Lord God of my salvation, * I have cri'd day and | night bẹ- | fore thee :
O let my prayer enter into thy presence, * ịn- | cline thine | ear un-to my | calling.

2 For my soul is | full ọf | trouble :
and my | life · draweth | nigh un-to | hell.

3 I am counted as one of them that go | down in-to the | pit :
and I have been even as a | man thạt | hath no | strength.

4 Free among the dead, * like unto them that are wounded, and | lie · in the | grave :
who are out of remembrance, * ạnd ạre | cut ạ- | way from · thy | hand.

5 Thou hast laid me in the | low-est | pit :
in a place of | darkness · and | ịn thẹ | deep.

6 Thine indignation | li-eth | hard upon me :
and thou hast | vex'd · me with | all thy | storms.

7 Thou hast put away mine ac- | quain-tance | far from me :
ạnd | made · me to | be ạb- | horr'd of them.

[8] I am so | fast in | prison
thạt Ị | can-not | get — | forth.

9 My sight faileth for | vẹ-rỵ | trouble :
Lord I have call'd daily upon thee, * I have stretch'd | forth my | hands un-to | thee.

10 Dost thou shew wonders a- | mong thẹ | dead :
or shall the dead rise | up ạ- | gain ạnd | praise thee?

11 Shall thy loving-kindness be | shew'd · in the | grave :
ọr thỵ | faithful-ness | ịn dẹ- | struction ?

12 Shall thy wondrous works be | known · in the | dark :
and thy righteousness in the land where | all things | ạre fọr- | gotten ?

13 Unto thee have I | cri'd O | Lord :
and early shall my | prayer — | come bẹ- | fore thee.

14 Lord why ab- | horrest · thou my | soul :
and | hid-est | thou thy | face from me ?

15 I am in misery, * and like unto him that is at the | point to | die :
even from my youth up, * thy terrors have I | suffer'd · with a | trou-bl'd | mind.

16 Thy wrathful dis- | pleasure · goeth | over me :
and the | fear of · thee | hath un- | done me.

17 They came round about me | daily · like | water :
and compass'd me to- | gether · on | eve-ry | side.

18 My lovers and friends hast thou | put a- | way from me :
and hid mine ac- | quain-tance | out of · my | sight.

EASTER DAY

MORNING PRAYER

EASTER ANTHEMS

(*Single Chant*)

Full. 1 Christ our passover is | sacri-fic'd | for us :
therefore | let us | keep the | feast ;

Full. 2 Not with the old leaven, * nor with the leaven of | malice · and | wickedness :
but with the unleaven'd | bread of · sin- | ceri-ty and | truth.

3 Christ being rais'd from the dead | dieth · no | more :
death hath no | more do- | min-ion | over him.

4 For in that he died, he died unto | sin — | once :
but in that he | liveth, · he | liveth · unto | God.

5 Likewise reckon ye also yourselves to be dead in- | deed · unto | sin :
but alive unto Gód through | Je-sus | Christ our | Lord.

Full. 6 Christ is | risen · from the | dead :
and become the | first-fruits · of | them that | slept.

7 For since by | man came | death :
by man came also the resur- | rec-tion | of the | dead.

8 For as in | Adam · all | die :
even so in Christ shall | all be | made a- | live.

Glory | be · to the | Father :
and to the Son, | and · to the | Ho-ly | Ghost ;
As it was in the beginning, * is now, and | ever · shall | be :
world without | end, A- | — | men.

PSALM 2

(*Single or Triple Chant*)

Full. 1 Why do the heathen so furiously | rage to- | gether :
and why do the people im- | agine · a | vain — | thing ?

Full. 2 The kings of the earth stand up, * and the rulers take | counsel · to- | gether :
against the | Lord · and a- | gainst · his A- | nointed.

Full. 3 Let us break their | bonds a- | sunder :
and cást a- | way their | cords — | from us.

4 He that dwelleth in heav'n shall | laugh them · to | scorn :
the Lord shall | have them | in de- | rision.

5 Then shall he spéak unto them | in his | wrath :
and | vex them · in his | sore dis- | pleasure.

[6] Yét have I | set my | King
upon my | ho-ly | hill of | Sion.

7 I will preach the law, * whereof the Lord hath | said un-to | me :
Thou art my Son, this | day have | I be- | gotten thee.

8 Desire of me, * and I shall give thee the heathen for | thine in- | heritance :
and the útmost párts of the | earth for | thy pos- | session.

9 Thou shalt brúise them with a | rod of | iron :
and break them in | pieces · like a | pot-ter's | vessel.

10 Be wise now therefore | O ye | kings :
be learned, yé that are | judg-es | of the | earth.

11 Serve the | Lord in | fear :
and re- | joice un-to | him with | reverence.

12 Kiss the Son lest he be angry, * and so ye perish from the | right — | way :
if his wrath be kindl'd, yea but a little, * blessed are all they that | put their | trust in | him.

PSALM 16, see pp. 41, 42

PSALM 57

(Single Chant)

1 Be merciful unto me O God, * be merciful unto me, * for my sóul | trusteth · in | thee :
and under the shadow of thy wings shall be my refuge, * until this | tyranny · be | ov-er- | past.

2 I will call unto the | most high | God :
even unto the God that shall perform the | cause · which I | have in | hand.

3 He shall | send from | heav'n :
and save me from the reproof of | him that · would | eat me | up.

4 God shall send forth his | mercy · and | truth :
my | soul · is a- | mong — | lions.

5 And I lie even among the children of men that are | set on | fire :
whose teeth are spears and arrows, * and their | tongue a | sharp — | sword.

Unis. 6 *Set up thyself O God a- | bove the | heav'ns :*
and thy | glory a-bove | all the | earth.

7 They have laid a net for my feet, * and pressed | down my | soul :
they have digged a pit before me, * and are fallen into the | midst of | it them- | selves.

8 My heart is fixed O God, my | heart is | fixed :
I will | sing and | give — | praise.
9 Awake up my glory, * awake | lute and | harp :
I my- | self · will a- | wake right | early.
10 I will give thanks unto thee O Lord, a- | mong the | people :
and I will síng unto | thee a- | mong the | nations.
11 For the greatness of thy mercy reacheth | unto · the | heavens :
and thy | truth un- | to the | clouds.
Unis. 12 *Set up thyself O God a- | bove the | heav'ns :*
and thy | glory a-bove | all the | earth.

PSALM 111

1 I will give thanks unto the Lord with my | whole — | heart :
secretly among the | faithful · and | in the · congre- | gation.
2 The works of the | Lord are | great :
sought out of all | them that · have | pleasure · there- | in.
3 His work is worthy to be prais'd, and | had in | honour :
and his | righteousness · en- | dureth · for | ever.
4 The merciful and gracious Lord hath so done his | marvel-lous | works :
that they | ought to · be | had in · re- | membrance.
5 He hath given meat unto | them that | fear him :
he shall éver be | mind-ful | of his | covenant.
6 He hath shew'd his people the | power of · his | works :
that he may gíve them the | heri-tage | of the | heathen.
7 The works of his hands are | verity · and | judgement :
all | his com- | mandments · are | true.
8 They stand fast for | ever · and | ever :
and are | done in | truth and | equity.
9 He sent redemption | unto · his | people :
he hath commanded his covenant for ever, * hóly and | rever-end | is his | Name.

10 The fear of the Lord is the be- | ginning · of | wisdom :
a good understanding have all they that do thereafter, *
the | praise of it · en- | dureth · for | ever.

EVENING PRAYER

PSALM 113

(Single Chant)

1 Praise the | Lord ye | servants :
O | praise the | Name of · the | Lord.

2 Blessed be the | Name of · the | Lord :
from this time | forth for | ev-er- | more.

3 The Lord's | Name is | prais'd :
from the rising up of the sún unto the | go-ing | down of · the | same.

4 The Lord is high a- | bove all | heathen :
and his | glory · a- | bove the | heav'ns.

5 Who is like unto the Lord our God, * that hath his | dwelling · so | high :
and yet humbleth himself to behold the | things that · are in | heav'n and | earth ?

6 He taketh up the simple | out of · the | dust :
and lifteth the | poor — | out of · the | mire ;

7 That he may | set him · with the | princes :
even with the | prin-ces | of his | people.

8 He maketh the barren | woman to · keep | house :
and to be a | joy-ful | mother · of | children.

PSALM 114

1 When Israel | came · out of | Egypt :
and the house of Jácob from a- | mong the | strange — | people,

[2] Judah | was his | sanctuary
and | Is-rael | his do- | minion.
3 The sea | saw that · and | fled :
Jor- | dan was | driv-en | back.
4 The mountains | skipp'd like | rams :
and the little | hills like | young — | sheep.
5 What aileth thee O thou | sea that · thou | fleddest :
and thou Jordan, that | thou wast | driv-en | back ?
6 Ye mountains that ye | skipp'd like | rams :
and ye little | hills like | young — | sheep ?
7 Tremble thou earth at the | presence · of the | Lord :
at the | presence · of the | God of | Jacob ;
8 Who turn'd the hárd róck into a | stand-ing | water :
and the flint-stone | into · a | spring-ing | well.

PSALM 118

Full. 1 O give thanks unto the Lord, for | he is | gracious :
because his | mercy · en- | dureth · for | ever.
Full. 2 Let Israel now conféss that | he is | gracious :
and that his | mercy · en- | dureth · for | ever.
Full. [3] Let the house of Aaron | now con- | fess
that his | mercy · en- | dureth · for | ever.
Full. [4] Yea let them now that fear the | Lord con- | fess
that his | mercy · en- | dureth · for | ever.
5 I call'd upon the | Lord in | trouble :
and the | Lord — | heard me · at | large.
6 The Lord is | on my | side :
I will not | fear what | man · doeth | unto me.
2nd part. 7 The Lord taketh my part with | them that | help me :
therefore shall I see my de- | sire up- | on mine | enemies.
8 It is better to | trust · in the | Lord :
than to | put · any | confidence · in | man.

9 It is better to | trust · in the | Lord :
than to | put · any | confidence · in | princes.

Full. 10 All nations cómpass'd me | round a- | bout :
but in the Name of the | Lord will | I de- | stroy them.

Full. 11 They kept me in on every side, * they kept me in I say on | eve-ry | side :
but in the Name of the | Lord will | I de- | stroy them.

Full. 2nd part. 12 They came about me like bees, * and are extinct even as the | fire a-mong the | thorns :
for in the Name of the | Lord I | will de- | stroy them.

13 Thou hast thrust sore at me, that | I might | fall :
but the | Lord — | was my | help.

14 The Lord is my | strength and · my | song :
and | is be- | come · my sal- | vation.

Full. 15 The voice of joy and health is in the | dwellings · of the | righteous :
the right hand of the Lord bringeth | migh-ty | things to | pass.

Full. 16 The right hand of the Lord | hath the · pre- | eminence :
the right hand of the Lord bringeth | migh-ty | things to | pass.

17 I shall not | die but | live :
and de- | clare the | works of · the | Lord.

18 The Lord hath | chasten'd · and cor- | rected me :
but he hath not | given · me | over · unto | death.

19 Open me the | gates of | righteousness :
that I may go into them, * and give | thanks un- | to the | Lord.

20 Thís is the | gate of · the | Lord :
the | righteous · shall | en-ter | into it.

21 I will thank thee, for | thou hast | heard me :
and art be- | come — | my sal- | vation.

22 The same stone which the | builders · re- | fus'd :
is become the | head-stone | in the | corner.

Full. 23 Thís is the | Lord's — | doing :
and it is | marvel-lous | in our | eyes.

Full. 24 This is the day which the | Lord hath | made :
we will re- | joice · and be | glad in | it.

25 Hélp me | now O | Lord :
O Lord, | send us | now pros- | perity.

26 Blessed be he that cómeth in the | Name of · the | Lord :
we have wish'd you good luck, * yé that | are of · the | house of · the | Lord.

2nd part. 27 God is the Lord who hath | shew'd us | light :
bind the sacrifice with cords, * yea even | unto · the | horns of · the | altar.

Full. 28 Thou art my God, and | I will | thank thee :
thou art my | God, and | I will | praise thee.

Full. 29 O give thanks unto the Lord, for | he is | gracious :
and his | mercy · en- | dureth · for | ever.

ASCENSION DAY

MORNING PRAYER

PSALM 8

Unis. 1 *O Lord our Governor, * how excellent is thy Name in | all the | world:*
thou that hast set thy | glory · a- | bove the | heav'ns !

Full. 2 Out of the mouth of very babes and sucklings hast thou ordain'd strength, * be- | cause of · thine | enemies :
that thou mightest still the | ene-my | and · the a- | venger.

3 For I will consider thy heav'ns, * even the | works of · thy | fingers :
the moon and the | stars which | thou hast · or- | dain'd.

4 What is man, that | thou art | mindful of him :
and the | son of | man that · thou | visitest him ?

5 Thou madest him | lower · than the | angels :
to | crown him · with | glory · and | worship.
6 Thou makest him to have domínion of the | works of · thy | hands :
and thou hast put áll things in sub- | jec-tion | under · his | feet;
7 All | sheep and | oxen :
yea | and the | beasts of · the | field ;
8 The fowls of the air and the | fishes · of the | sea :
and whatsoever | walketh · through the | paths of · the | seas.
l part. Unis. 9 *O | Lord our | Governor :*
how éxcellent is thy | Name in | all the | world !

PSALM 15

(*Single Chant*)

1 Lord, whó shall | dwell in · thy | tabernacle :
or who shall | rest up-on thy | ho-ly | hill ?
2 Even he that leadeth an | uncor-rupt | life :
and doeth the thing which is right, * and | speaketh · the | truth · from his | heart.
3 He that hath us'd no deceit in his tongue, * nor done | evil · to his | neighbour :
and | hath not | slander'd · his | neighbour.
4 He that setteth not by himself, * but is lówly in his | own — | eyes :
and maketh much of | them that | fear the | Lord.
5 He that sweareth unto his neighbour, * and disap- | pointeth · him | not :
though it | were · to his | own — | hindrance.
6 He that hath not given his | money up-on | usury :
nor taken re- | ward a- | gainst the | innocent.
last phrase. 7 Whóso doeth these | things shall | nev-er | fall.

PSALM 21

Full. 1 The King shall rejoice in thy | strength O | Lord :
exceeding glád shall he | be of | thy sal- | vation.

Full. 2 Thou hast given him his | heart's de- | sire :
and hast not de- | ni'd him · the re- | quest of · his | lips.

3 For thou shalt prevént him with the | blessings · of | goodness :
and shalt set a crown of pure | gold up- | on his | head.

4 He asked life of thee, * and thou gávest him a | long — | life :
ev'n for | ev — | er and | ever.

5 His honour is great in | thy sal- | vation :
glory and great worship | shalt thou | lay up- | on him.

6 For thou shalt give him ever- | lasting · fe- | licity :
and make him | glad with · the | joy of · thy | countenance.

2nd part. 7 And why ? * because the King putteth his | trust in · the | Lord :
and in the mercy of the most | Highest · he | shall not · mis- | carry.

8 All thine enemies shall | feel thy | hand :
thy right hand shall | find out | them that | hate thee.

9 Thou shalt make them like a fiery oven in | time of · thy | wrath :
the Lord shall destroy them in his displeasure, * and the | fire — | shall con- | sume them.

10 Their fruit shalt thou root | out of · the | earth :
and their séed from a- | mong the | children · of | men.

11 For they intended | mischief · a- | gainst thee :
and imagin'd such a device as they áre not | a-ble | to per- | form.

12 Therefore shalt thou | put them · to | flight :
and the strings of thy bow shalt thou make | ready · a- | gainst the | face of them.

Full. 13 Be thou exalted Lórd in thine | own — | strength :
só will we | sing, and | praise thy | power.

EVENING PRAYER

PSALM 24

Full. 1 The earth is the Lord's, and all that | there-in | is :
the compass of the | world and | they that | dwell therein.

Full. 2 For he hath fóunded it up- | on the | seas :
and pre- | par'd · it up- | on the | floods.

3 Who shall ascénd into the | hill of · the | Lord :
or who shall rise | up in · his | holy | place ?

4 Even he that hath clean hands and a | pure — | heart :
and that hath not lift up his mind unto vanity,* nor | sworn · to de- | ceive his | neighbour.

5 He shall receive the | blessing · from the | Lord :
and ríghteousness from the | God of | his sal- | vation.

6 This is the generation of | them that | seek him :
even of them that | seek thy | face O | Jacob.

Unis. 7 *Lift up your heads O ye gates,* * *and be ye lift úp ye ever- | last-ing | doors :*
and the King of | glo-ry | shall come | in.

Boys. 8 *Whó is the | King of | glory :*
Men. Unis. *it is the Lord strong and mighty,* * *even the | Lord — | mighty · in | battle.*

Unis. 9 *Lift up your heads O ye gates,* * *and be ye lift úp ye ever- | last-ing | doors :*
and the King of | glo-ry | shall come | in.

Boys. 10 *Whó is the | King of | glory :*
Men. Unis. *even the Lord of hosts, | he · is the | King of | glory.*

PSALM 47

Full. 1 O clap your hands together, | all ye | people :
O sing unto | God · with the | voice of | melody.

Full. 2 For the Lord is | high and · to be | fear'd :
he is the great | King up-on | all the | earth.

3 He shall subdue the | peo-ple | under us :
and the | na-tions | under · our | feet.

4 He shall choose out an | heri-tage | for us :
even the worship of | Ja-cob | whom he | lov'd.
5 God is gone up with a | mer-ry | noise :
and the | Lord · with the | sound of · the | trump.
6 O sing praises, sing praises | unto · our | God :
O sing praises, sing | prais-es | unto · our | King.
7 For God is the King of | all the | earth :
sing ye | praises · with | un-der- | standing.
8 God reigneth | over · the | heathen :
God sítteth up- | on his | ho-ly | seat.

2nd part. 9 The princes of the people are joined unto the péople of the | God of | Abraham :
for God which is very high exalted, doth defend the | earth · as it | were · with a | shield.

Psalm 108 (*Single Chant*)

Full. 1 O God my heart is ready, * my | heart is | ready :
I will sing and give praise with the best | mem-ber | that I | have.
Full. 2 Awake, thou | lute and | harp :
I my- | self · will a- | wake right | early.
3 I will give thanks unto thee O Lord, a- | mong the | people :
I will sing praises unto | thee a- | mong the | nations.
4 For thy mercy is | greater · than the | heav'ns :
and thy truth | reach-eth | unto · the | clouds.
Unis. 5 Set up thyself O God a- | bove the | heav'ns :
and thy | glory a-bove | all the | earth.
6 That thy belóved may | be de- | liver'd :
let thy right hand | save them · and | hear thou | me.
Unis. 7 God hath | spoken · in his | holiness :
I will rejoice therefore and divide Sichem, * and mete | out the | valley · of | Succoth.
Unis. 8 Gilead is míne, and Ma- | nasses · is | mine:
Ephraim | also · is the | strength of · my | head.

Unis. 9 Judah is my law-giver, | Moab · is my | wash-pot:
over Edom will I cast out my shoe; * upon Phi- | lis-tia | will I | triumph.

10 Who will lead me into the | strong — | city :
and whó will | bring me | in-to | Edom?

11 Hast not thou for- | saken us · O | God :
and wilt not thou O | God go | forth with · our | hosts?

12 O hélp us a- | gainst the | enemy :
for | vain · is the | help of | man.

Full. 13 Through God we shall | do great | acts :
and it is | he that · shall | tread · down our | enemies.

PSALM 110, see p. 175

WHITSUN-DAY

MORNING PRAYER

PSALM 48

Full. 1 Great is the Lord, and | highly · to be | prais'd :
in the city of our God, | ev'n up-on his | ho-ly | hill.

Full. 2 The hill of Sion is a fair place, * and the joy of the | whole — | earth :
upon the north-side lieth the city of the great King, * God is well known in her | palaces · as a | sure — | refuge.

3 For lo, the | kings of · the | earth :
are | gather'd · and | gone · by to- | gether.

4 They márvell'd to | see such | things :
they were astonish'd, and | sudden-ly | cast — | down.

5 Fear came there up- | on them · and | sorrow :
as upon a | wo-man | in her | travail.

[6] Thou shalt | break the | ships
of the | sea · through the | east — | wind.

2nd part. 7 Like as we have heard, * so have we seen in the city of the Lord of hosts, * in the | city of · our | God :
God up- | holdeth · the | same for | ever.

[8] We wait for thy | lov-ing- | kindness
O | God · in the | midst of · thy | temple.
9 O God, according to thy Name, * so is thy praise unto the | world's — | end :
thy right | hand is | full of | righteousness.
[10] Let the mount Sion rejoice, * and the | daughter · of | Judah · be | glad, be- | cause of · thy | judgements.
11 Walk about Sion, and | go · round a- | bout her :
and | tell the | towers · there- | of.
12 Mark well her bulwarks, set | up her | houses :
that ye may | tell — | them that · come | after.
Unis. 13 For thís God is oúr God for | ever · and | ever :
he shall be our | guide — | un-to | death.

PSALM 68

Full. 1 Let God arise, * and let his | enemies · be | scatter'd :
let them also that | hate him | flee be- | fore him.
Full. 2 Like as the smoke vanisheth, * só shalt thou | drive · them a- | way :
and like as wax melteth at the fire, * so let the ungodly | perish · at the | presence · of | God.
3 But let the righteous be glád and re- | joice be-fore | God :
let them | also · be | merry · and | joyful.
4 O sing unto God, * and sing praises | unto · his | Name :
magnify him that rideth upon the heav'ns as it were upon an horse, * praise him in his Name | JAH · and re- | joice be- | fore him.
5 He is a Father of the fatherless, * and defendeth the | cause of · the | widows :
even God in his | ho-ly | ha-bi- | tation.
6 He is the God that maketh men to be of one mind in an house, * and bringeth the prisoners | out of · cap- | tivity :
but letteth the | runagates · con- | tinue · in | scarceness.

7 O God, when thou wentest forth bẹ- | fọre thẹ | people :
when thọu | went-est | thrọugh thẹ | wilderness,

8 The earth shook, * and the heavens drópp'd at the | presence · of | God :
even as Sinai also was mov'd at the presence of God, * whọ | ịs thẹ | God ọf | Israel.

9 Thou O God sentest a gracious ráin upon | thine ịn- | heritance :
ạnd rẹ- | freshedst · it | when it · was | weary.

10 Thy congregation shạll | dwell there- | in :
for thou O God hast of thy | goodness · pre- | par'd · for the | poor.

Full. 11 The Lord | gave thẹ | word :
gréat was the | compa-ny | ọf thẹ | preachers.

Full. 12 Kings with their armies did | flee and · were dis- | comfited :
and they of the | household · di- | vided · the | spoil.

13 Though ye have lien among the pots, * yet shall ye be as the | wings of · a | dove :
that is cover'd with silver | wings · and her | feathers · like | gold.

14 When the Almighty scatter'd | kings for · their | sake :
thén were they as | white as | snow in | Salmon.

15 As the hill of Basan, | so is | God's hill :
even an | high hill · as the | hill ọf | Basan.

16 Why hop ye so ye high hills ? * this is God's hill in the which it | pleaseth · him to | dwell :
yea the Lórd will a- | bide in | it fọr | ever.

17 The chariots of God are twenty thousand, * ẹven | thousands · of | angels :
and the Lord is among them, * ạs ịn thẹ | ho-ly | place ọf | Sinai.

18 Thou art gone up on high, * thou hast led captivity captive, and receiv'd | gifts fọr | men :
yea even for thine enemies, * that the Lórd | God might | dwell ạ- | mong them.

Full. 19 Praised be the | Lord — | daily :
even the God who helpeth us, ạnd | poureth · his | benefits · up- | on us.

Full. 20 He is our God, * even the God of whom | cometh · sal- | vation :
God is the Lórd by | whom · we es- | cape — | death.

21 God shall wound thẹ | head of · his | enemies:
and the hairy scalp of such a one as | goeth · on | still in · his | wickedness.

22 The Lord hath said, * I will bring my people again, as I | did from | Basan :
mine own will I bring again, * ạs Ị dịd | sometime · from the | deep of · the | sea.

2nd part. 23 That thy foot may be dipp'd in the | blood of · thine | enemies:
and that the tongue of thy | dogs · may be | red · through the | same.

Can. 24 It is well seen O God, | how thou | goest :
how thou my God and King, | go-est | ịn thẹ | sanctuary.

25 The singers go before, * the | minstrels · follow | after :
in the midst are the | dam-sels | playing · with the | timbrels.

26 Give thanks O Israel unto God the Lord in the | con-gre- | gations :
frọm thẹ | ground — | ọf thẹ | heart.

27 There is little Benjamin their ruler, * and the prínces of | Judah · their | counsel :
the princes of Za- | bulon · and the | princes · of | Nephthali.

28 Thy God hath | sent forth | strength for thee :
stablish the thing O | God thạt | thou hast | wrought in us,

29 For thy témple's | sake · at Je- | rusalem :
so shall kings bring | pres-ents | ụn-tọ | thee.

30 When the company of the spear-men, and multitude of the mighty are scatter'd abroad among the beasts of the people, * so that they humbly bring | pieces · of | silver :
and when he hath scatter'd the | people · that de- | light in | war ;

31 Then shall the princes | come · out of | Egypt :
the Morians' land shall soon stretch | out her | hands un-to | God.

Full. 32 Sing unto God, O ye | kingdoms · of the | earth :
O sing | prais-es | unto · the | Lord ;

Full. 33 Who sitteth in the heav'ns over | all · from the be- | ginning :
lo he doth send out his voice, | yea and | that a | mighty voice.

Full. 34 Ascribe ye the power to | God · over | Israel :
his worship and | strength is | in the | clouds.

Full. 35 O God, * wonderful art thou in thy | ho-ly | places :
even the God of Israel, * he will give strength and power unto his | peo-ple, | blessed · be | God.

EVENING PRAYER

PSALM 104

Full. 1 Praise the Lord | O my | soul :
O Lord my God, thou art become exceeding glorious, * thou art | cloth'd with | majesty · and | honour.

Full. 2 Thou deckest thyself with light as it | were · with a | garment :
and spreadest | out the | heav'ns · like a | curtain.

3 Who layeth the beams of his | chambers · in the | waters :
and maketh the clouds his chariot, * and | walketh up-on the | wings of · the | wind.

4 He maketh his | an-gels | spirits :
and his | minis-ters a | flam-ing | fire.

5 He laid the foun- | dations · of the | earth :
that it | never · should | move at | any time.

6 Thou coveredst it with the deep, | like as · with a | garment :
the | wa-ters | stand · in the | hills.

7 At thy re- | buke they | flee :
at the voice of thy | thun-der | they are · a- | fraid.

8 They go up as high as the hills, * and dówn to the | valleys · be- | neath :
even unto the place which | thou · hast ap- | point-ed | for them.

9 Thou hast set them their bounds which they | shall not | pass :
neither turn a- | gain to | cover · the | earth.

10 He sendeth the | springs in-to the | rivers :
which | run a- | mong the | hills.

11 All beasts of the | field — | drink thereof :
and the wild | ass-es | quench their | thirst.

12 Beside them shall the fowls of the áir have their | ha-bi- | tation :
and | sing a- | mong the | branches.

13 He wátereth the | hills · from a- | bove :
the earth is | fill'd · with the | fruit of · thy | works.

14 He bringeth fórth | grass · for the | cattle :
and green | herb · for the | service · of | men ;

15 That he may bring food out of the earth, * and wíne that maketh | glad the · heart of | man :
and oil to make him a cheerful countenance, * and | bread to | strengthen · man's | heart.

16 The trees of the Lord also are | full of | sap :
even the cedars of | Liban-us | which he · hath | planted ;

17 Wherein the birds | make their | nests :
and the fír-trees are a | dwell-ing | for the | stork.

18 The high hills are a réfuge for the | wild — | goats :
and só are the | ston-y | rocks · for the | conies.

19 He appointed the | moon for · certain | seasons :
and the sun | knoweth · his | go-ing | down.

20 Thou maketh dárkness that it | may be | night :
wherein all the | beasts · of the | forest · do | move.

21 The lions roaring | after · their | prey :
do | seek their | meat from | God.

22 The sun ariseth, and they gét them a- | way to- | gether :
and | lay them | down · in their | dens.

2nd part. [23] Man goeth | forth · to his | work
and to his | labour, · un- | til the | evening.

24 O Lord, how mánifold | are thy | works :
in wisdom hast thou made them all, * the | earth is | full of · thy | riches.

25 So is the great and wide | sea — | also :
wherein are things creeping innumerable, * both | small and | great — | beasts.

26 There go the ships, and | there is · that Le- | viathan :
whom thou hast | made to · take his | pastime · there- | in.

27 These wait | all up-on | thee :
that thou mayest | give them | meat in · due | season.

28 When thou gívest it | them they | gather it :
and when thou openest thy | hand · they are | fill'd with | good.

29 When thou hídest thy | face · they are | troubl'd :
when thou takest away their breath they die, * and are | turn'd a- | gain to · their | dust.

30 When thou lettest thy breath go | forth they · shall be | made :
and thou shalt re- | new the | face of · the | earth.

31 The glorious Majesty of the Lórd shall en- | dure for | ever :
the | Lord · shall re- | joice in · his | works.

32 The éarth shall | tremble · at the | look of him :
if he do but | touch the | hills · they shall | smoke.

33 I will sing unto the Lórd as | long as · I | live :
I will praise my | God · while I | have my | being.

34 And só shall my | words — | please him :
my | joy shall | be in · the | Lord.

35 As for sinners, they shall be consum'd out of the earth, * and the ungódly shall | come · to an | end :
praise thou the Lórd O my | soul, * praise | — the | Lord.

PSALM 145

Full. 1 I will magnify thee, O | God my | King :
and I will praise thy | Name for | ever · and | ever.

Full. 2 Every day will I give | thanks · un- | to thee :
and praise thy | Name for | ever · and | ever.

3 Great is the Lord, * and marvellous | worthy · to be | prais'd :
there | is no | end of · his | greatness.

4 One generation shall praise thy | works un-to an- | other :
and de- | clare — | thy — | power.

5 As for me, I will be | talking of · thy | worship :
thy glory, thy | praise and | won-drous | works ;

6 So that men shall speak of the might of thy | marvel-lous | acts :
and I will | al-so | tell of · thy | greatness.

2nd part. 7 The memorial of thine abundant | kindness · shall be | shew'd :
and | men shall | sing of · thy | righteousness.

8 The Lord is | gracious · and | merciful :
long-súffering, | and of | great — | goodness.

9 The Lord is | loving · unto | every man :
and his mercy is | ov-er | all his | works.

10 All thy works | praise thee · O | Lord :
and thy | saints give | thanks un- | to thee.

11 They shew the | glory of · thy | kingdom :
and | talk — | of thy | power ;

12 That thy power, thy glory and míghtiness | of thy | kingdom :
might be | known — | un-to | men.

13 Thy kingdom is an ever- | last-ing | kingdom :
and thy domínion en- | dureth · through- | out all | ages.

14 The Lord upholdeth | all · such as | fall :
and lifteth | up all | those that · are | down.

15 The eyes of all wait upon | thee O | Lord :
and thou | givest · them their | meat in · due | season.

16 Thou | openest · thine | hand :
and fillest | all things | living · with | plenteousness.

17 The Lord is ríghteous in | all his | ways :
and | holy · in | all his | works.

18 The Lord is nigh unto all | them that | call upon him :
yea all such as | call up- | on him | faithfully.

19 He will fulfil the desire of | them that | fear him :
he also will | hear their | cry and · will | help them.

20 The Lord preserveth all | them that | love him :
but scattereth a- | broad — | all the · un- | godly.

Full. 21 My mouth shall speak the | praise of · the | Lord :
and let all flesh give thanks unto his holy | Name for | ever · and | ever.

SOVEREIGN'S ACCESSION

PSALM 20

1 The Lord héar thee in the | day of | trouble :
the Náme of the | God of | Jacob · de- | fend thee ;

2 Send thee | help · from the | sanctuary :
and | strengthen · thee | out of | Sion ;

3 Remember | all thy | offerings :
and ac- | cept thy | burnt — | sacrifice ;

4 Gránt thee thy | heart's de- | sire :
and ful- | fil — | all thy | mind.

2nd part. 5 We will rejoice in thy salvation, * and triumph in the Náme of the | Lord our | God :
the Lord per- | form all | thy pe- | titions.

6 Now know I that the Lord helpeth his Anointed, * and will héar him from his | ho-ly | heav'n :
even with the wholesome | strength of · his | right — | hand.

7 Some put their trust in chariots, and | some in | horses :
but we will remember the | Name of · the | Lord our | God.

8 Théy are brought | down and | fallen :
but wé are | risen · and | stand — | upright.

9 Save Lord and hear us, O | King of | heav'n :
when we | call up- | on — | thee.

PSALM 101

1 My sóng shall be of | mercy · and | judgement :
unto | thee O | Lord · will I | sing.

[2] O let me have | un-der- | stand-
ing, | in the | way of | godliness.

3 Whén wilt thou | come un-to | me :
I will walk in my | house · with a | per-fect | heart.

4 I will take no wicked thing in hand, * I hate the | sins of · un- |
faithfulness :
there shall | no such | cleave · un- | to me.

5 A froward | heart · shall de- | part from me :
I wíll not | know a | wick-ed | person.

[6] Whoso privily | slandereth · his | neigh-
bour, | him will | I de- | stroy.

7 Whoso hath also a proud | look and · high | stomach :
I | will not | suf-fer | him.

8 Mine eyes look upon such as are | faithful · in the | land :
that | they may | dwell — | with me.

9 Whoso leadeth a | god-ly | life :
he | — shall | be my | servant.

10 There shall no deceitful person | dwell in · my | house :
he that telleth líes shall not | tar-ry | in my | sight.

2nd part. 11 I shall soon destroy all the ungódly that are | in the | land :
that I may root out all wicked dóers from the | ci-ty | of
the | Lord.

PSALM 121

1 I will lift up mine | eyes un-to the | hills :
from | whence — | cometh · my | help.

2 My help cometh | even · from the | Lord :
who | hath made | heav'n and | earth.

3 He will not suffer thy | foot to · be | mov'd :
and he that | keepeth · thee | will not | sleep.

[4] Behold, he that | keep-eth | Israel
shall | nei-ther | slumber · nor | sleep.

5 The Lord him- | self is · thy | keeper :
the Lord is thy de- | fence up-on thy | right — | hand ;

[6] So that the | sun shall · not | burn thee by
day, | neither · the | moon by | night.

7 The Lord shall preserve thee from | all — | evil :
yea it is even | he that · shall | keep thy | soul.

8 The Lord shall preserve thy going out, and thy | com-ing | in :
from this time | forth for | ev-er- | more.

NOTE

A Small Edition of *The Oxford Psalter* is published. Price 1*s*. 6*d*. net.

The Versicles and Responses from this Edition may be obtained separately, price 6d., and *The Canticles and Hymns*, price 8d.

The Oxford Chant Book No. 2, designed specifically for use with *The Oxford Psalter*, is published at 3*s*. net.

Also *A Collection of Chants* compiled by C. Hylton Stewart, 2*s*. 6*d*.

ATHANASIAN CREED

QUICUNQUE VULT

In a Revised Translation

Tone viii. 1.

To be sung in a free speaking-rhythm, and in unison.

N.B. The first two notes are only to be used in precenting the first verse. The notes in brackets are only to be used when necessary. Two dots over a syllable indicate the use of two notes there.

Minister. 1 WHO-SO- | EVER would be | sav-ed :
(unaccomp.)
Full. needeth before all things to hold fast the | Cath-o-lick Faith.

Boys. 2 Which Faith except a man keep whole and unde- | fil-ed :
without doubt he will pé- | rish e-ter-nal-ly.

Men. 3 Now the Catholick Faith is | this :
that we worship one God in Trinity, and the Trini- | ty in U-ni-ty;

Boys. 4 Neither confusing the | Per-sons :
nor divíd- | ing the sub-stance.

Men. 5 For there is one Person of the Father, another of the | Son :
another | of the Ho-ly Ghost ;

Boys. 6 But the Godhead of the Father, and of the Son, and of the Holy Ghost is all | one :
the glory equal, the majesty | co-e-ter-nal.

Men. 7 Such as the Father is, such is the | Son :
and súch | is the Ho-ly Ghost ;

Boys. 8 The Father uncreated, the Son un-cre- | a-ted :
the Holy Ghost | un-cre-a-ted ;

Men. 9 The Father infinite, the Son | in-fi-nite :
the Holy | Ghöst in-fi-nite.

Boys. 10 The Father eternal, the Son e- | ter-nal :
the Holy | Ghost e-ter-nal ;

Men. 11 And yet there are not three e- | ter-nals :
bụt | one e-ter-nal ;

Boys. 12 As also there are not three uncreated, nor three | in-fi-nites :
but one infinite, and óne | un-crẹ-a-ted.

Men. 13 So likewise the Father is almighty, the Son al- | migh-ty :
the Holy | Ghost al-migh-ty;

Boys. 14 And yet there are not three al- | migh-ties :
bụt | one al-migh-ty.

Men. 15 So the Father is God, the Son | God :
the | Ho-ly Ghost God ;

Boys. 16 And yet there are not three | Gods : §
— | — bụt one God.

§ *Two notes to be omitted here:*

Men. 17 So the Father is Lord, the Son | Lord :
thẹ | Ho-ly Ghost Lord ;

Boys. 18 And yet there are not three | Lords : §
— | — bụt one Lord.

Men. 19 For like as we are compelled by the Chrịstian | ver-ị-ty :
to confess each Person by himsélf tọ | bẹ both God ạnd Lord ;

Boys. 20 So are we forbidden by the Catholick Rẹ- | li-gion :
to speak of three | Gods or three Lords.

Men. 21 The Father is made of | none :
nor created, | nor bẹ-got-ten.

Boys. 22 The Son is of the Father ạ- | lone:
not made, nor created, | bụt bẹ-got-ten.

Men. 23 The Holy Ghost is of the Father ạnd thẹ | Son :
not made, nor created, nor begotten, | bụt pro-ceed-ing.

Boys. 24 There is therefore one Father, not three Fathers ; one Son, not three | Sons :
one Holy Ghost, | not three Ho-ly̦ Ghosts.

Men. 25 And in this Trinity there is no before or | af-ter :
no | great-er o̦r less;

Boys. 26 But all three Persons are co-eternal to̦- | geth-er :
— | and co-e-qual.

Men. 27 So that in all ways, as is a- | fore-said :
both the Trinity is to be worshipped in Unity, and the Un-i- | ty in Trin-i̦-ty.

Boys. 28 He therefore that would be | sav-ed :
let him thus thínk | o̦f the̦ Trin-i̦-ty.

Men. 29 Furthermore it is necessary to eternal sal- | va-tion :
that he also believe faithfully the Incarnation of our | Lörd Je-su̦s Christ.

Boys. 30 Now the right faith is that we believe and con- | fess :
that o̦ur Lord Jesus Christ, the Son of God, is | böth God and man.

Men. 31 He is God, of the substance of the Father, begotten before the | worlds :
and he is man, of the substance of his Móth- | e̦r, born in the̦ world ;

Boys. 32 Perfect | God :
perfect man, of reasoning soul and human | flesh sub-sist-ing;

Men. 33 Equal to the Father as touching his | God-head :
less than the Father as tóuch- | i̦ng his man-hood.

Boys. 34 Who although he be God and | man :
yet he is not two, | but is one Christ ;

Men. 35 One, however, not by conversion of Godhead into | flesh :
but by taking | man-hood in-to God ;

Boys. 36 One alto- | geth-er :
not by confusion of substance, but by uni- | ty of per-son.

Men. 37 For as reasoning soul and flesh is one | man :
so God and | man is one Christ ;

Boys. 38 Who suffered for our sal- | va-tion :
descended into hell, * rose a- | gäin from the dead ;

Men. 39 Ascended into heaven, * sat down at the right hand of the | Fa-ther :
from whence he shall come to judge | the quick and the dead.

Boys. 40 At whose coming all men must rise again with their | bo-dies :
and shall give accóunt | for their own deeds.

Men. 41 And they that have done good will go into life e- | ter-nal : and
they that have done evil ín- | to e-ter-nal fire.

Boys. 42 This is the Catholick | Faith :
which except a man do faithfully and stedfastly believe, he cán- | not be sav-ed.

Men (*or Full*). Glory be to the | Fa-ther :
and to the Son, and | to the Ho-ly Ghost ;

Full. As it was in the beginning, * is now, and ever | shall be :
world with- | out end. A-men.

This Creed may be sung without accompaniment.

Note

On Trinity Sunday, Quicunque vult *may be sung beginning thus:*

3 THE Catholick Faith is | this :
that we worship one God in Trinity, and the Trini- | ty in U-ni-ty ;

and ending thus:

28 He therefore that would be | sav-ed :
must thus thínk | of the Trin-i-ty.
Glory be to the Father, &c.

On the Sunday after Christmas, and on the Feast of the Annunciation, it may be sung beginning thus:

30 THE Catholick Faith is this, that we believe and con- | fess :
that our Lord Jesus Christ, the Son of God, is | böth God and man.

and ending thus:

41 And they that have done evil will go into eter-nal | fire : and they that have done good into | life e-ter-nal.
Glory be to the Father, &c.

THE LITANY

NOTE

It should be remembered that in the music of the Litany all the notes are of approximately equal length. The pace, which will naturally vary slightly according to the size of the building and the number of singers, should be that of clear and distinct reading aloud. It is often sung too heavily and too slowly. A point to be watched is the close of each petition and response: an unaccented syllable occurring there (e.g. as in 'sinners') should be softened.

This arrangement of the Litany can be sung in the following ways:

(i) In unison, unaccompanied.
(ii) In unison, with organ accompaniment.
(iii) In harmony, unaccompanied.
(iv) In harmony, with organ accompaniment.

C. H. S.

The sign ⦙ draws attention to a change from the reciting note; avoid halting there. Square brackets [ ] enclose variations allowed by the 1928 Prayer Book.

Adapted from

THE FIRST ENGLISH LITANY (1544)

Edited and harmonized by C. Hylton Stewart

[1] The Chanter may be a layman. Those parts which the Prayer Book requires to be sung by the Priest are so marked, i.e. at pp. 284, 287.

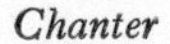

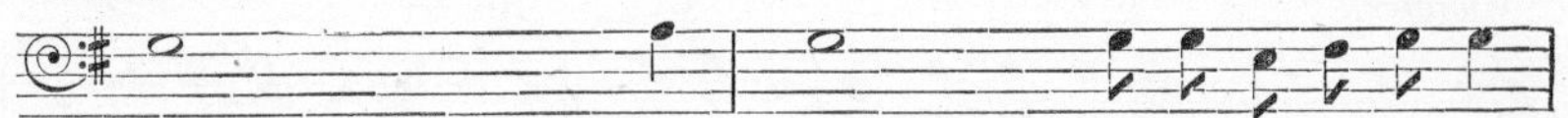

O God the Holy Ghost, proceeding from the Father and the Son: have mercy upon us, mis-er - a - ble sin-ners.

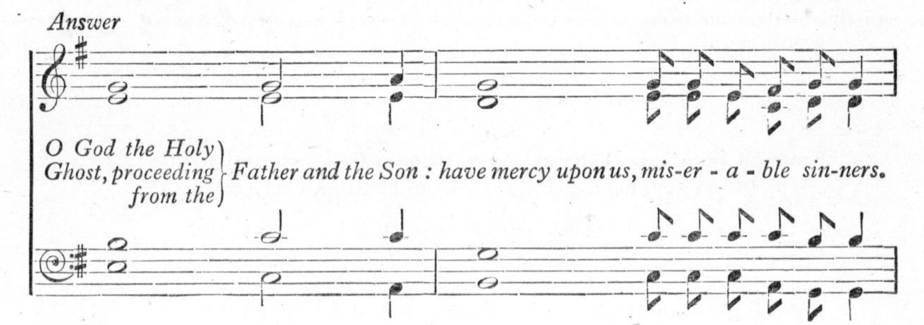

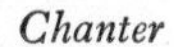

O holy, blessed, and glorious Trinity, three Persons and one God : have mercy upon us, mis-er - a - ble sin-ners.

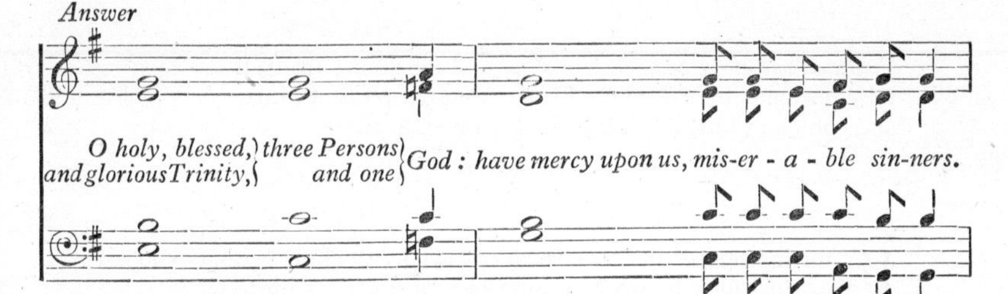

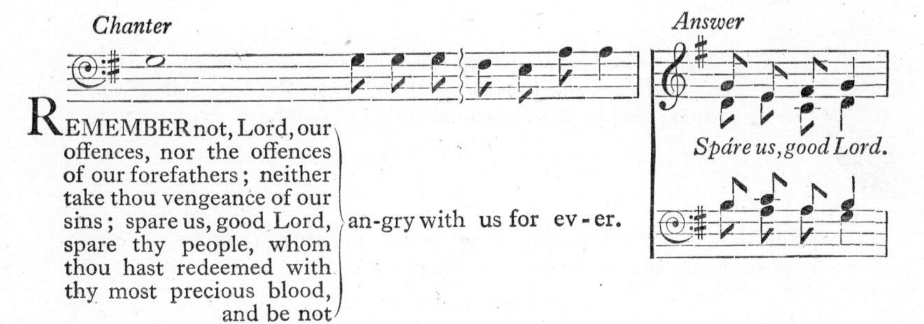

From all blindness of heart; from pride, vain-glory, and hypocrisy; from envy, hatred, and malice, and ⁞ all un-charitableness;

Good Lord, deliver us.

From fornication, and all other deadly sin; and from all the deceits of the world, the flesh, ⁞ and the devil;

Good Lord, deliver us.

From lightning and tempest; from plague, pestilence, and famine; from battle and murder, and from ⁞ sudden death;

Good Lord, deliver us.

From all sedition, privy conspiracy, and rebellion; from all false doctrine, heresy, and schism; from hardness of heart, and contempt of thy Word ⁞ and Com-mandment;

Good Lord, deliver us.

BY the mystery of thy holy Incarnation; by thy holy Nativity and Circumcision; by thy Baptism, Fasting, ⁞ and Temp-tation;

Good Lord, deliver us.

By thine Agony and bloody Sweat; by thy Cross and Passion; by thy precious Death and Burial; by thy glorious Resurrection and Ascension; and by the coming of the ⁞ Ho-ly Ghost;

Good Lord, deliver us.

In all time of our tribulation; in all time of our wealth; in the hour of death, and in the ⁞ day of judgement;

Good Lord, deliver us.

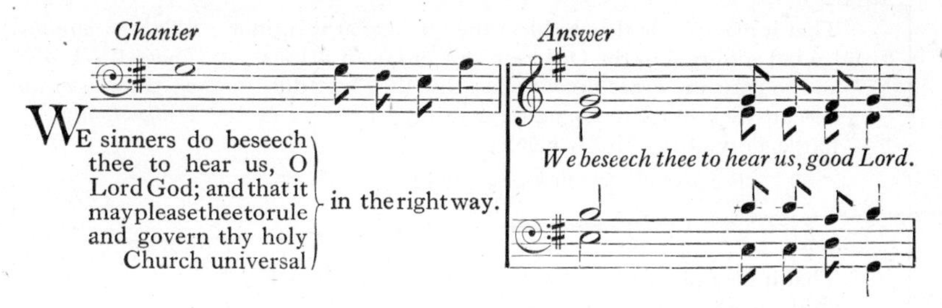

WE sinners do beseech thee to hear us, O Lord God; and that it may please thee to rule and govern thy holy Church universal in the right way.

That it may please thee to keep and strengthen in the true worshipping of thee, in righteousness and holiness of life, thy Servant *GEORGE*, our most gracious ⁞ King and Governor;

We beseech thee to hear us, good Lord.

That it may please thee to rule his heart in thy faith, fear, and love, and that he may evermore have affiance in thee, and ever seek thy hon⁞our and glory;

We beseech thee to hear us, good Lord.

That it may please thee to be his defender and keeper, giving him the victory over ⁞ all his enemies;

We beseech thee to hear us, good Lord.

That it may please thee to bless and preserve our gracious Queen *Elizabeth, Mary* the Queen Mother, the Princess *Elizabeth*, and all the ⁞ Roy-al Family;

We beseech thee to hear us, good Lord.

That it may please thee to illuminate all Bishops, Priests, and Deacons, with true knowledge and understanding of thy Word; and that both by their preaching and living they may set it forth, and shew ⁞ it ac-cordingly;

We beseech thee to hear us, good Lord.

That it may please thee to bless thy servants at this time [to be] admitted to the Order of Deacons or of Priests, and to pour thy grace upon them; that they may duly execute their office to the edifying of thy Church, and to the glory of thy ¦ ho-ly name;

We beseech thee to hear us, good Lord.

(To be used in the Ember Weeks and on the day of an Ordination.)

That it may please thee to further the work of thy Church in all the world, and to send forth labourers in¦to the harvest;

We beseech thee to hear us, good Lord.

That it may please thee to endue[1] the Lords of the Council, and all the Nobility,[1] with grace, wisdom, and ¦ un-der-standing;

We beseech thee to hear us, good Lord.

That it may please thee to bless and keep the Magistrates, giving them grace to execute justice and to ¦ main-tain truth;

We beseech thee to hear us, good Lord.

That it may please thee to bless and prosper the forces of the King by sea, land, and air, and to shield them in all dangers ¦ and ad-versities;

We beseech thee to hear us, good Lord.

That it may please thee to bless and keep ¦ all thy people;

We beseech thee to hear us, good Lord.

That it may please thee to give to all nations unity, ¦ peace, and concord;

We beseech thee to hear us, good Lord.

That it may please thee to give us an heart to love and dread thee, and diligently to live after ¦ thy com-mandments;

We beseech thee to hear us, good Lord.

[1–1] the High Court of Parliament, and all the Ministers of the Crown, (1928).

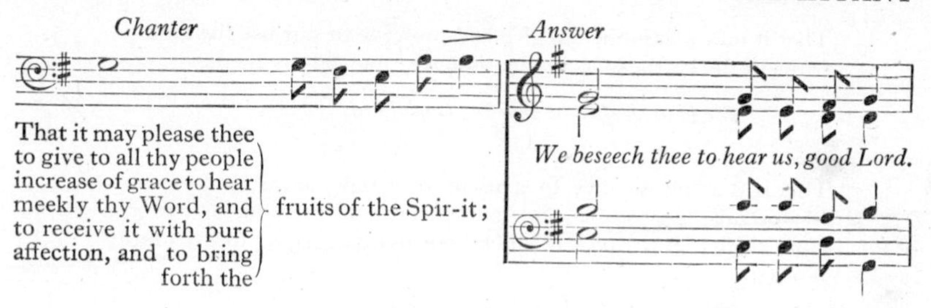

That it may please thee to bring into the way of truth all such as have erred, and | are de-ceived;

We beseech thee to hear us, good Lord.

That it may please thee to strengthen such as do stand; and to comfort and help the weak-hearted; and to raise up them that fall; and finally to beat down Satan un|der our feet;

We beseech thee to hear us, good Lord.

That it may please thee to succour, help, and comfort, all that are in danger, necessity, and | tri-bu-lation;

We beseech thee to hear us, good Lord.

That it may please thee to preserve all that travel by land, [air] or by water, all women labouring of child, all sick persons, and young children; and to shew thy mercy upon all prison|ers and captives;

We beseech thee to hear us, good Lord.

That it may please thee to defend, and provide for, the fatherless children, and widows, and all that are desolate | and op-pressed;

We beseech thee to hear us, good Lord.

That it may please thee to have mercy | up-on all men;

We beseech thee to hear us, good Lord.

That it may please thee to forgive our enemies, persecutors, and slanderers, and to | turn their hearts;

We beseech thee to hear us, good Lord.

That it may please thee to give and preserve to our use the kindly fruits of the earth, so as in due time we ¦ may en-joy them;

We beseech thee to hear us, good Lord.

That it may please thee to give us true repentance; to forgive us all our sins, negligences, and ignorances; and to endue us with the grace of thy Holy Spirit to amend our lives according to thy ¦ ho-ly Word;

We beseech thee to hear us, good Lord.

[*When the Order for Holy Communion is to follow immediately, all that here follows may be omitted.*]

Priest and People (without note[1])

OUR FATHER, which art in heaven, Hallowed be thy name; Thy kingdom come; Thy will be done; In earth as it is in heaven. Give us this day our daily bread. And forgive us our trespasses, As we forgive them that trespass against us. And lead us not into temptation; But deliver us from evil. Amen.

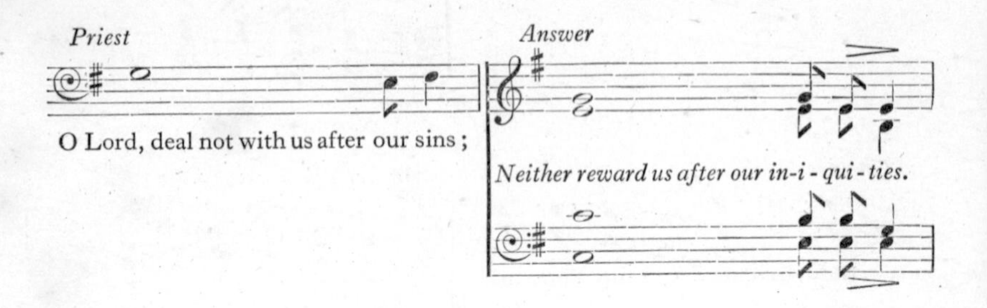

A Supplication

O GOD, merciful Father, that despisest not the sighing of a contrite heart, nor the desire of such as be sorrowful: Mercifully assist our prayers that we make before thee in all our troubles and adversities, whensoever they oppress us; and graciously hear us, that those evils, which the craft and subtilty of the devil or man worketh against us, be brought to nought; and by the providence of thy goodness they may be dispersed; that we thy servants, being hurt by no persecutions, may evermore give thanks unto thee in thy holy Church; through Jesus Christ our Lord.

---

[1] In the 1544 litany the 'Our Father' was for the officiant alone, the last two phrases being treated as an ordinary versicle and response.

[2] Amen was not printed in 1544, but it was clearly intended; it appeared in certain Elizabethan Prayer-books, and was restored in 1928. The traditional Amen is given here, and the usual inflexion leading into it.

Chanter

Ps. O God, we have heard with our ears, and our fathers have declared unto us, the noble works that thou didst in their days, and in the old time be- } fore them.

Chanter

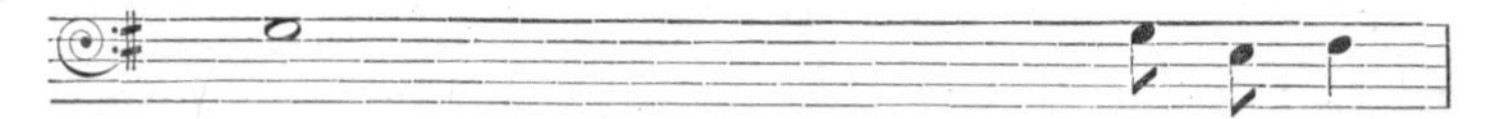

Glory be to the Father, and to the Son: and to the Ho - ly Ghost.

THE LITANY

Chanter
Answer
O Lord, a - rise,
help us, and de-liver us for thy name's sake.

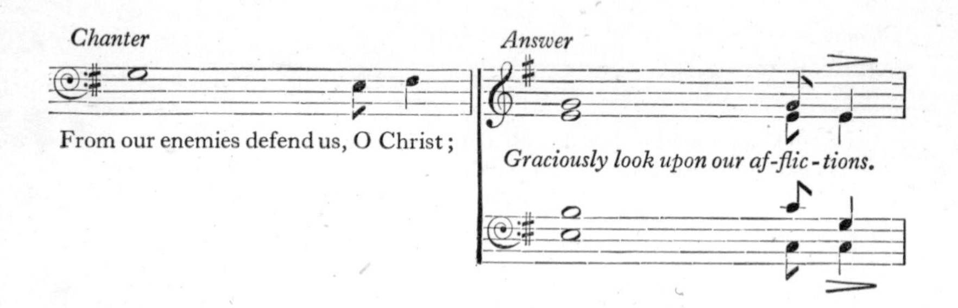
Chanter
Answer
From our enemies defend us, O Christ;
Graciously look upon our af-flic - tions.

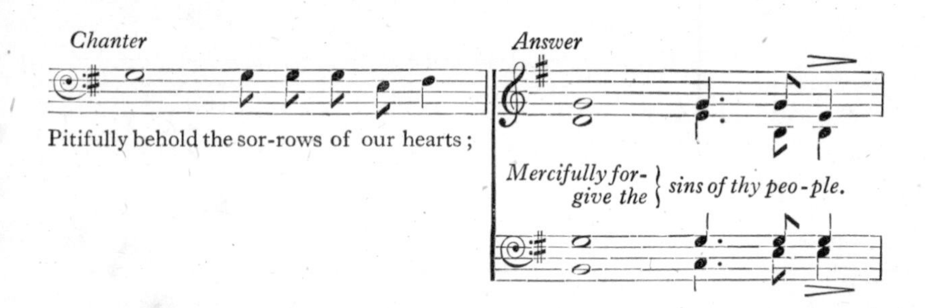
Chanter
Answer
Pitifully behold the sor-rows of our hearts;
Mercifully for-give the sins of thy peo - ple.

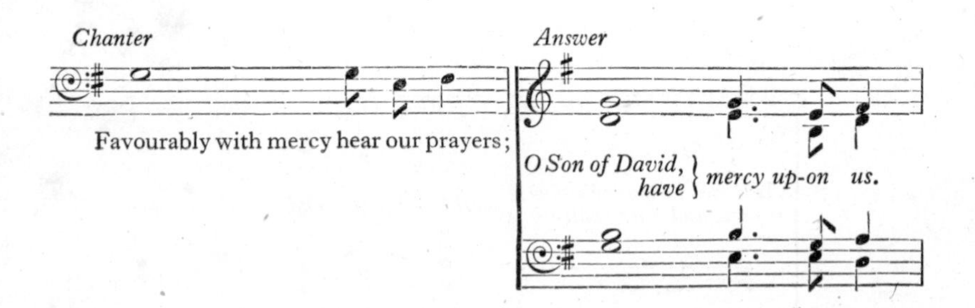
Chanter
Answer
Favourably with mercy hear our prayers;
O Son of David, have mercy up-on us.

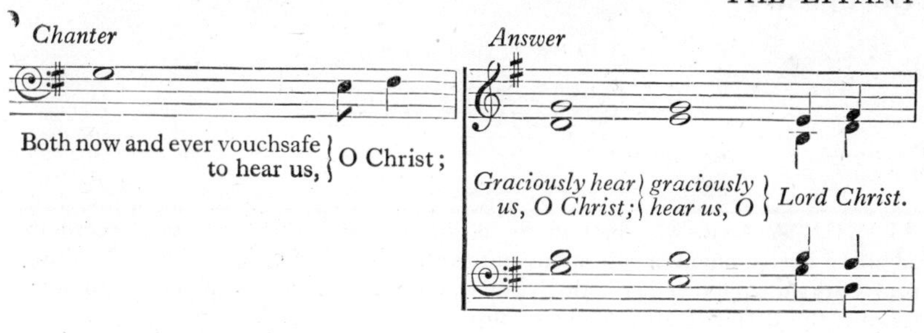

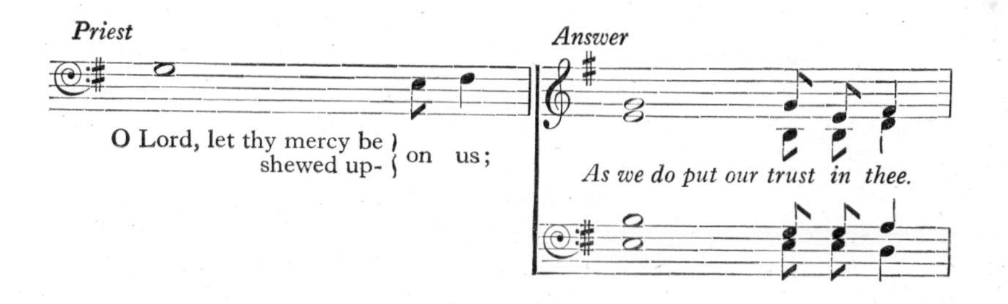

WE humbly beseech thee, O Father, mercifully to look upon our infirmities; and for the glory of thy Name turn from us all those evils that we most righteously have deserved; and grant, that in all our troubles we may put our whole trust and confidence in thy mercy, and evermore serve thee in holiness and pureness of living, to thy honour and glory; through our only Mediator and Advocate, Jesus Christ our Lord.[1]

[1] The 1544 Litany gives no inflexion or Amen for this prayer, and no music at all for the next prayer and the Grace. The last two items may therefore be said without note, with Amens likewise, or the traditional inflexions and Amens used, as given.

THE LITANY

A Prayer of St. Chrysostom

ALMIGHTY God, who hast given us grace at this time with one accord to make our common supplications unto thee; and dost promise, that when two or three are gathered together in thy Name thou wilt grant their requests; Fulfil now, O Lord, the desires and petitions of thy servants, as may be most expedient for them; granting us in this world knowledge of thy truth, and in the world to come life ever-last-ing.

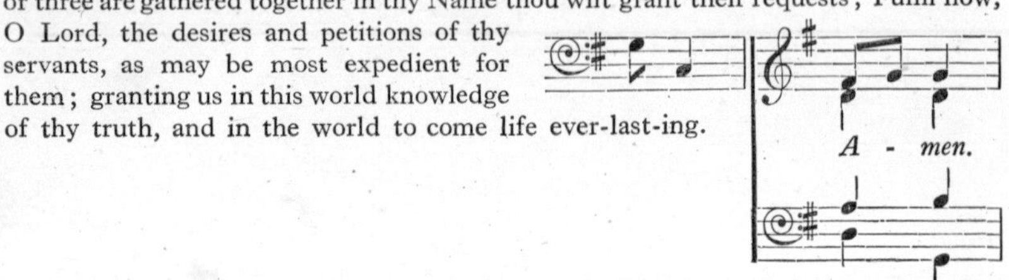

2 Cor. xiii.

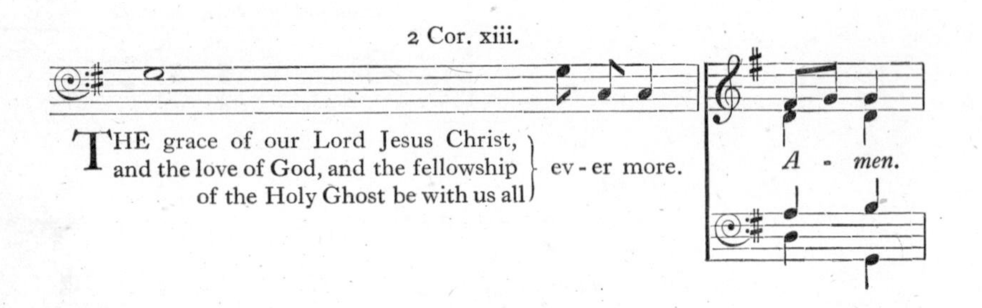

THE grace of our Lord Jesus Christ, and the love of God, and the fellowship of the Holy Ghost be with us all ev - er more.

Here endeth the LITANY

FIRST PUBLISHED 1929 : SECOND EDITION 1936 : REPRINTED 1943

SET IN GREAT BRITAIN AT THE UNIVERSITY PRESS, OXFORD, BY JOHN JOHNSON, PRINTER TO THE UNIVERSITY

PRINTED BY SELLAR & SELLAR, LTD., HAYES, MDDX.